The National Environmental Policy Act

The National Environmental Policy Act

AN AGENDA FOR THE FUTURE

Lynton Keith Caldwell

Indiana University Press

BLOOMINGTON AND INDIANAPOLIS

This book is a publication of

Indiana University Press
601 North Morton Street
Bloomington, IN 47404-3797 USA

http://www.indiana.edu/~iupress

Telephone orders 800-842-6796
Fax orders 812-855-7931
Orders by e-mail iuporder@indiana.edu

The paper used in this publication meets the minimum requirements of
American National Standard for Information Sciences—Permanence of
Paper for Printed Library Materials, ANSI Z39.48-1984.

MANUFACTURED IN THE UNITED STATES OF AMERICA

Library of Congress Cataloging-in-Publication Data

Caldwell, Lynton Keith, date
    The National Environmental Policy Act : an agenda for the future /
Lynton Keith Caldwell.
        p.   cm.
    Includes bibliographical references and index.
    ISBN 0-253-33444-6 (cloth : alk. paper)
    1. Environmental law—United States.   2. Environmental policy—
United States.   3. United States. National Environmental Policy Act
of 1969.   I. Title.
KF3775.C35   1998
344.73'046—dc21   98-38666
1 2 3 4 5   03 02 01 00 99 98

In Recognition of the
Foresight and Statesmanship
of Henry M. Jackson
1912–1983
Senator, United States Congress
1953–1983

CONTENTS

PREFACE

This book has been written in the belief that the National Environmental Policy Act (NEPA) offers a set of goals that could guide the nation toward an economically and environmentally tolerable, sustainable future. To this end NEPA is presented on a trajectory in time and space — from what its authors intended it to be in 1970 to what it could become in the 21st century. This requires placing NEPA into context, identifying major environmental issues to which NEPA has always been relevant but which are now acquiring major transnational and global dimensions. The space dimension has thus expanded, not because of textual changes in the Act, but because the extent of its practical relevance is beginning to be understood. While the scope of its concern has always been as broad as the human environment, occasions for its application have increased.

The book does not offer a legal or legislative analysis, or a detailed history, of NEPA. These have been covered in other books. *The National Environmental Policy Act* emphasizes the intent of the Act, its prescriptive declaration, and its unrealized potential. It deals with redirecting national policy through procedural reform, but the emphasis is on policy. It is concerned less with how NEPA has been administered than with its potential for guidance of American policy in the interacting, globalizing world of nations in the 21st century. Its documentation is limited to sources that illustrate, elaborate, or differ from arguments advanced in the text, as well as confirm direct quotations. The Notes and References do not offer a comprehensive bibliography of the subject matter. Such a listing could easily exceed the volume of the present text. General accessibility was one criterion for inclusion, and the omission of pertinent books and articles does not indicate a judgment on their quality or importance. It should be unnecessary to note that the human species is identified alternatively as man, mankind, humans, humanity, and the human species. Within the context of this book gender distinctions are irrelevant.

While Congress has made numerous exceptions to NEPA's application (at least twenty-eight indicated in the U.S. Code as of 1997), there has been virtually no change in its text since its enactment in 1969. But during the past thirty years, significant changes have occurred in the circumstances to which it is applicable. On a space-time trajectory the position of NEPA has changed; the rapid interrelating and globalizing of international affairs during the latter decades of this century have involved the United States in actions all over the world, and where Federal action occurs, NEPA applies. In brief, the space dimension of NEPA's applicability has expanded. The time dimension has also changed as history accelerates and moves ever more swiftly toward an uncertain future. NEPA does not impose American values and requirements on other people. Its purposes and procedures apply only to actions by the Federal government of the United States.

Americans are divided over how the future should be approached, and this division affects the future of NEPA and the nation. The general—and hence imperfect—division is between an optimistic laissez-faire, market-directed ideology and a contrasting cautionary opinion arguing the need for forecasting, anticipatory planning, and adaptive management. This latter implies an effort to project a preferred future embracing the goals set forth in Section 101(b) of NEPA. The laissez-faire followers are largely cornucopians who foresee a future of "progress" and "abundance" if governments do not interfere. The contrasting opinion, held by most "environmentalists" (among many others), is doubtful regarding the future. Some are called "catastrophists"—the so-called gloom and doom school of foreboding. More, however, take a precautionary viewpoint, unpersuaded that individuals pursuing their private interests will contribute to the public good. From the environmentally concerned viewpoint, NEPA provides an agenda for society-wide participatory planning toward a preferred future. Trend analysis and forecasting are authorized under NEPA's Title II, Section 204, but beyond the *Global 2000 Report* of 1980/81, the Council on Environmental Quality has been unable to fulfill this part of its mandate.

For more than 300 years a unifying goal for the European colonists and their American descendants had been the "conquest," "subjugation," and domestication of the continent. Today this purpose has been recast as economic growth and expanding development—but it no longer has a unifying force, and it provides no guidance toward a quality of life in the future. The historic unifying factor for Americans was the continental frontier. Since the closure of that frontier at the end of the 19th century, Americans have had no surrogate or replacement. In 1945 a report to the president from the U.S. Office of Scientific Research and Development was titled *Science: The Endless Frontier*. Following the launching of the Russian Earth Orbiting Satellite (Sputnik) in 1957, outer space represented a new frontier. But these and other evocations of the frontier ethos have never offered an opportunity for the participation of all Americans; neither have they influenced the ethos and expectations of the nation comparable to the westward-moving land frontier.

Whether the environmental principles and goals declared in NEPA can or will become a unifying factor in the civic life of Americans is uncertain. It may be an integrative possibility. Probabilities are uncertain, but evidence from the sciences, along with statistical projections from measured trends, indicates serious trouble ahead for humankind and the biosphere. Perceived threats of disaster have sometimes had a unifying effect on societies. The 1993 *World Scientists' Warning to Humanity* (Union of Concerned Scientists) reported that "Human beings and the natural world are on a collision course." Many similar, highly informed assessments have been made. A prudent and rational response to these forecasts would be recognition of NEPA as a protective national strategy for a sustainable and enhanced future.

That NEPA offers this possibility is the principal thesis of this book. Environmental protection measures adopted thus far have done little more than slow the rate of adverse trends, and seem to be inadequate to prevent an ecological impoverishment of the Earth. It may be that the processes of global climate change, thinning of the protective ozone layer, increase in human populations, loss of biodiversity, and deterioration of agricultural productivity are now built irreversibly into the world system. Future generations may perforce adapt to a world more crowded, more polluted, less stable ecologically, and more vulnerable to disruption than is the world we live in now *(Global 2000 Report).* Humankind is a highly adaptive species, doubtless capable of shaping a civilization very unlike our own, in response to conditions that we today would find unacceptable.

But humans also have the capacity to respond to possibilities, once the benefits and costs are understood. NEPA declares an agenda for the possible. If a heavy cost to the quality of the environment cannot be avoided, it can hopefully be diminished—and in time the destructive trends may be stopped, and some even reversed. For this to happen in America and throughout the world, a change in human perspective as great as that following the Copernican revolution of the 17th century will be necessary. Earth is no longer seen as the center of the cosmos, and humanity is neither center nor master of the biosphere. NEPA and the UN Agenda 21 set out what should be done to attain a tolerable, sustainable future. A reciprocal relationship between collective learning and catalytic leadership throughout all sectors of society would be necessary—and indeed essential at the highest levels of political responsibility.

The need for a national agenda for the future is not new. In 1968, Secretary of the Interior Stewart L. Udall published an *Agenda for Tomorrow;* and in 1985 "Leaders of America's Foremost Environmental Organizations" co-authored *An Environmental Agenda for the Future.* Their *Agenda* set forth a series of recommendations consistent in substance with NEPA's precepts and principles, but did not invoke NEPA as mandating its recommendations. I argue that NEPA provides a statutory rationale for specific national goals and targets for the environmental future corresponding to a revised and extended version of the 1985 Leaders' *Agenda.* To develop a credible agenda responsive to America's long-term needs would require collective and considered contributions from many sources. It is not a task appropriate for a single author.

Fulfillment of the intent behind NEPA implies an agenda for the possible. The probable requires a joining of informed foresight and popular comprehension to political will. In 1970, the year that NEPA became law, I wrote in a report on environmental education in America that "Our country faces a crisis of the mind and spirit more profound and threatening than the crisis of the environment." I called it "a crisis of will and rationality." Now nearly 30 years later, I find no reason to revise my assessment. But I still retain hope.

ACKNOWLEDGMENTS

Because this book is a culmination of more than 30 years' involvement with environmental policy and law, it is impossible for me to identify all of the people who, in various ways, contributed to it. To attempt to again thank all who have influenced or informed this effort would risk missing some whose assistance was significant. It is possible, however, to recognize principal contributors to the actual production of the book. The suggestion that this book would be timely came from A. James Barnes, Dean of the School of Public and Environmental Affairs, Indiana University. Financial support to assist its preparation was provided to the School by the Henry M. Jackson Foundation. Efficient and expeditious typing of the manuscript was provided by Jennifer Mitchner and also by Eve Alexander. William Plummer assisted with reference searches. The reference staff services of the Indiana University libraries were an indispensable source of assistance, notably in the Research Collection, Government Publications, School of Law, and School of Public and Environmental Affairs.

Also indispensable for information and factual review of the manuscript was the staff on the Council on Environmental Quality in the Executive Office of the President, especially General Counsel Dinah Bear and Senior Policy Analyst Ray Clark. I am also indebted for review of the manuscript to Richard N. L. Andrews, Daniel A. Dreyfus, Philip Emmi, Kristin Shrader-Frechette, James M. McElfish Jr., and Paul Wieland, and to my wife Helen Caldwell for perceptive and practical editorial advice. Finally, I am grateful for the enthusiastic response of Indiana University Press, its Director, John Gallman, and its editorial and production staff. Authors may prepare manuscripts, but the work of many more people is necessary to produce books.

None of the conclusions of the author or his interpretations of NEPA are fairly attributed to any Federal agency or personnel.

INTRODUCTION
REAFFIRMING NEPA

The purpose of this book is twofold: *first,* to enlarge understanding of a unique and undervalued declaration of national policy for the environment and *second,* to show how this policy provides the foundation for a future national program of action.

The thesis of this book is that the National Environmental Policy Act (NEPA) expresses a maturing of values that are widely but not yet universally shared by Americans. But to realize in practice the principles declared in NEPA requires a strategic long-term effort toward enhancing and sustaining the quality of national life. I argue that NEPA's substantive precepts (including directives to the Federal agencies) have the status of legal principles which may be implemented by executive action, or by statutory measures enforceable through the courts.

NEPA is more than rhetoric—it mandates coordinative procedures by the Federal agencies and it democratizes Federal planning and decision-making that significantly affect the environment. However, the greater significance of NEPA may lie in its articulation of *values* and *goals* which could guide the nation from its present condition toward coping with problems converging in the 21st century. To fully comprehend this potential of NEPA it is necessary to understand the Act's historical context. It is also necessary to project NEPA's potential significance into a broad range of national and international social, economic, and political affairs.

Substantial parts of the text will identify some major environmental issues that created the climate of concern in which NEPA emerged. Since NEPA became policy, the number and magnitude of serious environmental hazards have increased or belatedly been discovered, and its relevance has been enlarged and extended beyond our national boundaries.

As I use the term, *environment* implies more than the relationship between man and nature—and the interactive effects of technology. While these considerations are indeed central to national and international policy, they do not convey the ultimate scope and depth of the environment as the condition for life on Earth. Despite demonstrable progress in retarding or reversing specific environmental degradations, the global environment in the aggregate is deteriorating at a pace that should be alarming. Failure to appreciate these dangers follows, at least in part, from a myopic, narrowly bounded view of the environment.

Environment in its larger sense should not be defined as a "special interest" or regarded as a category on a spectrum of issues including those defined as ecologic, economic, political, physical, aesthetic, and ethical. In reality, environment embraces all of these in various ways. In its larger sense, the environment is not less than the totality of interrelationships between the human species and the cosmos. The ultimate environment extends from the infinitely small (the microcosmos) to the infinitely vast (the universe). As Carl Sagan explains, "We are, in a very real and profound sense, a part of that cosmos, born from it, our fate deeply connected with it."[1] While this concept reflects physical reality and philosophic authenticity it is not manageable. Awareness of this ultimate dimension is important to perspective on human affairs, but the concept of environment must be broken down into discrete yet interrelated parts amenable to human purposes.

This larger comprehension of environment is implicit in the text of NEPA, which declares a national policy that will encourage productive and enjoyable harmony between man and his environment; create and maintain conditions under which man and nature can exist in productive harmony; and fulfill the social, economic, and other requirements of present and future generations of Americans. The environment and the economy are not dichotomies requiring "balance." Conflicts may indeed occur between economic and ecologic values—but the economy is an integral part of the larger human environment. The appropriate relationship is *synthesis*—not balance.

Economist Herman E. Daly suggests that this relationship can be illustrated by two diagrams—one labeled "economy" within a larger one labeled "environment."[2] I regard this as the right way to look at the relationship. The environment in its fundamental sense is all-inclusive—it embraces cosmic and microcosmic reality. Humans can manage only defined increments of it. They risk error and defeat if in efforts to manage some of the parts they fail to relate those efforts to the whole—to the ascertainable elements of the whole that set the parameters for human achievement.

FIVE ASPECTS OF NEPA

NEPA is a coordinative response to the larger dimension of the environmental issue. Its meaning should not be considered obscure or isolated from other legislation. Its text is short and free from jargon. Nevertheless the Act has too often been misunderstood and misrepresented. To fully comprehend its purpose and to correct its misinterpretation there are five points that need to be considered—and which will be revisited in the following chapters. They are summarized here as an aid to understanding NEPA as a declaration of purpose and commitment. NEPA's simplicity, however, is in some measure deceptive. The Act itself is an unusual piece of legislation—a declaration of policy requiring long-term implementation and the modification of some long-standing national priorities.

First, NEPA is a *policy* act—it sets a course for governmental action; it is not a regulatory statute. It does include and by extension provides a number of action-forcing features—primarily in Section 102—that mandate identification and assessment of environmental impacts by the Federal agencies responsible for major environment-affecting proposals. Under presidential authority, the Council on Environmental Quality (CEQ) issues regulations to the Federal agencies regarding the preparation and content of impact statements. The Environmental Protection Agency (EPA) initially reviews impact statements for adequacy and conformity to NEPA requirements—and unresolved questions are referred for further review to the CEQ.

The communicative function of NEPA is to articulate national environmental goals and values which the Federal government is directed to honor in cooperation with State and local governments and other concerned public and private organizations. The language of NEPA, understood as a declaration of policy, is principled and general—appropriate to a complex and comprehensive area of public policy. Yet its practical significance may be overlooked because while the Act declares values to be expressed in public policy, it does not confer individual rights, nor regulate private behavior. Senator Henry M. Jackson recognized its significance for value choice, observing that

> A statement of environmental policy is more than a statement of what we believe as a people and as a nation. It establishes priorities and gives expression to our national goals and aspirations. It serves a constitutional function in that people may refer to it for guidance in making decisions where environmental values are found to be in conflict with other values.[3]

The extent to which NEPA actually affects the policies of the Federal agencies is not easily generalized. For many people, "law" implies court-enforced rights or regulations, and NEPA has been interpreted as justiciable primarily in relation to environmental impact statements. For those with a limited concept of the environment, there is more implied in NEPA than is readily apparent. Federal Judge Henry J. Friendly understood the difficulty in interpreting NEPA better than did its short-sighted critics. In his opinion in the case of *City of New York v. United States* (331 F Supp. 150, 159) he observed that NEPA "is so broad, yet so opaque that it will take even longer than usual to comprehend its impact." The language of NEPA is simple, but its larger implications are far-reaching. Policy *declared* is inoperative until activated through legitimized procedure or positive law. NEPA, as policy, is a "template" against which decisions affecting the environment can be compared for consistency with its declared principles.

Second, the procedural requirements of NEPA are intended to force attention to the policies declared in the Statement of Purpose (Section 2) and in Title I (Section 101) of the Act. The purpose of the Act is to write impact statements. To regard the action-forcing provision of Section 102 (the so-

called NEPA Process) as the essence of the Act is to misinterpret its purpose—the substance of which had been under consideration in the Congress
for at least a decade before the concept of the environmental impact statement (EIS) was introduced in 1969. Impact analysis is an important aspect
of planning and decision-making and has been applied to a wide range of
policy determinations—but it ought not be substituted for the declared policies which it is intended to activate. Environmental impact analysis and
assessment is a discovery function for ascertaining the range of risks and
benefits of proposals that have major environmental consequences. It therefore has a disclosure function, democratizing the policy process and identifying alternatives to the proposed action in relation to NEPA's principles.
The April 16, 1969, hearing before the Committee on Interior and Insular
Affairs on NEPA (Senate Bill 1075) makes clear its intended linkage between
policy and procedure.

Third, NEPA is future-directed, furthering values that in some measure
have long been present in American society, and to which in principle, it seems
safe to say a plurality of Americans today adhere. In the historic settlement
and economic development of the continent, material growth was the governing value, and little thought was given to the long-term consequences of the
reshaping and manipulation of nature or the building of urban environments.
Francis Bacon's dictum that "Nature, to be commanded, must be obeyed"
(*Novum Organum*, 1620) was only half understood. By the mid-20th century
the quality-of-life objective of material growth was being frustrated by excess
and misapplication in economic activities and technology. The environmental
movement emerged as it became apparent that the quality of life sought
through economic growth and technological innovation would not be achieved
or sustained without a reorientation of values and a reconsideration of behaviors. NEPA expresses this realization, and provides an agenda for harmonizing
legitimate sustainable economic goals with larger environmental values.

The need for a reevaluation of public policy priorities has been sensed
by many people who nevertheless have been slow to understand the underlying causes of a perceived threat to the quality of life. Comprehension and
implementation of the principles declared in NEPA, as Judge Friendly observed, will take time to be realized. There is a NEPA process larger than
impact statement procedure. It is a process of policy leadership, social learning, and reconsideration of values—of scientific advancement and psychological and behavioral change reflected in the ends and operations of society,
government, and the economy. There is a growing worldwide perception
that the ways in which humans have been exploiting their environment in
its many dimensions may no longer be sustainable—but there is less agreement as to what should be done about these problems and when. NEPA
provides a foundation for America's role in meeting the global challenge to
humanity's environmental future.

Fourth, NEPA is not self-executing. The EIS is intended to force attention to NEPA's declared goals and principles. But the action that the EIS forces does not determine the outcome expressed in an agency's Record of Decision. That decision may be influenced not only by the statutory mission and priorities of the agency but also by the weight of organized interests, priorities of the president, committees of Congress, and opinions of the courts. The information and rational analysis provided by the EIS have caused some proposals to be revised or withdrawn. The NEPA Process has been more corrective or preventive than enhancing. There are numerous issues declared or implied in NEPA upon which neither Congress nor the president has acted and, in addition, there are recommendations by several national commissions (e.g. on population, forecasting, and material resources) which if implemented or even seriously considered could further the realization of the NEPA intent.

Fifth, the distinction between NEPA and the larger volume of environmental policy and law (Federal, State, and local) is the difference in their focus, scope, and emphasis. The environmental law of case books and the courts is essentially *remedial, facilitating,* or *prohibitive,* intended to remove or retard specific environmental threats to human health, safety, and a preferred quality of life. These policies address fragments or pieces of the underlying problems. They are nevertheless necessary to realize the NEPA intent.

NEPA, in distinction, addresses comprehensively the *greater* environmental problem. Conventional statutory law, as applied by lawyers and judges, appears contrastingly (sometimes deceptively) explicit because it is usually case-specific and procedural. NEPA is unconventional in its purpose to broaden understanding and to assist in a reorientation of values, beliefs, and behaviors. It legislates values not by imposing them, which no statute can do, but by giving them national visibility and assisting in their implementation. This task is more fundamental than is the controlling of industrial effluents and emissions or disposing of noxious wastes. The implementation of NEPA requires a new and widespread coevolution of beliefs and behaviors, consistent with the way the world works. This is why NEPA has been difficult to comprehend. People have not been accustomed to perceiving the "environment" in its holistic context. It is not the immediate environment to which they daily relate. Even so, change is occurring in human perceptions of environmental circumstances, and the change is becoming worldwide. Growth and understanding of interactive effects within the terrestrial environment, along with discoveries in outer space may establish recognition of the ultimate unity between the domestic environment of mankind and the cosmic environment within which the Earth exists.

The success or failure of legislative initiatives is always to some extent circumstantial. In the case of NEPA, the political response to the nation's awakening environmental consciousness came in the right form at the right time, and with important implications for the future.

NEPA'S FUTURE

There remains the question of NEPA's future. NEPA declares a policy for harmonizing environmental and economic values. To achieve this goal, a synthesis of values will be necessary. Balancing equities may achieve political compromise but is unlikely to find lasting solutions to the greater problems of mankind's environmental relationships. NEPA does not mandate any particular way of reconciling sustainable environmental quality with economic or other interests, but it does express the environmental values to be served—values broadly defined that should enhance the quality of America's future.

A large amount of social learning may yet be required before the significance of the environment for life on Earth is universally understood and consensus is achieved in our highly diverse, short-focused, personal-centered society. Social learning requires informed and persuasive teaching—a quality sometimes, but not often, found in political leadership. There can hardly be a more important goal for human learning and public policy than appreciation of the time-space dimensions of the environment as manifest in the inanimate and living systems of the Earth. This is a very large order for education through formal schooling and experience in public affairs. We discount the significance of interactions between man and nature in the environment when we fail to recognize their interconnectedness to an infinite whole. We can deal only with specifics, but will do so wisely and successfully only if, so far as possible, we comprehend them in context. NEPA set goals for America toward which the nation moved for two decades, leading the world in most areas of environmental policy. However, in 1996, an environmental performance review of member countries by the Organization for Economic Cooperation and Development (OECD) found uncertainty in the commitment of the United States toward environmental action—notably in relation to international issues.[4]

Certainly in an evermore interdependent, interactive world, no nation can separate itself from global trends. NEPA defines and legitimizes the active concern of the United States in protecting and enhancing the human environment and the biosphere. To regard the environment as a "special interest" is to misconceive the human situation. The environment is pervasive; it embraces all humanity. It is no less a human "interest" than is life itself, of which it is an inseparable part. NEPA underscores the need for knowledge and foresight in guiding human behavior in relation to the environment and in providing direction toward a sustainable future.

The principle thesis of this book—that NEPA's declaration of policy sets a substantive agenda for the future—is essentially that of an Environmental Law Institute Research Report, *Rediscovering the National Environmental Policy Act: Back to the Future* (September 1995), prepared by James McElfish and

Elissa Parker. In its introductory chapter the authors present the following concept of NEPA, which is also mine:

> The conventional wisdom about NEPA is that it is a flowery preamble attached to a single—and wholly procedural—requirement to prepare environmental impact statements for a small subset of federal decisions. This conventional wisdom is wrong. Like a classic of literature read when one is too young, what one remembers about NEPA is not, in fact, what is most important about it. NEPA is not just an environmental impact statement law. It is, rather, a vision of this nation's future, coupled with an intensely practical strategy for action.

Notwithstanding the important contributions of Senators Edmund Muskie, Gaylord Nelson, and Representative John Dingell to the legislation which became NEPA, I have drawn most heavily on the leading role of Senator Henry M. Jackson. He was the most articulate and effective advocate of this legislation in the 91st Congress, and in my view had the deepest insight into its scope and significance. Having had the privilege of consulting Senator Jackson and the Senate Interior Committee in the development of NEPA, I was able to observe the determination and legislative skill that enabled Senate Bill 1075 to become law. NEPA was, and is, extraordinary legislation, and I doubt that it could have been enacted without the leadership of Henry Jackson and the capability of his staff.

The National Environmental Policy Act

1

Environmental Policy: Values and Perceptions

TO DECLARE A NATIONAL POLICY WHICH WILL ENCOURAGE
PRODUCTIVE AND ENJOYABLE HARMONY BETWEEN MAN AND HIS
ENVIRONMENT; TO PROMOTE EFFORTS WHICH WILL PREVENT OR
ELIMINATE DAMAGE TO THE ENVIRONMENT AND BIOSPHERE AND
STIMULATE THE HEALTH AND WELFARE OF MAN; TO ENRICH THE
UNDERSTANDING OF THE ECOLOGICAL SYSTEMS AND NATURAL
RESOURCES IMPORTANT TO THE NATION; AND TO ESTABLISH A
COUNCIL ON ENVIRONMENTAL QUALITY.

—PURPOSE: THE NATIONAL ENVIRONMENTAL
POLICY ACT OF 1969, SECTION 2.

With this declaration of purpose the 91st Congress sought to establish a national policy responsive to values widely held in American society and endangered by the deteriorating quality of the environment. In a hearing on April 16, 1969, before the Senate Committee on Interior and Insular Affairs, on S.1075 (the bill which evolved to become NEPA), Committee Chairman Henry M. Jackson offered the following statement:

> I introduced this measure because it is my view that our present knowledge, our established policies, and our existing institutions are not adequate to deal with the growing environmental problems and crises the nation faces.
>
> The inadequacy of present knowledge, policies, and institutions is reflected in our nation's history, in our national attitudes, and in our contemporary life. We see this inadequacy all around us: haphazard urban growth, the loss of open spaces, strip-mining, air and water pollution, soil erosion, deforestation, faltering transportation systems, a proliferation of pesticides and chemicals, and a landscape cluttered with billboards, powerlines, and junkyards.
>
> Traditional government policies and programs weren't designed to achieve these conditions. But they weren't designed to avoid them either. And, as a result, *they were not avoided.*
>
> As a nation, we have failed to design and implement a national environmental policy which would enable us to weigh alternatives, and to anticipate the undesirable side effects which often result from our ongoing policies, programs and actions.

Today it is clear that we cannot continue to perpetuate the mistakes of the past. We no longer have the margins for error and mistake that we once enjoyed.

It was in view of this background and these considerations that I introduced S.1075, my bill to establish a national environmental policy. The purpose of this legislation is threefold: *First,* to establish a national policy on the environment; *Second,* to authorize expanded research and understanding of our natural resources, the environment, and human ecology; and *Third,* to establish in the Office of the President a properly staffed Council of Environmental Quality Advisors.[1]

In legislating this intent the Congress faced a need not only to respond to the values underlying the growing concern over a deteriorating environment but as much as possible to reconcile and harmonize the diversity of values and concepts present in American society that related to the environment. Not everyone saw environment in the same light or valued it in the same way. The reconciliation of differences regarding the place of the environment in public policy thus became—and remains—a problem that is political, juridical, administrative and, at its base, ethical. The principles and purposes declared by NEPA are widely shared and offer few causes for conflict. It is in their implementation (chiefly in other environmental statutes) that political difficulties arise when values and interests conflict.[2] Commenting on the Report of the Conference Committee on S.1075 before its final passage, Senator Jackson observed that NEPA "provides a statutory foundation to which administrators may refer . . . for guidance in making decisions which find environmental values in conflict with other values."[3]

Nearly 30 years after enactment of NEPA (S.1075), an implementing bill (S.399), introduced by Senator John McCain of Arizona, The Environmental Policy and Conflict Resolution Act (Public Law 105-156), was signed into law by President Clinton on February 11, 1998. The Act creates the United States Institute for Environmental Conflict Resolution "to assist the Federal Government in implementing section 101 of the National Environmental Policy Act of 1969." The legislation authorizes federal agencies to use the Institute in matters of disputes or conflicts relating to the environment, public lands, or natural resources. The Institute is associated with the Center established by the Morris K. Udall Foundation at the University of Arizona. The chairman of the CEQ is designated as a non-voting member of the Foundation.[4]

TO DECLARE A POLICY

Basic to an understanding of NEPA is that it is a declaration of *policy* with action-forcing provisions—a policy act—*not* a regulatory statute comparable to environmental legislation relating to air, water, hazardous substances, endangered species, wetlands, wilderness, and historic preservation.

Also important to its comprehension is its place in a progressive worldwide shifting in values during the latter half of the 20th century.

The NEPA Purpose was restated in the Declaration which followed: "to foster and promote the general welfare, to create and maintain conditions under which man and nature can exist in productive harmony, and fulfill the social, economic, and other requirements of present and future generations of Americans." The Congress legislates only for the United States, but its acts cover the actions of individuals and agencies within its jurisdiction, regardless of whether the impact of those actions fall within or beyond its territorial limits. The broad scope of NEPA is "to promote efforts which will prevent or eliminate damage to the environment and the biosphere."

Interpreting this commitment, Senator Jackson declared "that we do not intend, as a government or as a people, to initiate actions which endanger the continued existence or the health of mankind."[5] From these statements a logical inference might be drawn that NEPA declared a policy for actions by the government of the United States, extending to those programs and projects of Federal agencies that have environmental impact on the whole Earth and its inhabitants. The environment and the biosphere for which NEPA declares a responsibility are planetary in scope. America is not a "sphere," and "mankind" is far more inclusive than the people of the United States. It seems clear that the drafters of NEPA intended it to have a global relevance. A successful policy to "encourage productive and enjoyable harmony between man and his environment" must reconcile and mediate a diversity of values at the national level before the United States can contribute cooperation and leadership to world environmental affairs.

EMERGING ENVIRONMENTAL CONSCIOUSNESS

The state of the environment as an international concern emerged during the latter half of the 20th century, initially in Western Europe and North America[6] and spread globally, leading to the United Nations Conference on the Human Environment in 1972 and again in 1992 to the United Nations Conference on Environment and Development. This growth of environmental consciousness was prominent within a larger transformation in social values, but required reconciliation with traditional assumptions in which environmental quality—aside from public health and sanitation (e.g. urban smog and sewage) had been confined largely to limited urban aesthetics (e.g. city planning and beautification). This transformation is still ongoing and some decades may be required before it becomes universal.

Recognition of environmental influences has been slow and uneven because of (1) insufficient understanding of environmental interrelationships, (2) concepts contrary to traditional assumptions, and (3) failure to distinguish between conceptualizing the environment in its totality and those aspects of the environment amenable to human management. This latter distinction is fundamental to environmental impact assessment—to ascertain what aspects of the environment interact with human actions and to what effect. Differences in comprehension of the environment complicate implementation of environmental policies. For example, a professor of environmental resources declared, "My position on environment is simple, it is that there isn't one. There are as many environments as there are living things in the world; each has its own."[7] True, each living and inanimate thing has a unique environmental relationship. But all are affected by environmental forces and phenomena—ubiquitous and cosmic. It is a major misconception to regard personal or particular aspects of the environment in disregard of the larger context of the whole insofar as its relevant effects can be ascertained.

In the UN Conferences, behavior in relation to the environment was widely recognized as encompassing local to international dimensions (e.g. think globally, act locally). The natural world is a complex total system organized politically as an artificial system of separate sovereign nations. There being no worldwide legislative authority, environmental policy for all mankind and the planet can be initiated only by the concerted action of national governments. International environmental policy requires the collective action of nations, but it is necessary that individual governments act for their own nations in order to collaborate with others. National action may precede international action, but it may sometimes follow in response to international initiatives.

Although specific aspects of environmental policy had been addressed in the United States and in other countries (as in the British Town and County Planning Acts and land use regulations in the Netherlands), the United States appears to have been the first nation to respond comprehensively to an insistent (though inchoate) public demand for action to protect the quality of the environment. Comprehensive legislation was needed, but the Congress had no model or precedent for a national environmental policy. The closest similarity appeared to be the Employment Act of 1946, which dealt with a more definable aspect of the economy. The principal impediment to formulating, legislating, and administering environmental policy is *perception*—the differences in the ways in which people understand the meaning and significance of "environment." For example, environmental policy has been variously conceived as primarily an antipollution issue, has been confused with conservation of natural resources, has aroused controversy over rights of property owners, and has led to political conflict over these and many other areas of policy. The values which people acknowledge may reflect traditional principles, but practical interests are limited by lifetimes and personal circumstances. Principled values and practical interests are often segregated, if not conflicted. Reconciliation of environmental values and economic interests is a major objective of NEPA.

But its achievement is a long-term process, one which is—from a pessimists' perspective—too long to avert avoidable disasters toward which humanity is tending.

The need for action to reverse environmental deterioration was voiced by numerous critics during the 1950s and 1960s, but the means to action were not systematically addressed. However, in April 1963 with the article "Environment: A New Focus for Public Policy" (*Public Administration Review,* Vol. 23), I called for a reconceptualization of the environment in relation to the responsibilities and functions of government. In March 1966 I followed with the article "The Human Environment: A Growing Challenge to Higher Education" (*Journal of Higher Education,* Vol. 37). It seemed evident that if a major change in national values and priorities were to be effective, changes in public administration and education would be necessary. Changes in popular values anticipate changes in public institutions.

Early in 1968, through an arrangement between Russell Train, president of the Conservation Foundation, and Senator Jackson, I was asked to assist in developing the substance of a national environmental policy act. In a report prepared for the Senate Interior Committee, with the assistance of William Van Ness, I offered the following observations regarding legislation that would respond to the national concern:

> To be effective, a national policy for the environment must be compatible and consistent with many other needs to which the Nation must respond. But it must also define the intent of the American people toward the management of their environment in terms that the Congress, the President, the administrative agencies and the electorate can consider and act upon. A national policy for the environment—like other major policy declarations—must be concerned with principle rather than with detail; but it must be principle which can be applied in action. The goals of effective environmental policy cannot be counsels of perfection; what the Nation requires are guidelines to assist the government, private enterprise and the individual citizen to plan together and to work together toward meeting the challenge of a better environment.[8]

A year later NEPA did provide principles, short of operational guidelines, to assist the government, private enterprise, and the individual citizen to plan together and work together toward meeting the challenge of a better environment. But implementation of the principles set forth in the NEPA Declaration was confronted by the reality of significant differences in people's perceptions of the environment. Although opinion analysis confirmed a strong concern for environmental protection and improvement, individuals held differing values, beliefs, and interests regarding the role of government and the importance of the environment in relation to other public priorities. NEPA legislated a declaration of broadly conceived principles intended to elevate attitudes and actions relating to the environment to the level of national policy.

The Congress could not impose the values implicit in its declaration upon individual Americans, and this was not its purpose. It might raise the national consciousness concerning the environment, but it could mandate conformity with NEPA values on only the Federal agencies. Actions by the Federal agencies today extend throughout the national economy and have both direct and indirect impacts upon the environment. Almost every aspect of the economy is affected by public law and administration, e.g. agriculture (including forestry), energy, commerce, transportation, health and safety, education, science research and development, and military defense among the more prominent.

The environment emerged as a significant concern for public policy after 1969 but was subordinate to legacies of a past in which economic development of land and all other natural resources was the nation's primary goal. Government programs and agencies were established to "develop" the nation's material assets; education and research were enlisted with public support to advance development in farming, forestry, mining, and engineering. Professional attitudes and values in these (as in other fields of practice, e.g. law and medicine) were instilled in the schools and applied in the administration of government programs. And so it was necessary in realizing national environmental policy objectives to lay unequivocal mandatory requirements on the Federal bureaucracies whose inbred attitudes were resistant to the new environmental objectives. But bureaucracies everywhere and historically have been notoriously artful in evading policy prescriptions which they perceive as disadvantageous to their interests.

VALUES AND PERSPECTIVES

Problems with communication and consensus in environmental policy arise in those diverse and often conflicting ways in which people and their public officials perceive and evaluate "the environment." What ought to be generally understood (and is not) is that NEPA is basically legislation *about* values. But NEPA does not seek to *impose* values. The 91st Congress did what it was competent to do—it set forth environment-related values in the form of principles to guide the actions of the Federal agencies in pursuit of their missions. Environmental values implicit in NEPA are preferred relationships between people and their surroundings, which today may extend from home to the whole Earth. The term "value" cannot be precisely defined, but it expresses an attitude rather than identify an object or condition.[9] But legislation to declare and implement environmental values has not been pleasing to some Americans. There are values in American society, some strongly held, that are counteractive to environmental quality values and concerns. While they do not cancel out a widespread concern for environmental quality and sustainability, they retard the achievement of a national consensus sufficient to extend NEPA principles to programs for action. A publication of the conservative American Enterprise Institute severely criticized NEPA as "special values legislation" not representative of the values of most Americans.[10] This opinion, expressed by "antienvironmentalists," contrasts unaccountably with conservative emphasis on "family values" and values associated with traditional morality for which government intrusion into private lives is condoned—but regulation of economic activities is often condemned.

Because of the scope and reach of Federal action in the American economy, the effects of a policy mandating the implementation of environmental values in Federal actions could multiply throughout American society. Beyond America, and as early as the 1960s, environmental consciousness was beginning to emerge throughout the world. In 1968 while the legislation antecedent to NEPA was being drafted, the first world conference on the biosphere, sponsored by a number of international agencies under the leadership of UNESCO, was occurring in Paris.[11] The drafters of NEPA could not have foreseen the internationalizing of the environmental movement in the ensuing decades, but Senator Jackson recognized America's responsibilities in relation to the world environment, and NEPA may have been the first national statute to declare a purpose "to promote efforts which will prevent or eliminate damage to the environment and biosphere." A worldview of man's place in nature implies the need for a common consensual set of environmental values for all mankind.

Ernest Becker stated the essence of the relationship of values to policy when he wrote, "[The] fundamental question of values in any culture can be phrased in simple terms—what kind of control over what kind of environment?"[12] True values are deeply embedded in the human psyche; intuitive perceptions of the human relationship to life on Earth have an emotional character not easily accessible to reasoned discourse or to political fiat. Values may be understood as hierarchal, some being as fundamental as the preservation of one's life, whereas others may change with changes in knowledge and experience.

ETHICAL IMPERATIVE

Environmental policy addresses a large complex human problem—the attempt to understand, rationalize, and formalize relationships with the world life-support system of which humans are themselves a part. Human beliefs and behaviors in relation to the environment are mediated by values and perceptions that are cultural in design and increasingly influenced by science. The limited life span of humans and pursuit of their necessities leads

to an introverted short-term view of the environment. The future is dis-
counted in meeting the needs and purposes of the present. Continuity of the
environment is tacitly assumed and accordingly is ignored. The dominant
historic ethos of Americans (and of many other people) has contributed to
the attrition and degradation of the environment. Human mastery of technology has contributed to a delusion of mastery over nature. To be com-
mended, nature must be obeyed. NEPA provides an alternative to past assumptions which experience has shown to be beyond realization in a world
of limits—an alternative subjected to unprecedented human demands upon
the environment, and magnified by powerful technologies. The future presents a challenge to human will and rationality in creating an ethos that will
reconcile the improvement of human life with the sustainability of the life-
support system of the environment.

The essence of such an ethos is an ethic much larger than environmental
relationships in the conventional sense.[13] It can be no less than the sense of
humanity's relationships within the cosmos. And these relationships include
those between and among human beings. To ascertain and interpret these
relationships has been a function of all major religions. After thousands of years
of speculation and revelations we are left with a profound mystery, seemingly
beyond the human mind to fathom. Of the origin of the universe, and hence
of life on Earth, science today postulates an immense explosion of energy into
matter (the Big Bang). And before that? Can something come from nothing?
We are left with questions which science today has no means to address.

The ultimate mystery—the origin and meaning of reality—may never
have been better expressed than in the opening lines of the New Testament
Gospel According to St. John:

> In the beginning was the Word, and the Word was with God and the Word
> was God.

The biblical scholar, Dr. James Moffett, identifies the Word (Logos) as the
"divine principle of creation apart from which the universe is unintelligi-
ble—"[14] in our perception of the universe, we can comprehend the Word no
better than is manifest in the creative imperative from which physical, biological, cultural, and ethical evaluation have followed. The mystery may
forever be beyond the limitations of human mind, but its implications, which
have infused all great religions, are not. They imply humility, forbearance,
and respect for the immense process of creation of which humanity is a part.
This does not mean that humans should not act against other life forms that
threaten their existence (e.g. lethal microorganisms). Rather it means that
ethics, morality, equity, and justice are not preordained, but are for mankind
to discover. The urge toward realization of these values seems implanted in
the human psyche by the creative force that infuses our natures, but is beyond our understanding. To realize these values in the practical business of

life is a goal implicit in the Declaration of the National Environmental Policy Act. Serious pursuit of its agenda could raise greatly the level of civic life throughout the nation, and raise our sense of the significance and qualitative aspects of human life.

CONCEPTS AND PERSPECTIVES

A fundamental difficulty in evaluating the true reality of the environment lies in its complexity, comprehensiveness, and changing character. In the abstract, the *concept* of environment as a total system is as simple as it is fundamental. Although this holistic concept is operationally unmanageable beyond providing a general perception and perspective on "how the world works," it may have a cautionary value in causing people to consider possible inadvertent consequences of working against nature. Human actions taken in ignorance of collateral effects and consequences have resulted, for example, in "plagues" of zebra mussels in the Great Lakes, rabbits in Australia, water hyacinths in Florida, and the burdensome costs of their control.

This perception of an interactive world system is important because it is the context within which rational decisions affecting the environment must be made. But it is seldom the viewpoint of people preoccupied with their immediate day-to-day concerns. In its infinite interrelating detail, the holistic environment seems to exceed human comprehension. This complexity is perhaps the most obdurate obstruction to defining and implementing a policy for the environment where large issues, such as global climate change, are beyond ordinary expectation, evaluation, and behavior. Rational environmental policy requires an understanding of "natural" systems, which is the business of science, but it is with the behavior of human social systems in relation to environmental interactions that policy and law are ultimately concerned.

In his book *The Image* (1956) Kenneth Boulding observed that people see the world as they do because it has paid them, and continues to pay them, to do so. This being the case, people hold to perceptions that protect their values and deny interpretations that threaten their perceived interests. Many objectives of the environmental movement and legislation do conflict with expectations regarding profit-making and property rights. Beliefs about the way things ought to be that characterize materialistic and self-centered interests in modern society are sources of opposition to "environmentalism." Vocal opposition to NEPA (chiefly to environmental impact statements) and to many other environmental protection statutes may be "rear-guard" actions, persisting for some time and gaining some victories. But the growth of knowledge along with coercive forces and limitations of the natural environment on the socio-economic order will make improbable the persistence of anti-environmental attitudes into the future. Meanwhile they obstruct constructive solutions to many environmental problems and may cause irretrievable losses.[15]

At present, some self-styled conservatives regard environmental education as indoctrination based on pseudoscience. Others regard environmentalism as preferring "nature" to people, and obstructing human progress. To the extent that these beliefs are regarded as true, they are perceptions of a virtual reality that need not be true to be believed. These negative attitudes do not reflect informed and comprehending conservatism. They generalize from particulars which may sometimes be misinterpreted and unrepresentative. They also fail to recognize that understanding the environment has been, and continues to be, a learning process. As might be expected, new knowledge may change perceptions and may lead to a reassessment of assumptions and values. Even religious doctrines are not immune to reconsideration.

For the past 2000 years the moral and practical beliefs expressed in monotheistic religions which took root in Europe and the Middle East have been characterized by the assumption that the Earth and all it contains was made for man. Although doctrines of compassion and stewardship for the living world have been preached by theological moralists—notably by St. Francis—"abuse of nature" has seldom been regarded as a religious sin. Not only was human dominion over all things Earthly ordained by divinity, but humanity was set apart from the rest of the Earth called *nature*. The dichotomy of man and nature has for centuries been an assumption basic to Western civilization. Ingrained in religion, economy, and governance, this assumption (until recently rarely questioned) has not been readily effaced by expanding knowledge of the interrelationships among all living species and the physical elements of Earth and cosmos.

In recent years, however, many religious bodies have adopted or resurrected an ethic of respect for nature and environmental stewardship. In 1986 an ecumenical ethical-ecological alliance among the world's leading religions was initiated at a World Wildlife Fund for Nature anniversary celebration at Assisi, Italy, home of St. Francis. How deeply the respect for nature ethic is internalized in how many communicants, and how religious doctrine affects behavior are unanswered questions. But ecological consciousness and ethics are expressed in the world's major religions and were related in a 1993 International Summer Institute on Population and the Environment: Population Pressures, Resources, Consumption, Religions and Ethics, organized by the Centre for Religion and Society at the University of Victoria, British Columbia.[16]

When humans encounter environmental disaster, the dichotomy still governs perception, and it is often to an erroneous view of cause-effect relationships that public policy responds. Too often environmental disasters have been attributed to accident or to the malevolence of nature, whereas a proclivity of humans for putting themselves at risk to natural hazards may be the real cause of catastrophe.[17] Only during the latter half of the 20th century has popular perception of the true nature of human-environment relationships grown strong enough to permit environment to become a political issue and to allow—but not always to attain—a reality-oriented focus of public policy. Even today, people find difficulty in believing that many environmental problems are in reality *people* problems.

Efforts to protect, restore, or enhance the quality of the environment invariably involve the beliefs and behaviors of people. But the view that humanity is part of a holistic reality called the biosphere does not yet appear to be fully comprehended by most people and their governments. A holistic concept of the environment may be articulated by some political leaders, yet has little effect upon their practical decisions. In issuing a call for the 1965 White House Conference on Natural Beauty, President Lyndon Johnson declared:

> Our conservation must be—a creative conservation of restoration and innovation. Its concern is not with nature alone, but with the total relation between man and the world around him.[18]

Yet many of Johnson's subsequent acts as president reveal a disconnection between his "philosophic" recognition of the holistic character of the environment and his practical actions as a politician. This dichotomy of professed belief and inconsistent action (cognitive dissonance) has perhaps been more visible among politicians than among most people, presumably as an attempt to accommodate conflicting values and practical interests. There are differences of information and opinion in all areas of public concern, and the economy may be no better understood than is the environment, but there is consensus that the economy is fundamental, regardless of differences over economic policy. There is greater ambivalence regarding the importance of environment as a public issue, and this explains the cautious approach by public authorities toward implementing a rhetorical declaration of environmental policy.

Section 101(b) of NEPA declares in general terms the provisions, principles, goals, or values which "it is the continuing responsibility of the Federal Government to use all practicable means, consistent with other essential considerations of national policy," to achieve. Six admonitions are listed and each would require interpretation and evaluation in any given case. As expressions of values they are unavoidably general, yet they are recognizable in action and especially in the results of action. The Federal Government is instructed:

> to improve and coordinate Federal plans, functions, programs, and resources to the end that the Nation may—
>
> (1) fulfill the responsibilities of each generation as trustee of the environment for succeeding generations;

(2) assure for all Americans safe, healthful, productive, and esthetically and culturally pleasing surroundings;

(3) attain the widest range of beneficial uses of the environment without degradation, risk to health or safety, or other undesirable and unintended consequences;

(4) preserve important historic, cultural, and natural aspects of our national heritage, and maintain, wherever possible, an environment which supports diversity and variety of individual choice;

(5) achieve a balance between population and resource use which will permit high standards of living and a wide sharing of life's amenities; and

(6) enhance the quality of renewable resources and approach the maximum attainable recycling of depletable resources.

A purpose which the administration of NEPA has not yet fully achieved is the voluntary integration of these environmental values into Federal policy. The identification of environmental effects required under Title I, Section 102(2)(c), the EIS provision, lays no explicit obligation on the agencies to reconcile their decisions with the principles (or values) declared in Section 101. But a preceding section clearly does so, stating that "the policies, regulations and public laws of the United States shall be administered and interpreted in accordance with the policies set forth in this Act." Obviously the six provisions under Section 101(b) would not apply equally to particular Federal actions. As NEPA now stands, it may deter an agency from doing demonstrable harm to environmental values, but it provides no program or project for enhancing the future quality of life and the environment as declared in Section 101(b). For example, transgenerational equity is a consideration mandated by Section 101(b)(1) and by the concept of sustainable development promoted by the Clinton administration. Yet there is nothing compelling in the statute or regulations to cause the agencies to evaluate the implication of their actions for sustainability beyond possibly estimating long-term effects.

The closest, clear, but apparently unpersuasive linkage between the Section 101(b) precepts and the 101(2)(c) detailed statement may be found in Part 1502.2(d) of the CEQ Regulations:

> Environmental impact statements shall state how alternatives considered in it and decisions based on it will or will not achieve the requirements of Sections 101 and 102(1) of the Act and other environmental laws and policies.

Section 102(1) states, "The Congress authorizes and directs that to the fullest extent possible: (1) the policies, regulations, and public laws of the United States shall be interpreted and administered in accordance with the policies set forth in the Act . . ." To persons unfamiliar with the folkways of bureaucracies, this admonition might seem sufficiently explicit. But apparently it is not. Specific and verifiable evidence of conformity to the 1502 regulation seems necessary to confirm agency observance of the NEPA intent. One way of disclosing the extent to which the values articulated in Section 101 are honored in agency action would be a set of questions resembling a checklist (noted in chapter 3) provided as guidance to preparers of environmental assessments and statements, and to ensure that important considerations were not overlooked.

ENVIRONMENT AND ENVIRONMENTALISM

The advent of the *whole environment* as an issue of global concern marks the beginning of a new era in history. How it will develop in the 21st century cannot be predicted with confidence. As previously noted, different people have different perceptions of the environment, and it is probable that relatively few see the environment whole, extending far beyond their immediate personal awareness. Great world ideologies (notably Christianity and Islam) grew gradually from insignificant beginnings before expanding exponentially. But unlike religion, which finds its truths in transcendental revelation, the environmental movement has a foundation in empirical evidence—cause-effect relationships discovered through science. The environmental movement has emotional, aesthetic, and ethical aspects, and is increasingly influenced by science-based revelation. Ethical values, sometimes approximating a natural religion, underlie the commitment of many environmentally concerned individuals. The broader vision of the environmental movement is the place of the human species on the planet—a temporary tenant in the biophysical system of the Earth in cosmos. The environmental perspective may be described as "biocentric"—life-centered—in contrast to an exclusively "anthropocentric" or man-centered view of the world dominant in modern civilization. Biocentrism is not indifferent to humanity; rather, it seeks a relationship which will sustain human life on Earth.

The changing concept of the relationship of man to Earth is as revolutionary as was the Copernican "revelation" in the 17th century—that the Earth was not the center around which the universe revolved. Humanity has preempted and presumed to manage the Earth but ultimately is confronted by conditions and limits inherent in the cosmos called "nature." Yet in the 30 years since NEPA was drafted, the biospheric concept of the world environment as a total interrelating system, while widely held, is not an active dominant assumption in American society. Uncomprehending "conservatives" continue to complain that the environmental movement is antipeople—that "nature" is preferred over people. However, in defending NEPA Senator Jackson declared that

an environmental policy is a policy for people. Its primary concern is with
man and his future. The basic principle is that we must strive, in all that
we do, to achieve a standard of excellence in man's relationship to his
physical surroundings.[19]

In a general consensus on the way the world works and man's place in
the system, conservation of the environment for transgenerational equity
would be a value held by nearly everyone. But that consensus has not yet
been reached, and many environmental issues are controversial—at odds
with traditional concepts of entitlement and values. Consequently, concern
for the state of the environment is still viewed by some economy-centered
critics as a "special interest." This so-called special interest has been given
a name—"environmentalism." Regard for the importance of the economy
in American life is seldom described as "economism." Yet concern for the
equally important state of the environment is still condescendingly labeled
"environmentalism."

The suffix "ism" is a common but imprecise grammatical device. It is
often used for generalizations when specificity or discrimination would be
awkward and might undercut the argument that the user wishes to make.
The Dictionary Companion, compiled by C. O. Sylvester Mawson (1932), lists
five different meanings of "ism." The meaning relevant to environmentalism is commitment to "system, doctrine, policy, or practice." "Isms" are
almost always omnibus terms, often obscuring differences in viewpoint and
intensity within a common area of concern. "Environmentalism" as a generality implies a broad commitment to environmental integrity and sustainability. The term may mislead, however, if applied without discrimination to the varied perspectives and priorities comprising the environmental
social movement.

For each "ism" there is an "ist," which Mawson identifies as "one who
does or makes a practice of, or is an adherent of a creed, system, or cult."
The expression "environmentalist" is usually intended to imply a high, active, or professional concern for the environment. To make the designation
more emphatic, the expression "activist" refers to persons engaged in political advocacy or overt action on behalf of environmental issues. Although
these terms are now in common usage, they are characteristically journalistic,
with little concern for accuracy or significance; they are intended to identify
"actors" and to arouse reactions. To this extent they are harmful to the NEPA
objectives because they carry an implicit suggestion of "environment" as a
"special interest."

But environmentalism is not a "special interest" in the invidious sense
of particular groups seeking advantages for their own members, regardless
of costs to society. Environmentalists are for the most part not an organized
cohesive group. Their common concern is for all society and the biosphere

and a sustainable future. They see their concern as in the public interest.[20] As "environmentalists" they seek harmonization of economic and environmental objectives. Their values and agendas, however, could deprive others of opportunities for economic gain through actions that disregard public interests for personal advantage. Interests that are "special" need not be harmful. Some could be beneficial—some neutral. However, there are economic, behavioral, and recreational activities which in effect diminish the quality and sustainability of the environment now and for the future, and are opposed by "environmentalists."

Evaluating the significance of environmentalism, sociologist Robert Nisbet conjectured, "It is entirely possible that when the history of the twentieth century is finally written, the single most important social movement of the period will be judged to be environmentalism."[21] But he also declared that "environmentalism has become, without losing its eliteness of temper, a mass socialist movement of, not fools, but sun worshipers, macrobiotics, forest druids and nature freaks generally committed by course if not by fully shared intent to the destruction of capitalism." Nisbet's remarks are from a book entitled *Prejudices* and failed to account for the sober concern of many participants in the environmental movement who are neither opponents of capitalism in its more benign modes nor "true believers" of socialist ideology. He did, however, place the force of the movement in historical perspective, comparing it to redemptionist and revolutionary movements in the past.

In the earlier years of the environmental movement in America most critics failed to recognize its international character. It was not another ephemeral American fad, soon to give way to some other temporary enthusiasm.[22] That environmentalism was becoming a persisting and growing value in America was evidenced by the establishment, survival, and successes of public interest law firms such as the Natural Resources Defense Council (1970), the Environmental Defense Fund (1967), and the Sierra Club Legal Defense Fund (1971). The number and membership of nongovernmental environmental organizations grew exponentially after 1960, and many of the older conservation and outdoor sportsmen's organizations adopted environmental agendas. Business firms were beginning to advertise their concern for environmental values. Concern for the environment, however conceived, was becoming a core value for growing numbers of Americans.[23]

Both before and after the enactment of NEPA, a sense that history had reached a critical point beyond which change would be necessary was expressed in numerous publications. Representative of a larger number were *Sand County Almanac*, by Aldo Leopold (1949); *The Limits to Growth*, by Donella W. Meadows et al. (1972); *Silent Spring*, by Rachel Carson (1962); *The Quiet Crisis*, by Stewart Udall (1963); *Overshoot: The Ecological Basis of Revolutionary Change*, by W. R. Catton Jr. (1980); *The Turning Point: Science*,

Society and the Rising Culture, by Fritjof Capra (1984); *Environmentalists: Vanguard for a New Society,* by Lester W. Milbrath (1984); and *The New Environmental Age,* by Max Nicholson (1987).

The transnational extent of environmental concern was demonstrated by the establishment in 1968 of the Club of Rome, initiated by Italian industrialist Aurelio Peccei and British scientist Alexander King. The Club, consisting of invited scientists, politicians, and business leaders, addressed the growing environmental "predicament of mankind" as the world "problematique." It commissioned a series of reports, e.g. *The Limits to Growth* (1972), *Mankind at the Turning Point* (1973), and published a report by the Council of the Club of Rome, *The First Global Revolution,* by Alexander King and Bertrand Schneider (1991).

If these perceptions of a turning point in history are correct—as the weight of evidence increasingly suggests—then preservation of the quality of human life and of the biosphere itself has gained salience as a social value which governments in most advanced industrial countries feel obligated to address. The implication of these expressions of concern was that environmentalism was more than a transitory anxiety to be alleviated by antipollution regulations. It was a response, often inchoate, to accumulating perceptions that industrial civilization was approaching a point beyond which reassessment of its priorities would be necessary if the sustainability of the economy and quality of life were to be preserved. The NEPA initiative, developing in 1968 and 1969, proceeded on the assumption that legislation for a fundamental change toward the future would be required to cope with conditions recognized as "the predicament of mankind."

CRISIS OR CLIMACTERIC?

Although the causes of environmental disorder were deeper than its visible manifestation, American environmentalism of the 1960s and 1970s grew (as Senator Jackson noted) out of cumulative public perception of deterioration in many aspects of the environment. Nuclear contamination was a continuing source of apprehension; Lake Erie was pronounced "dead"; the oil-slicked Cuyahoga River caught fire; oil and chemical spills contaminated shorelines in California, France, and England, and rivers in many countries. Outdoor recreation areas were becoming overused and overcrowded. The growing pressure upon them was reported by the Outdoor Recreation Resources Review Commission in 1961. Risks to health, safety, and declines of wildlife, especially among birds, were attributed to misuse and abuse of toxic chemicals. A growing list of environmental insults could be expanded almost indefinitely. The frequency and diversity of environmental disasters was described as a "crisis." In certain circumstances this term was not a misnomer, but the environmental situation was fundamentally of greater scope, significance, and duration than the concept of a crisis would suggest.

Unfortunately politics in the United States tend to be dominated by a crisis mentality. Regardless of its intrinsic importance as measured by its ultimate consequences, an issue is seldom a priority unless it is a "crisis." For example, the prospect of global climate change might be regarded as having great policy significance. Yet a White House spokesman explaining the American refusal to commit to positive measures to reduce carbon dioxide emissions that were believed to contribute to global warming was quoted as saying: "Americans should take some comfort in the fact that we are not dealing with economic or security crises. This is not a moment of high drama."

Historians in the future will doubtless see the late 20th century as a "watershed" in human history. The assumptions and values that have dominated man-Earth relationships during modern times are beginning to be perceived as no longer sustainable. One-time-only fixes—technical or legal to overcome a crisis—will not suffice to meet the continuing challenge to humanity. There has persisted a belief that "the environmental crisis" of the late 1960s and early 1970s was a temporary circumstance, resulting from inadvertent neglect but correctable by targeted laws and regulations. As he signed NEPA on January 1, 1970, President Nixon declared:

> The nineteen-seventies absolutely must be the years when America pays its debt to the past by reclaiming the purity of its air, its waters and our living environment. It is literally now or never.[24]

Misconception of the "environmental problem" has been a major deterrent to a serious effort to implement NEPA. Acceptance of the environmental problem as an indefinitely continuing task for society would imply a major rearrangement of policy priorities. In 1977 in an address at Stanford University, Sir Eric Ashby set forth the environmental circumstances with which humanity will have to live henceforward. The following paragraph states the case:

> I believe that man's attitude to nature in Western societies has been changing almost imperceptibly over the last hundred years, and that the change is for the better. . . . I do not underestimate the perils threatening industrial society, though I think that some of the people who warn us about environmental crisis have got their perspectives wrong. Indeed, I think they are wrong to call it a crisis at all. A crisis is a situation that will pass; it can be resolved by temporary hardship, temporary adjustment, technological and political expedients. What we are experiencing is not a crisis: it is a climacteric. For the rest of man's history on earth, so far as one can foretell, he will have to live with problems of population, of resources, of pollution. And the seminal problem remains unsolved: Can man adapt himself to *anticipate*

environmental constraints? Or will he (like other animal societies) adapt himself only in *response* to the constraints after they have begun to hurt?[25]

If Lord Ashby's interpretation of a turning point in the relationship between modern society and the terrestrial environment is accepted, there follows an implied need to reconsider the values and perceptions that have brought humanity to this historical climacteric. Critical examination of values and perceptions relating to the natural world were undertaken decades before environmentalism emerged as a social and political movement. But the essentially economistic ethos that has dominated modern values and assumptions has not yet been replaced; rather, it has been modified and to some extent redirected.

A NEED FOR LEARNING

Misconceptions of virtual (apparent) reality have historically led to degradation, impoverishment, and collapse of environmental life-support systems as human societies have been confronted by the limits of veritable (verifiable) reality. Many miscalculations in human assumptions and behaviors are really attributable to lack of knowledge and may in part be corrected through experience (sometimes costly), or prevented through applications of scientific knowledge. A sustainable society will seek to learn which apparent barriers may be safely breached or extended and which limits cannot be transgressed—or which transgressions lead to unwanted consequences. In the world of veritable reality not all things are possible, and incidents of nonintentional environmental destruction should be infrequent.

A requisite for living and surviving within limits—some limits only apparent, others unsurmountable—is *learning*.[26] A basic task of implementing the principles of the National Environmental Policy Act is learning how they may be realized in action. This task is essential to NEPA's role in shaping a national agenda for the future and will be emphasized throughout this book. The most important but often unacknowledged purpose of environmental impact analysis and the resulting statement is to learn the effects of proposed action before experiencing its consequences. This purpose applies the old homily of "looking before leaping," and looking implies learning.

Human ingenuity in devising useful technologies has not always been matched by wisdom in application, and enthusiasm for innovation has seldom been tempered by insight and foresight. Progress toward these attributes of learning is necessary for realization of the values declared in NEPA and are more than implicit in Title II, Section 204(5) and (6), which authorize the CEQ:

> (5) to conduct investigations, studies, surveys, research, and analyses relating to ecological systems and environmental quality;

(6) to document and define changes in the natural environment, including plant and animal systems, and to accumulate necessary data and other information for a continuing analysis of these changes or trends and an interpretation of their underlying causes.

As a charter for shared learning, NEPA provides a convening and coordinating process under Title II, Section 205, which states that:

> In exercising its powers, functions, and duties under this Act, the Council shall—
>
> (1) Consult with the Citizens' Advisory Committee on Environmental Quality established by Executive Order No. 11472, dated May 29, 1969, and with such representatives of science, industry, agriculture, labor, conservation organizations, State and local governments and other groups, as it deems advisable; and
>
> (2) Utilize, to the fullest extent possible, the services, facilities and information (including statistical information) of public and private agencies and organizations, and individuals, in order that duplication of effort and expense may be avoided, thus assuring that the Council's activities will not unnecessarily overlap or conflict with similar activities authorized by law and performed by established agencies.

If these provisions have seldom been realized in action the fault is not in the legislation but in the secondary, and controversial status of the environment in American politics. In this respect NEPA appears to be ahead of present time—its time may yet come as educational efforts change the presently prevailing dominant view of reality. Although environmental education has been criticized by some miscalled conservatives who regard it as unsubstantiated and subversive, it has nevertheless accompanied the growth of environmental research, and may influence priorities in public opinion in future years.

The environmental education movement, worldwide in scope, has been sponsored by UNESCO, which reports activities and developments in the publication *Connect*. The North American Association for Environmental Education (NAAEE) is focused on learning at the primary and secondary levels. In the United States, the Environmental Education Act (Public Law 91.516, October 17, 1970) followed the enactment of NEPA, establishing the Office of Environmental Education, which provides for grants and contracts, and the Advisory Council on Environmental Education. This legislation was repealed in the Reagan antienvironmental reaction by PL 97-35 (August 13, 1981). But the office was restored by PL 101-619 (November 16, 1990), and a National Environmental Education and Training Partnership was established between the North American Association for Environmental Education and the Environmental Protection Agency.

At more advanced educational levels, schools of the environment and programs of environmental studies have been established in many colleges and universities. At least sixty American colleges and universities as of May 21, 1997, were listed on the Directory of Higher Education Environmental Programs (DHEEP), and a World Wide Web database of undergraduate and graduate interdisciplinary programs is maintained by the Committee for a National Institute for the Environment. Over eighty academic and professional education programs have been reported, a circumstance which augurs well for the future of environmental priorities in America. Among professional and scientific organizations formed for environmental concerns have been the National Association of Environmental Professionals, established in 1975; the International Association for Impact Assessment (which includes more than environmental impacts) in 1981; the International Society for Ecological Economics in 1988; and earlier, the International Council of Scientific Unions Scientific Committee on Problems of the Environment (SCOPE) in 1969. Nevertheless in the early years of the environmental movement many scientists (characteristically specialists) were skeptical of the factual soundness of environmentalism. By 1992, however, when the Union of Concerned Scientists issued the *World Scientists' Warning to Humanity*, signed by 1600 members of national or international science academies and 104 Nobel laureate scientists, all but a minority of professional contrarians accepted the proposition that serious problems were confronting humanity in its relationship with the world environment.[27]

But perhaps the most compelling force for environmental learning and legislation is political pressure from nongovernmental environmental membership organizations (NGOs). These volunteer associations now number in the hundreds throughout the world and are active in both national and international policy-making. Some, especially the World Conservation Union (IUCN), have worked with governments and United Nations agencies to develop a World Conservation Strategy. It has been estimated that at least 400 NGOs participated in an Environmental Forum co-incident with the United Nations Conference on the Human Environment convened in Stockholm in 1972; and at the United Nations Conference on Environment and Development meeting in Rio de Janeiro in 1992, at least 1800 NGOs were reported to have been present. Since Rio there has been an explosive growth of NGOs in "developing countries." A 1993 estimate places the number of NGOs in the world at 35,000. Not all are environmentally concerned, but many are and this may make a difference in international environmental affairs.[28]

In retrospect NEPA may now be seen as a major commitment to American involvement in a social and intellectual movement of worldwide dimensions. Unlike many policy pronouncements, NEPA's substantive provisions are not realizable at some fixed date. NEPA declares what should be done, but the diversity of circumstances requires that implementing action be authorized through other statutes, as in some cases has already happened (e.g. American Antiquities, Historic Preservation, Endangered Species, Coastal Zone Management, Wilderness Areas, etc.). Federal agencies are instructed to act in accord with NEPA's declared principles, and the action-forcing provisions under Section 102(2) are intended to assure agency attention to the precepts and values declared in the Preamble and Section 101 of the Act. However, as has been noted, there are impediments to translating NEPA values into agency practice.

Implementing NEPA requires a process of social learning which, although not in NEPA's text, implies a process of "public" education and persuasive teaching. How to achieve the outcomes declared in Section 101(b) is a task for the Federal agencies, the CEQ, and the nation. From our perspective one should not look for the precision and specificity that legalistic critics fault NEPA for failure to provide. NEPA is a summons to do what the nation has not yet done, and in order to realize the Act's objectives, the American people must learn how to translate its precepts into action.

The genius of NEPA is its potential for linkage of principle and process in legislation to transform the national ethos from the pioneer ethic to one of environmental custody and care. To use a convenient metaphor, NEPA is a statute of four dimensions:

(1) *Substantive*—a declaration of goals, principles, and values for Americans, to which their governments are expected to adhere;

(2) *Operative*—instructions to the Federal agencies of principles and procedures to be followed in plans, programs, and decisions having major impacts on the human environment—but not linked explicitly in the statute to the principles declared in Section 101.

(3) *Evaluative*—a means to reinforce and, where needed, to reform the values, perceptions, and behaviors of the American people in relation to their environment, which must henceforth be understood to encompass the planetary future.

(4) *Progressive*—its goals and principles, global and transgenerational, provide a foundation agenda for the future.

These dimensions summarize the significance of the unknown NEPA—a statute not to impose values on individual citizens, but to declare those environmental values that are necessary to sustain the quality of life along with a viable economy for present and future generations of Americans. Because the intent of NEPA has not been fully realized during the decades following its enactment does not justify its dismissal as substantially ineffectual. To evaluate NEPA solely on what it has thus far accomplished, or failed to accomplish, does not address its greater potential—to provide a foundation and agenda for America's future. The CEQ in January 1997 published a retrospective on NEPA—*The National Environmental Policy Act: A Study of Its Effectiveness After Twenty-Five Years.* The focus of this study was on "the effectiveness and efficiency of the NEPA process." In another review and assessment of NEPA, Richard N. L. Andrews has addressed the need to "spell out more specific criteria" to make the substantial goals of NEPA operational and to establish measurable benchmarks toward their attainment.[29] It is not the purpose of this book to "spell out" specific criteria for translating NEPA goals and precepts into action. That task, which requires inquiry into the urgency and interrelating of environmental problems, fulfills the purpose of NEPA but is beyond the scope of this book.

2

NEPA: Enactment and Interpretation

IN THE LAST FEW YEARS, IT HAS BECOME INCREASINGLY CLEAR
THAT SOON SOME PRESIDENT AND SOME CONGRESS MUST FACE THE
INEVITABLE TASK OF DECIDING WHETHER OR NOT THE OBJECTIVE OF
A QUALITY ENVIRONMENT FOR ALL AMERICANS IS A TOP-PRIORITY
NATIONAL GOAL WHICH TAKES PRECEDENCE OVER A NUMBER OF
OTHER, OFTEN COMPETING, OBJECTIVES IN NATURAL RESOURCE
MANAGEMENT AND THE USE OF THE ENVIRONMENT. IN MY JUDG-
MENT, THAT INEVITABLE TIME OF DECISION IS CLOSE UPON US.

—SENATOR HENRY M. JACKSON INTRODUCING A REPORT ON *A
NATIONAL POLICY FOR THE ENVIRONMENT*, JULY 11, 1968.

Few statutes of the United States are intrinsically more important
and less understood than is the National Environmental Policy Act of 1969.[1]
This comprehensive legislation, the first of its kind to be adopted by any
national government, and now widely emulated throughout the world, has
achieved notable results, yet its basic intent has not been fully achieved.[2] Its
purpose and declared principles have not yet been thoroughly internalized
in the assumptions and practices of American government. Nevertheless
there appears to be a growing consensus among the American people that
environmental quality is a public value, and that development of the economy does not require a trade-off between environmental quality and economic well-being. Voluntary compliance with NEPA principles may one day
become standard policy and procedure for government and business; meanwhile it is in the national interest to understand the historical developments
that led to NEPA and the subsequent course of its implementation. There
have been numerous and often contradictory evaluations of its intent and
effectiveness.

The legislative history of NEPA and the policy concepts it declared are
more extensive and accessible than some of its critics recognize. Treating
NEPA as if it were a special application of the Administrative Procedures
Act of 1946 misreads its principal purpose and misdirects criticism. NEPA
declares public values and directs policy, but it is not "regulatory" in the

ordinary sense. A decade of thought, advocacy, and negotiation in and out of Congress preceded the legislation of 1969. Dissatisfaction with NEPA and its implementing institution—the Council on Environmental Quality—should not be directed against this innovative and well-considered statute, but rather toward those authorities who have not seriously attempted to understand its purpose, to reinforce its administration, or to support its intent. This does not imply that a more explicit and extended revision of NEPA could never be enacted. But it cannot be successfully undertaken until a critical mass of the voting public acquiesces.

Through the judicially enforceable process of impact analysis, NEPA has significantly modified the environmental behavior of Federal agencies and, indirectly, of State and local governments and private undertakings. Relative to many other statutory policies, NEPA must be accounted an important success. But implementation of the substantive principles of national policy declared in NEPA requires a degree of political will not yet evident in the Congress or the White House. The public-at-large, which has received little help in understanding the purpose of the Act or the requirements for its implementation, has not audibly demanded that NEPA be put into effect.

A quarter-century, however, is a very short time for a new aspect of public policy—the environment—to attain the importance and priority accorded such century-old concerns as taxation, defense, education, civil liberties, and the economy. The goals declared in NEPA are as valid today as they were in 1969. Indeed, perhaps more so, as the Earth and its biosphere are stressed by human demands to a degree that has no precedent. But "environment" in its full dimensions is not easily comprehended. Human perceptions are culturally and physically limited, but science has been extending environmental horizons from the cosmic to the microcosmic. Even so, the word "environment" does not yet carry to most people the scope, complexity, or dynamic of its true dimensions.

If NEPA continues to be interpreted narrowly and exclusively by the courts, more compelling legislation may be required. A statutory or constitutional amendment may be necessary to give its substantive provisions operational legal status. Some defenders of NEPA fear that opening the statute to textual amendment might result in its being weakened, for example, through statutory exclusions that limit class-action suits based on NEPA or that would deny its applicability to Federal action that has an environmental impact beyond U.S. territorial limits. Its text unchanged, NEPA has already in effect been amended to exclude its application to major environment-affecting projects popular with the Congress (e.g. the Alaska oil pipeline). As of 1997 the U.S. Code listed at least 28 exceptions to the application of NEPA. Some were for clarification, however, and did not significantly affect the substance or intent of the Act. An amendment to the United States Constitution might strengthen the applicability of NEPA's substantive provisions to judicial review and executive implementation. Meanwhile for the NEPA intent to be more fully achieved, two developments will be necessary.

First is greatly increased popular comprehension of the purpose and principles of environmental policy as expressed in NEPA—especially by conservation and environmental groups, civic organizations, religious denominations, and political parties at the grass roots, along with the recognition, now beginning to appear in the world of business, that economic and environmental objectives need not be incompatible. NEPA principles, if rationally applied, would help sustain the future health of both the economy and the environment.

Second is appreciation by the Congress, the executive branch, the courts, and the news media of the political responsibilities and institutional arrangements necessary to fulfill the NEPA mandate. More visible commitments in the White House and at the top policy levels of the Federal agencies, and especially in the Congress, are needed. As long as candidates for Federal office are dependent on financing from sources seeking exploitation of the environment, support for NEPA in Congress and the White House is unlikely to be more than symbolic, and seldom invoked.

NEPA, however, contains means to achieve its purpose. Institutional arrangements for coordinating policies for natural resources and, by implication, the environment, underwent extensive consultations for at least a decade preceding NEPA, within and between both houses of Congress, with the Federal agencies, and with nongovernmental representatives of public interests. NEPA incorporated most of the provisions upon which general agreement had been reached. For example, since 1959 an overview and advisory council characterized nearly every proposal to establish a national policy for natural resources, conservation, or the environment.

HISTORICAL BACKGROUND

To better understand the purpose, politics, and potential of the National Environmental Policy Act, a brief retrospective of its origins and legislative history is necessary.[3] Terence T. Finn, the author of the most detailed account of the enactment of NEPA, writes that "for over ten years the concepts incorporated in Public Law 91-190 were developed, expressed, explained, forgotten, revised, advocated, opposed, and finally accepted."[4] Although our focus here is primarily on the interpretation of NEPA, the circumstances under which this legislation took shape decisively influenced both the timing of its enactment and its subsequent history.

The historical record of innovative ideas or changes in popular perceptions shows a lag-time between the emergence of new ways of thinking and their ultimate acceptance. The decade between the introduction of Senator James E. Murray's Resources and Conservation Act of 1959 in the 86th

Congress and passage of the National Environmental Policy Act of 1969 in the 91st Congress, was a relatively short interval for a major change in public policy, law, and the role of government. Expediting the pace of this change was the emergence of the environmental movement as a popular political force.

A conceptual foundation for the environmental movement had been building for several decades. Parallel to and to some extent within the conservation movement, an ecological concern was growing. Unlike the conservation movement, the concerns of which were essentially those of economy and efficiency, the emphasis on the environmental movement was on ecological relationships between man and nature and with the protection and preservation of the life-support system of the biosphere. The "biosphere" as a concept had become barely current in the 1920s, and few Americans were aware of the term. "Environment," as understood today, had very limited meaning prior to the 1960s. To Americans generally (and there were of course exceptions), the natural world was seen as an inexhaustible storehouse of raw materials, intended for human economic purposes.

The conservation movement sought to ensure the "wise use" of the potential wealth of nature. Although assumptions and objectives differed, there was some overlap between conservation and the emerging environmental movement. In the absence of the term "environment" to identify the new ecological perspective, President Lyndon Johnson spoke of "the new conservation," and his 1965 White House Conference on Natural Beauty was essentially concerned with environmental quality without the name.[5]

From the 1930s through the 1960s a science-based literature began to lay a foundation for popular concern leading toward environmental legislation. In 1956, a 1193 page report of an international symposium on *Man's Role in Changing the Face of the Earth* was published for the Wenner-Gren and National Science Foundations,[6] and in 1964 a nearly forgotten book, *Man and Nature*, by George Perkins Marsh was reprinted by Harvard University Press. Also, in 1965, the Conservation Foundation convened a conference on Future Environments of North America, the proceedings of which were published in 1966.[7] Books by Paul Sears (1935), William Vogt (1948), Fairfield Osborn (1948), Aldo Leopold (1949), and especially by Rachel Carson (1962) and Stewart Udall (1963) contributed cumulatively to a heightened public awareness of an endangered environment.

Although aesthetic and ethical values were prominent in the early popular literature of environmental protest, science and health were more frequently invoked. Scientific instrumentation permitted increasingly refined analyses of environmental effects—notably measurements of contaminants and carcinogens in air, water, soil, and food. During the 1950s and thereafter, apprehension over nuclear fallout from atmospheric weapons testing and growing opposition to risks of radiation from nuclear reactors were catalytic factors in inducing environmental awareness. All of the emerging environmental values were enhanced by the Apollo VIII astronauts, who provided humanity on Christmas Eve of 1968 with the first view of planet Earth from outer space. The concept of the Earth as a spaceship, although oversimplified, had a pervasive psychological effect upon public attitudes.

During the 1950s, 1960s, and 1970s, Congress enacted and upgraded laws intended to reduce air and water pollution.[8] By the 1960s environmental pollution had become a major public health concern. Reports of the Public Land Law Review Commission (1964–1970) and the Outdoor Recreation Resources Review Commission (1958–1962) informed popular concern regarding threats to the quality of the public domain and natural environment. Between 1964 and 1969 the American Medical Association sponsored six major conferences on environmental health. Here was an issue that had personal impacts translatable into political action. Sportsmen's groups such as the Isaac Walton League and Ducks Unlimited were angry over the contamination and unsightliness of lakes and streams, the filling and draining of wetlands, and the declining populations of waterfowl.

To a large number of people, including many congressmen, environment was a surrogate term for antipollution measures. It seems probable that many congressional votes for NEPA were cast on the assumption that the Act was essentially an antipollution statute. The news media generally shared this misconception. Not until after NEPA and the antipollution measures of the 1970s came into effect did Congress, the Federal agencies, and the public begin to discover the larger dimensions and implications of environmental legislation. Short of virtual unanimity, "congressional intent" indicates the votes of congressional majorities on any legislative proposition, even as a five to four majority of Supreme Court justices determines the law of the Constitution. Intent in government means the political position that prevails but does not reveal differences in motives and opinions among legislators or judges.

The legislative history of NEPA goes back at least to 1959 with the effort of Senator James E. Murray (Montana) to obtain consideration in the 86th Congress of his Resources and Conservation Act (S.2549). The Murray Bill contained several elements ultimately incorporated in NEPA—a declaration of policy, an advisory council in the Executive Office of the President, and an annual report. A joint committee of Congress was included in this and several subsequent bills. A joint committee was also considered in the drafting of NEPA, but could not overcome objections by the several committees of Congress claiming jurisdiction over all or parts of the proposed statute. Hearings on the Murray Bill were held in January 1960, and although the bill had thirty co-sponsors, it was opposed by the Eisenhower administration, by many Federal agencies, and by organized business. The Republican vice-president, Richard M. Nixon, then a presidential candidate, proposed the alternative of a council composed of cabinet secretaries—a forecast of his action as president in 1969 that established a cabinet-level council to head off the one proposed for NEPA.

Senator Murray did not seek reelection in 1960, but his bill was reintroduced in the 87th Congress by Senator Clair Engle (California). A similar bill (S.1415) was also introduced by Senator Gale McGee (Montana) but did not include provision for a joint committee. Hearings on these bills were held in April 1961 with the Kennedy administration and Federal agencies opposing both measures; neither bill was reported out of the Senate Interior Committee. Similar bills, which were introduced again by Senator McGee in 1963 and by Senator George McGovern (South Dakota) in 1965, received hearings. An "environmental problem" was widely acknowledged during these years, but dissatisfaction with worsening conditions was not yet firmly linked to political solutions. Because the problem was defined as conservation of natural resources, and pollution caused by mismanagement of the externalities of material production, the solution was seen as economic and technological. The economic perspective was taken in a 1962 report to President Kennedy on natural resources by the Committee on Natural Resources of the National Academy of Sciences-Natural Resource Council.[9] This report introduced the concept of "environment" as a natural resource, observing that "perhaps the most critical and most often ignored resource is man's total environment." The distinction between natural resources and the environment had not yet been drawn.

As late as the early 1960s, ecology as a science had not been regarded seriously by many "mainstream" scientists. But during the 1960s, the relevance, volume, and influence of ecological studies increased. The terms ecology and environmental science appeared in legislative proposals beginning in 1965 with introduction of Senator Gaylord Nelson's Ecological Research and Surveys Bill (S.2282). This bill did not come to vote, but similar provisions were incorporated in Title II of NEPA. The establishment of a council of environmental/ecological advisors continued to appear in proposed legislation, notably in 1966 in those bills introduced by Senator Henry M. Jackson and by Representative John Dingell. A council of ecological advisors was recommended to the Department of Health, Education, and Welfare by a task force report on *A Strategy for a Livable Environment* (1967).[10] The task force, chaired by Ron Linton, urged that the president submit to Congress a proposal for an Environmental Protection Act.

By the years 1967 and 1968 the environment had become an active legislative issue, distinguished from natural resources and conservation. During the 90th and 91st Congresses as many as forty separate proposals relating to environmental policy and protection were introduced. Meanwhile a number of reports on environmental policy were issued by congressional committees.

On June 17, 1968, the House Subcommittee on Science, Research, and Development chaired by Emilio Q. Daddario transmitted a report to the Committee on Science and Astronautics titled *Managing the Environment*.[11] The report did not propose specific legislation, but summarized previous hearings and comments of staff and advisors, and listed the principal relevant legislative proposals before Congress. On July 11, 1968, the report *A National Policy for the Environment* was published for the Committee on Interior and Insular Affairs.[12] This report, which I prepared with assistance from William Van Ness, made the case for a national policy as expressed primarily in Senator Jackson's bill S. 2805 (subsequently reintroduced as S.1075).

On July 17, 1968, a Joint House-Senate colloquium was held on a National Policy for the Environment.[13] Its purpose was to avoid issues of congressional committee jurisdiction and to bring together members of the Congress with executive branch heads and leaders of industrial, commercial, academic, and scientific organizations. The colloquium helped to raise congressional awareness of the environmental policy issue and to legitimize it as a concern of the entire Congress as contrasted with the exclusive jurisdictional interests of specific committees. A *Congressional White Paper*[14] reported the proceedings of the colloquium and documented the broadening of legislative concern.

In the 91st Congress, Senator Jackson's S. 2805 was reintroduced as S.1075. The only Senate hearing on this bill occurred on April 16, 1969.[15] In retrospect, the notable event on this occasion was the introduction of the concept of an environmental impact statement. The need for an action-forcing provision to obtain compliance from the Federal agencies had been recognized by committee staff and other commentators on environmental protection legislation. As consultant to the committee and a committee witness, in response to a question by Senator Jackson, I said that a declaration of environmental policy must be operational to be effective—written so that its principles could not be ignored. I urged that "a statement of policy by the Congress should at least consider measures to require Federal agencies in submitting proposals, to contain within the proposals an evaluation of their effect upon the state of the environment."[16] This action-forcing provision (Section 102(2)(c)) could be reviewed by the courts, supplementing the anticipated questionable implementation of NEPA in the Executive branch. Detailed language for the impact statement requirement was drafted by Interior Committee staff member Daniel A. Dreyfus and counsel William Van Ness.

During 1969, strategic maneuvers occurred in the House and Senate between competing legislative proposals and rival legislative jurisdictions. In the Senate, disagreements between Jackson and Muskie and staffs of the Committee on Public Works and the Committee on Interior and Insular Affairs threatened delay of Jackson's bill S.1075, which was moving into a lead position. Senator Jackson and his principal counsel on environmental policy, William Van Ness, proved to be the better legislative tacticianers. On July 9, 1969, S.1075 was reported by the Interior Committee and placed on the Senate calender. With swiftness not anticipated by most members of the Senate, S.1075 was called up the next day, July 10, under the "consent calendar" during the "morning hour"—a period set aside for routine matters before the beginning of the principal business of the day. The Act was passed without debate and no amendments were offered. Similar legislation introduced by Representative Dingell was frustrated by jurisdictional conflict in the House which delayed action on his proposals. In May and June 1969, Dingell had held hearings on bills to establish a Council on Environmental Quality.[17] In subsequent negotiations and the House-Senate Conference on S.1075 a number of Dingell's ideas were incorporated in Public Law 91-190.

A House-Senate Conference Committee meeting in December 1969 resolved differences between Jackson's and Dingell's bills.[18] On December 20 the Conference Report on S.1075 passed the Senate, and on December 22, the day before the House adjourned sine die, the Conference Report passed the House. NEPA as enacted closely resembled the original S.1075.

On January 1, 1970, President Nixon signed NEPA into law, an Act that with remarkable coherence embodied the principles and institutional arrangements that had been proposed, debated, and redefined during the preceding decade. Of the leading proposals during these years only the Joint Committee of the Congress failed to be included. A new element, however, was added in the requirement of an environmental evaluation of all Federal agency proposals or actions having a significant impact upon the environment. This provision became the most influential and widely emulated feature of the Act. Its effectiveness, however, depended upon judicial review of agency compliance. As a mandatory procedure required of Federal agencies in actions having a major impact upon the environment, the courts could hold the agencies to strict compliance with the law, whereas on the policy or substantive provisions of NEPA, the courts have generally deferred to agency discretion.

DECLARATION OF NATIONAL POLICY

The most important and least appreciated provision of NEPA is the congressional declaration of national policy under Title I, Section 101, that

> it is the continuing policy of the Federal government, in cooperation with State and local governments, and other concerned public and private organizations, to use all practicable means and measures, including financial and technical assistance, in a manner calculated to foster and promote the general welfare, to create and maintain conditions under which man and nature can exist in productive harmony, and fulfill the social, economic, and other requirements of present and future generations of Americans.

Seven specific aspects of policy are enumerated, and while necessarily stated in general terms, they are hardly vague in purpose. Section 101(b) states that:

> in order to carry out the policy set forth in this Act, it is the continuing responsibility of the Federal government to use all practicable means, consistent with other essential considerations of national policy, to improve and coordinate Federal plans, functions, programs, and resources to the end that the nation may
>
> (1) fulfill the responsibilities of each generation as trustee of the environment for succeeding generations;
>
> (2) assure for all Americans safe, healthful, productive, and aesthetically and culturally pleasing surroundings;
>
> (3) attain the widest range of beneficial uses of the environment without degradation, risk to health or safety, or other undesirable and unintended consequences;
>
> (4) preserve important historic, cultural, and natural aspects of our national heritage, and maintain, wherever possible, an environment which supports diversity, and variety of individual choice;
>
> (5) achieve a balance between population and resource use which will permit high standards of living and a wide sharing of life's amenities; and
>
> (6) enhance the quality of renewable resources and approach the maximum attainable recycling of depletable resources.

In addition the Congress recognized that "each person should enjoy a healthful environment and that each person has a responsibility to contribute to the preservation and enhancement of the environment."

These six goals were formulated through staff discussions in the Congress. They reflected a range of popular concern and the need and purpose of a national policy set forth in *A National Policy for the Environment: A Report on the Need for a National Policy for the Environment: An Explanation of Its Purpose and Content; An Explanation of Means to Make It Effective; and a Listing of Questions Implicit in Its Establishment* (July 11, 1968). In the event that a statutory policy should not prove feasible, a *Draft Resolution on a National Policy for the Environment* was appended to the *Report* and listed the following four objectives:

> 1. To arrest the deterioration of the environment.
>
> 2. To restore and revitalize damaged areas of our Nation so that they may once again be productive of economic wealth and spiritual satisfaction.
>
> 3. To find alternatives and procedures which will minimize and prevent future hazards in the use of environment-shaping technologies, old and new.

4. To provide direction, and if necessary, new institutions, and new technologies designed to optimize man-environment relationships and to
minimize future costs in the management of the environment.

The NEPA Declaration clearly implies that economic and environmental
quality are or should be compatible. A key to understanding NEPA may be
found in the phrase "to create and maintain conditions under which man
and nature can exist in productive harmony, and fulfill the social, economic,
and other requirements of present and future generations of Americans."
This statement has often been interpreted to require a balancing of equities,
primarily economic and environmental. But the intent of NEPA would not
be achieved by off-setting (but still retaining) an economic "bad" with an
environmental "good," as mitigating measures may attempt. More consistent
with the spirit of the Act would be a synthesis in which "productive harmony" is attained and transgenerational equity is protected.

Beneath the language of the Declaration there are fundamental questions
of jurisprudence and constitutional responsibility that, bearing upon the implementation of NEPA, have not generally been addressed: Does the Declaration establish a policy by law? If the statute, in fact, is a declaration of law
as well as policy, what then are the responsibilities of the president under
Article II of the Constitution that "he shall take care that the laws be faithfully
executed?" And what are the responsibilities of the Congress to see that a
policy declared by a Congress and not repealed, is not sabotaged or neglected
in the Executive branch or by its own committees?

Critics of NEPA have found its substantive provisions nonjustifiable, and
by implication not positive law. The courts have refrained generally from
overturning administrative decisions that could be interpreted as incompatible with the substantive provisions of NEPA. However, in the case of *Calvert
Cliffs Coordinating Committee v. Atomic Energy Commission,* Judge Skelly Wright
of the U.S. Circuit Court of Appeals of the District of Columbia declared:

> The reviewing courts probably cannot reverse a substantive decision on its
> merits, under Section 101, unless it can be shown that the actual balance of
> costs and benefits that was struck was arbitrary or clearly gave insufficient
> weight to environmental values. But if the decision was reached procedur-
> ally without individualized consideration and balancing of environmental
> factors, conducted fully and in good faith, it is the responsibility of the
> courts to reverse.[19]

The generally recessive posture of the courts on the policy provisions of
NEPA contrasts markedly with their activist policymaking in constitutional
civil and property rights cases. In these cases Federal judges have not hesi-
tated to assert sweeping jurisdiction over all levels of government in which
official action or inaction was found to be at variance with judicial opinion.

A plausible explanation for this contrast is the absence of any direct provision in the Constitution of the United States for environmental protection, in contrast to explicit provisions for property rights and civil rights in the Fifth and Fourteenth Amendments. Where the Congress has mandated or prohibited specific actions affecting air and water pollution or endangered species and provided penalties for violations, the courts have reviewed and enforced if no infringement of constitutional rights is found. Presumably they would do so for any of NEPA's substantive policy mandates for which Congress provided specific procedures and penalties not subject to judicial reversal.

Section 101 of NEPA establishes the principles and goals of environmental policy and is, in essence, a declaration of values. It is difficult to adjudicate values, but legislation implementing principles also expressed in NEPA and applied to specific tangible policies has been reviewed and upheld in the courts. The Historic Preservation Act (PL 89-665, October 15, 1966) and the Endangered Species Act (PL 93-205, December 28, 1973) are examples. Substantive mandates in these and other environmental statutes are or could be reinforced by the substantive and procedural provisions of NEPA.

Beyond the judiciary there is another recourse to enforce the principles of NEPA—in the constitutional obligation of the president "to take care that the laws be faithfully executed." The president rarely needs a court opinion to use residual executive power to apply the law; the presidency possesses broad executive discretion over implementation of the laws by the Federal agencies. A president whose priorities coincided with NEPA's principles, absent blocking in the Congress or the courts, could by executive action go a long way toward fulfilling the NEPA mandates.

THE CASE FOR A NATIONAL POLICY

From the viewpoint of traditional constitutional conservatism, environment in the broad sense was not a comprehensible subject for public policy—at least for national policy. Strict constitutional constructionist Thomas Jefferson did not even believe that highway construction was an appropriate function of the Federal government. For environmental nuisances, such as air or water pollution, common law remedies were available under state police powers, and prior to the 1960s were widely regarded as local issues.

Emergence of environment as a public and national issue followed from profound changes in the population and economy of the United States in the course of the 20th century. These changes were accompanied by unprecedented growth of scientific knowledge and technology. Progress of this new industrial society increasingly encountered and created environmental problems with which neither local government nor the market economy could cope. Quality-of-life values in health, amenities, and opportunities were being lost or threatened and the causes transcended artificial political jurisdictions.

Only the Federal government had the geographic scope and institutional structure able to deal with the growing array of interrelating problems now called "environmental." These problems of air, water, resource conservation, and the biosphere were soon seen to be transnational, but national government was the only available institution sufficiently inclusive and authoritative to deal with them. International cooperation depended upon the ability and willingness of national governments to address common regional and global environmental problems, and so by the mid-20th century, environment began to emerge as a new focus for public policy.

Broad statements of policy and principle that are not perceived to affect personal interests or property rights seldom arouse much public concern or response. Issues that do elicit popular concern almost always affect the present and personal advantages or apprehensions of people. Attitudes relating to the environment in modern American society have been largely issue-specific and subjective. People do not live lives of generality and objectivity; they live in the present and are concerned primarily with matters directly affecting their interests and values, which may range from local to international. But effective response to circumstances in the larger societal and biospheric environments necessarily must be collective, with whole communities or an organized "critical mass" of the society activated. Stratospheric ozone depletion, global climate change, or tropical deforestation are hardly neighborhood or personal issues which people might feel that their actions could influence. And while nongovernmental organizations may help in many ways to assist environmental protection, the ultimate agent of public interests affecting all of the United States is the Federal government. State and county boundaries are environmentally artificial, corresponding to neither ecosystems nor bioregions, and seldom to economic activities that are increasingly interstate, nationwide, and transnational in scope.

NEPA, supplementing the legislative powers of the Federal government over interstate commerce, navigable waters, and public lands, creates an obligation to apply its provisions where relevant. Thus applications for Federal permits, licenses, purchases, concessions, and grants may require the preparation of environmental impact assessments required by NEPA. This application of NEPA is weakened, however, by interpretations of the EIS requirement as not applying to state licensing or permitting, implementing so-called "delegated programs." Thus the greater number of permits issued by the states are exempt from NEPA. Wetland 464 permitting, however, is subject to NEPA. For other environmental policies the president, through Executive Orders, may instruct the agencies in the performance of their functions, as President Carter did in giving legal status to the NEPA Regulations of the CEQ (EO 11991, May 24, 1977) and, paralleling NEPA in Federal activities abroad, in EO 12114, January 4, 1979.

The volunteer conservation and environmental organizations have seldom made effective use of the NEPA Declaration and Section 101. It may be that not all officers of these nongovernmental organizations have fully understood the Act or appreciated its potential beyond the impact statement requirement. Nevertheless, NGOs have played major roles in protecting environmental quality. Without referring to NEPA, their actions have often promoted NEPA objectives. But as voluntary civic organizations they depend upon dues-paying members for funding and credibility. Their appeals for membership and money are intended to mobilize opposition to specific threats that can be easily comprehended and communicated. The principled, generalized, and (to some) abstract provisions of the NEPA Declaration do not rally constituents who more readily respond to action appeals to stop that dam, ban timbering in the Tongass, save the Everglades, preserve the rain forests, or prohibit toxic substances.

The issue-specific focus on environmental policy may offer at least a partial explanation for the initial support (later retracted) by most of the nation's large volunteer environmental organizations for the Clinton administration's intention to abolish the CEQ and transfer its oversight of NEPA to a cabinet-level Department of Environmental Protection in 1993. A nonstatutory environmental policy office administered by White House staff was proposed, presumably eliminating most of the functions specified for the CEQ under Title II of the Act. The leaders of environmental organizations were motivated to support a Democratic administration that appeared more responsive to their concerns than the preceding Republican administrations, and they hoped to see a cabinet-level department for the environment.

Although "mainstream" environmental nongovernmental organizations tacitly supported Senator Jackson's bill at the time of its enactment, they subsequently showed interest in NEPA primarily as the environmental impact requirement that enabled them to stop or delay specific government programs or projects to which they objected. It is not apparent that the CEQ consistently reached out to these organizations or undertook to explain its purpose or functions to them. Accordingly, when on April 1, 1993, the Senate Committee on Environment and Public Works held a hearing on "Abolishing the Council on Environmental Quality,"[20] no environmental organization appeared in protest—and statements from them were introduced in support of the president's action. Had the CEQ met periodically with the heads of the principal environmental organizations (and also with representatives of the news media) the purpose of NEPA and the role of the CEQ might have been better understood. A tactical problem for CEQ outreach, however, is that its constituency is nationwide and the immediate political concerns of most citizens are "local," although in principle many show concern for the nation's environmental legacy. Contrary to the allegations of some critics of environmental policy, the CEQ is not the particular agent of "environmentalists." It represents widely held values and a national interest; the environment in its many aspects is everyone's business.

INTENTION OF THE FRAMERS

The argument for a national policy, and hence an indicator of intent, was set forth in the report on *A National Policy for the Environment*, which, assisted by William Van Ness, I prepared in the summer of 1968 at the request of Senator Jackson for the Senate Committee on Interior and Insular Affairs. This document was reprinted in the report on a *Joint House-Senate Colloquium to Discuss the Need for a National Policy for the Environment* (July 17, 1968).[21] At that time there were three options for establishing a national policy for the environment: (1) a joint resolution of the Congress, (2) a statute, and (3) a constitutional amendment. A statute appeared to be the most effective and attainable choice, and bills were already being drafted in the House and Senate.

A constitutional bill of rights (several had been proposed) was rejected as requiring a protracted process of uncertain result, and doubt regarding whether right to a "healthful" or "decent" environment could be judicially defined. A joint resolution would not bind government agencies to compliance although a suggested draft was appended to the 1968 Senate report on *A National Policy for the Environment*. The most reliable strategy for a realizable national policy was through the authority of Congress and the president over the actions of the Federal agencies. The Congress had no explicit constitutional authority to legislate environmental policy per se. But Congress and the president did have the authority to define and direct the policies and actions of the Federal agencies. Because Federal missions collectively impinged directly or indirectly upon almost every aspect of American society, an environmental protection statute could be enacted that would be both effective and constitutional. Moreover, a statutory declaration of national policy could at least in theory be morally binding upon the Legislative and Executive branches. But it was not foreseen that the substantive intent declared in NEPA would not be binding on the judiciary or regarded as obligatory by the Congress or the president.

In various ways and degrees many members of Congress participated in the framing of NEPA. Critical roles were played by Senators Jackson, Nelson, and Muskie, and Representatives Dingell, George Miller, and Daddario. Legislation in both the Senate and the House was complicated by rivalries over committee jurisdiction. Faced with complications and procrastination by House leadership, Dingell, through perseverance, obtained jurisdiction over a bill (HR 6750) which would have established an independent Council on Environmental Quality that was "free from partisan politics, free from Cabinet imperatives, and free from sectional viewpoints."

The framers of NEPA did not assume that placing the CEQ in the Executive Office would cause the president to embrace NEPA principles or give the environment a prominent place on his agenda. Richard Nixon had opposed locating the CEQ in the Executive Office and had appointed a Cabinet-level council to head off NEPA. Defeated in the effort, he accepted NEPA with good grace and appointed Council members whose qualifications matched those specified in Title II of the statute. Neither Congress nor the courts can determine the president's interests or priorities; Article II, Section 3 of the Constitution specifies among his duties that "he shall take care that the laws be faithfully executed." Thus the implementation of NEPA depends upon the role of the president in relation to the Executive Office of the President (notably to the CEQ), and the Environmental Protection Agency. Specific aspects of environmental policy are administered by other agencies (e.g. Agriculture, Interior, Defense, Transportation, and Energy) but NEPA is the overall "umbrella" environmental statute for the nation, and the CEQ and the EPA are its oversight agencies.

The language of the Act and location of the CEQ in the Executive Office were intended to ensure that the national policies declared by Congress were not ignored or subverted by successive presidential incumbents, their White House staffs, or the cabinet-level departments. An unsympathetic president may nevertheless diminish the effectiveness of NEPA and the CEQ by use of the presidential powers of appointment and budgetary initiative—as occurred under the administration of Ronald Reagan. The framers appeared to have assumed (or hoped) that successive congresses would be protective of a statute enacted by an earlier (91st) Congress. But the performance of the Congress has been mixed. It has declined (narrowly) to abolish the CEQ, but it has not acted to uphold Title II requirements of NEPA. Appointees to the Council have not always possessed the high qualifications stated in Title II of the Act and Presidents Reagan, Bush, and Clinton have failed to appoint councillors as provided by the law—and the Senate has acquiesced. Diminishing budget allocations to the CEQ seem intended to marginalize its effectiveness. A long-practiced political strategy to rid an administration of an unwanted agency is to deny it adequate personnel and funding, to veto its initiatives, and then to call for its abolition because it has been ineffective. It is a transparent policy that often works.

The framers of NEPA intended a consistent but evolving national policy that was nonpartisan and that drew upon the best available science. The 91st Congress by its own declaration established principles of environmental policy and administration with which subsequent Congresses and future presidents would be expected to comply. But it is beyond the competence of any Congress to ensure that subsequent Congresses or successive presidents will honor commitments which they have not made but have inherited.

Upon its enactment NEPA was widely misconstrued as an antipollution law. The *New York Times* headlined its report of the signing of NEPA by

President Nixon as "Nixon Promises an Urgent Fight to End Pollution."[22] Few news-media reporters appear to have even read the law despite its extraordinary brevity. With judicial enforcement of Section 102(2)(c), widespread opinion developed that the writing of impact statements was the primary purpose and intent of NEPA. Even the editors of the prestigious journal *Science* appeared to have concurred with this misinterpretation.

This limited understanding of NEPA has been reinforced by comment in many law journals and judicial opinions.[23] The concept of a policy act, as distinguished from regulatory legislation, appears to have been lost on these commentators. The substantive provisions of Section 101 have been dismissed, in effect, as idealistic rhetoric, as administratively inoperable and as judicially unenforceable. Yet the language of Section 101 is explicit and mandatory. Although the courts have generally conceded the interpretation of NEPA's substantive provisions to the Executive agencies, this judicial concession in no way removes these provisions from statutory law or from the responsibilities of the president. The substantive provisions of NEPA are enforceable through Executive Orders and through other statutes, judicially reviewable, as is presently the case with acts establishing mandatory obligations upon the agencies (e.g. protection of antiquities, endangered species, and wetlands).

PURPOSE AND FUNCTIONS OF THE CEQ

The Council on Environmental Quality is integral to the National Environmental Policy Act of 1969.[24] To margialize or to eliminate the role of the CEQ would be to diminish NEPA as an instrument of national policy. As adopted in 1969, NEPA initiated an unprecedented and comprehensive innovation. No other nation had enacted so comprehensive an environmental statute. No experience provided guidance in its implementation. As previously noted, popular concern for the environment had grown rapidly during the late 1960s and had been frequently expressed in demands for a council of ecological or environmental advisors to guide the development and implementation of government policy for the environment.

The Council of Economic Advisers (CEA) established by the Employment Act of 1946 was the model most often suggested and, since 1959, numerous bills had been proposed to establish a high-level natural resources or conservation council comparable to the CEA. It was intended that this council identify important natural resources issues, monitor environmental effects, assess trends, and advise the president and Congress on appropriate action. But no law could compel the president or the Congress to seek or receive advice, especially advice that could embarrass political priorities.

Most proposals for establishing a policy for natural resources and environment adopted the concept of the advisory council, and the Council of Economic Advisers provided an established model. On certain critical points the language of NEPA is identical to the language of Section 4 of the Employment Act. The requirement "with the advice and consent of the Senate" implies a Congressional concern for the actions of the councils. Neither the CEA nor the CEQ were constituted as the personal agents of the president, and they were not domiciled in the White House.

A significant difference between the two councils is the establishment of a Congressional Joint Committee on the Economic Report (of the CEA) and the absence of such a joint committee in NEPA. A Joint Committee on the Environment was urged by some of the drafters of NEPA but was opposed by the chairmen of existing committees with claims to jurisdiction over all or parts of NEPA and environmental policy. The joint committee concept was rejected by Senator Jackson, who could see that a jurisdictional fight over environmental policy-making could endanger enactment of his bill. Since 1980, presidents have not treated the CEQ as a council, appointing only a chairman, and from 1993 to 1995 no chairman. In as much as the CEQ serves at the pleasure of the president and there is no joint oversight committee in Congress with explicit responsibility for NEPA, there appears to be no compelling means to persuade the president to appoint a full council.

To accommodate the inconsistency between law and practice, the Congress stipulated in the 1988 appropriations bill that, notwithstanding the provisions of the National Environmental Policy Act, there would be for fiscal year 1988 just one member of the Council on Environmental Quality (instead of three), and that individual would act as chairman. The politics of the day prevails over the intent of the law. The operational functions of the CEQ appear to have been well administered under a single head. To the extent that the CEQ performs an interpretative or quasi-adjudicative function, there remains an argument for a full council. The supreme court has held that interpretations of NEPA by the CEQ are entitled to substantial deference.[25]

Political realities limit the functions of the CEQ in implementation of Title II of NEPA and the CEQ in relation to the economy. The CEA fares better in a Congress in which "economism" or the predominance of economic values is an ingrained ideology, whereas "environmentalism" is controversial. The chairman of the Federal Reserve Board may have more influence on national economic policy than the CEA, and many congressmen appear to regard the Environmental Protection Agency as sufficient to deal with such functions stipulated for the CEQ as they are willing to have performed (forecasting for the future is not one of them). Economic policy affects most people less directly than do environmental policies, many of which collide directly with economic expectations and interests that congressmen regard as the political life blood of their constituencies. Neither the president nor the Congress is easily persuaded to defer judgments on controversial environmental issues to an independent council.

The inference to be drawn from a comparison of the CEA and the CEQ is that the former represents a high presidential priority and the latter, regardless of claims to be "an environment president," has been relatively low on the scale of presidential attention. Great disparities in budget requests for Executive Office agencies show where presidential priorities lie. No president would think of abolishing the CEA, even when its members do not view the economy from precisely the same perspective as the president. But abolition of the CEQ was attempted in the Carter and Clinton administrations, and budgetary starvation severely limited its functions during the Reagan years.

Because environmental considerations cut across the jurisdictional boundaries of most cabinet level and independent agencies, and because presidential authority is necessary (and by the Constitution required) to execute the laws, the CEQ is located appropriately to fulfill its obligations under NEPA. But if the environment is perceived as a policy area of less than presidential significance, its location in the EOP may be regarded as inappropriate. The latter opinion appears to be held among some highly placed governmental and academic commentators.

An example of a narrowly focused and underinformed view of environmental policy among otherwise competent Washington officials and advisors appears in the report of a panel of the National Academy of Public Administration (NAPA) chaired by former Controller-General Elmer B. Staats. In a report on *The Executive Presidency: Federal Management for the 1990s* (1988), commenting on the future of the Executive Office of the President, the report declared:

> The Panel is concerned about the growth of special purpose offices in the EOP, such as the Council on Environmental Quality, which represent certain special functions or constituencies but contribute little to fulfilling the president's broad responsibilities for national policy making and implementation.

The Panel's report reveals incomprehension of the environmental issue. By the Panel's reasoning the departments of Agriculture, Commerce, and Labor might be misplaced at the cabinet level, having a more specialized clientele than does the environment which, like the economy, directly affects everyone regardless of interest. The Panel members were largely experienced and distinguished public officials, but the viewpoint expressed was that of conventional myopic bureaucratic conservatism.

The opinion of the Panel exemplifies the lack of institutional memory, indifference to legislative history, and disregard for prior experience that has too often characterized prominent political personalities. There is no evidence in the Academy Panel report that the staffers who prepared it made any serious inquiry into the history or rationale of the CEQ or that the panelists sought informed independent opinion on the subject. A similar "establishment" panel for advising the president—"Harnessing Process to Purpose" (1992), convened by the Carnegie Endowment for International Peace and the International Institute for Economics, also recommended abolition of the CEQ. An informed evaluation of these panel reports leads to the observation that prestige in the public milieu does not necessarily correlate with insight or comprehending judgment in all aspects of public policy. It appears that these panels concerned with reorganizing the presidential office conceived the proper role of advisor to the president to be performed by individual appointees subordinate to and answering to the president in preference to an independent council with deliberative responsibilities. At the April 16, 1969, hearing on S.1075, Senator Jackson in reference to the CEQ said, "It is my view that what is needed is an impartial, objective full-time Council of Environmental Advisors in the Executive Office of the President 'to provide the president with independent and impartial advice as to what action to take.'" "The Council I have proposed," Jackson said "would be properly staffed and equipped to provide this advice." Jackson's opinion reflected ten years of congressional inquiry and concurrence over the best way to coordinate Federal policy for natural resources and the environment. It seems doubtful if this experience was evaluated by or even known to the staff that drafted the reports of the blue-ribbon advisory panels.

The placement of the statutory CEQ in the Executive Office of the President was motivated by two considerations: first, the NEPA applied to all Federal agencies, cutting across departmental jurisdictions. It could not appropriately be administered by any one department which would be expected to apply its oversight provisions to other, presumably coequal, departments. Interagency conflict would be almost inevitable. Second, the president is the constitutional executor of Federal law and has the power and responsibility to direct compliance with the law by agencies within the Executive Branch. But American jurisprudence appears unclear concerning how the president fulfills his constitutional obligation to take care that laws be faithfully executed.

It is sufficient here to observe that locating the CEQ in the Executive Office of the President was intended to facilitate the advisory role of the CEQ to the president, the agencies, and the Congress. Agencies comprising the Executive Office were regarded by Franklin D. Roosevelt's President's Committee on Administrative Management as the central managerial and coordinative agencies of the Federal government encompassing budget, personnel, planning, and administrative management.[26] Although intended to facilitate the executive functions of the president in the implementation of national policies, appointees to the central managerial agencies were not regarded as his personal political aides. The White House staff was "invented" by the Committee for that function.

In recent years this distinction between the White House staff and the

Executive Office of the President appears to have been lost. Although intended to assist the president in the discharge of his managerial duties, a broader governmental responsibility was implied in the statutory specification of qualifications for appointment as the principal officers of these central agencies. For appointment to the CEQ (subject to confirmation by the Senate), Title II requires that

> Each member shall be a person who, as a result of his training, experience, and attainments, is exceptionally well qualified to analyze and interpret environmental trends and information of all kinds; to appraise programs and activities of the Federal government in the light of the policies set forth under Title I of this Act; be conscious of and responsive to scientific, economic, social, and cultural needs and interests of the Nation; and to formulate and recommend national policies to promote the improvement of the quality of the environment.

This language closely follows that establishing the CEA. No comparable standards are required for appointment by the president to the White House staff.

The CEQ is integral to the purpose and the intended implementation of NEPA. The legislative history of NEPA and its antecedents shows clearly that an advisory council with powers of initiative was regarded as advantageous to the shaping and monitoring of a national policy for natural resources and the environment. The reasons for a highly qualified deliberative council rather than a single nonstatutory administrator were spelled out repeatedly. They appear to have been overlooked by the Clinton proposal to replace the CEQ with a nonstatutory White House office. But the functioning of the tripartite council has been complicated by interpretation of the Government in the Sunshine Act (PL 94-409) of 1976. The cumbersome procedures required by this legislation handicap the Council's deliberations and advisory role to the president. The convenient presidential response (as previously noted) has been to reduce the Council to a single chairperson— hardly a council. This arrangement has proved convenient for presidential budget and political priorities but alters the intended role of the CEQ, effectively reducing its deliberative functions and Title II responsibilities.

IMPLEMENTING ACTION-FORCING PROVISIONS

The implementing and action-forcing provisions of NEPA are primarily in Title I, Section 102. Implementation is also provided for in Sections 103 and 105[27] and in the (largely unfulfilled) functions specified for the CEQ under Sections 204 and 205.[28] The provision requiring the President's *Environmental Quality Report* (Section 201) underscores NEPA as national policy. Implementing NEPA, in principle, does not appear to be a discretionary presidential policy, although how the president fulfills his constitutional responsibility in practice is largely, but not exclusively, a matter for his decision. Article I of the Constitution vests legislative power in the Congress and this would imply congressional power to ensure that the "legislative intent" is not ignored or transgressed. But a "legislative intent" does not transfer automatically from congress to congress.

Because Section 102(2)(c) imposes a mandatory performance requirement on Federal agencies, its implementation is reviewable by the courts. As noted, this action-forcing provision, the Environmental Impact Statement (EIS, considered in chapter 3), was not present in earlier drafts of NEPA. The concept was introduced in a public hearing on April 16, 1969, before the Senate Committee on Interior and Insular Affairs. Senator Jackson, Committee chairman and principal sponsor of the Senate bill, agreed with Committee staff that without a justifiable provision the Act might be no more than a pious resolve which the Federal bureaucracy could ignore with impunity. There was also a well-founded doubt that the president could be relied upon to enforce the Act.

Recognizing the novelty of the EIS, and lack of experience with its implementation, some Committee staff urged that provision be made and funds provided to help the agencies learn how to fulfill their responsibilities under Section 102. This proposal, however, was not accepted in the appropriation of funds for implementing NEPA. To have run up the initial cost of NEPA might have jeopardized its passage in the Congress.

After consultation with the agencies, the CEQ undertook to remedy this lack of experience with impact analysis by issuing guidelines. But the impact statement requirement was widely regarded in the agencies as extraneous to their mission functions regardless of the language of NEPA. As a consequence, action relating to the EIS was too often misdirected, inadequate, and irrelevant to agency planning and decision-making. Lacking effective interpretation, the purpose of NEPA was widely construed to be preparation of impact statements to avoid reversals in the courts. This was notably so after the judicial decision in the *Calvert Cliffs* (1971) case.[29] The agencies, in theory, were to be held to strict compliance with the EIS mandatory procedures specified by NEPA. And these mandates applied to all actions of major environmental significance subsequent to the date upon which NEPA became effective, January 1, 1970, and to projects and policies in effect as of that date regardless of their previous authorization or state of completion, as the court held in the *Gillham Dam* case in 1972.[30]

Some observers hailed NEPA as an environmental Magna Carta; others ridiculed the EIS as a "boondoggle" for underemployed ecologists and, dismissing its history and intent, declared it to be a disaster to the environmental protection movement. An adjunct scholar of the American Enterprise Institute opined, probably with regret, that "NEPA turned out to be much more than a symbol."[31] Following further experience with the EIS, Executive

Order 11991 (1977) was issued by President Carter, which enabled the CEQ to adopt uniform regulations to enhance the informative value of the EIS, to coordinate its implementation across agency lines, and to remedy earlier inadequacies and misuse—many of which resulted from inexperienced fumbling attempts to meet the NEPA mandate.

Some agencies made an early show of compliance; others sought to evade EIS requirements as irrelevant to their missions, or to satisfy the courts through minimal pro forma procedures. Unequivocal White House and Office of Management and Budget (OMB) support for NEPA might have moved the agencies to more serious efforts toward conformity with NEPA principles. But as often happens when a presidential administration is presented with a policy which it sees no political advantage in promoting, enforcement is largely left to the courts. Nevertheless, agency pro forma compliance with the EIS requirement was generally attained. Not all agency personnel were indifferent or opposed to NEPA principles and procedures. Some, notably younger employees, welcomed NEPA objectives.

PRESIDENTIAL RESPONSIBILITY

Although NEPA declared a national policy for the environment and created the CEQ to facilitate its implementation, this statute alone could not enable the CEQ to carry out its mandates. Commenting on the critical role of implementation in achieving the NEPA intent Senator Jackson observed that

> the declaration of a national environmental policy will not alone necessarily better or enhance the total man-environment relationship. The present problem is not simply the lack of a policy. It also involves the need to rationalize and coordinate existing policies and to provide a means by which they may be continuously reviewed to determine whether they meet the national goal of a quality life in a quality environment for all Americans. Declaration of a national environmental policy could, however, provide a new organizing concept by which governmental functions could be weighed and evaluated in the light of better perceived and better understood national needs and goals.[32]

Constitutional responsibility for action by the Federal government is placed in the three branches, legislative, executive, and judicial. In addition to the role of head of state, the presidency was established to oversee administration of the executive branch and the execution of the laws. But the status of the presidency has received two dissimilar interpretations. These differences are matters of emphasis, for both are inherent in the office. The first sees the presidential role as importantly institutional, overseeing the chief managerial functions within an interrelating system of public law, policy development, and governance.[33] The second emphasizes the role of the president as political leader, articulating goals and persuading action, largely independent of the legislative branch and with broad discretion in his selective attention to the multiplicity of Federal laws.[34] The institutional presidency subordinates the incumbent to the office and to the functions and duties specified under Article II of the Constitution; the personal presidency emphasizes political leadership and decision-making by the incumbent. These differences appear in tendencies that characterize particular presidencies, but are both inherent in the office. The difference that they appear to have made in relation to NEPA and the CEQ is in the ways that presidents have used the Executive Office of the President. In any case, however, the personal priorities of a president are doubtless the principal factors.

With some exceptions the concept of an institutional presidency prevailed in American politics prior to the election of John F. Kennedy. Thereafter a tacit assumption of a personal presidency gained ascendancy in the news media, in popular perception, and even in the Congress. The advent of television after the 1950s has been a major factor in personalizing the presidency. The dominant popular perception of the office at any one time has tended to reflect the preferred style and circumstances of the incumbent president. Placing oversight of NEPA in the Executive Office of the President rather than in the White House was intended to facilitate the institutional role of the president. Accordingly, the president could be expected to reinforce the implementation of NEPA regardless of his personal priorities. The personal style of a president is reflected in emphasis on either the political or on the managerial aspects of the office, but presidents have often subordinated their managerial responsibilities to their political agendas—a tendency noted especially in recent presidential administrations.

The institutional aspect of the presidency is administration of the public laws. The personal presidency is focused on the incumbent president's priorities and personal agenda. The history of the CEQ during the first term of the Clinton presidency illustrates a use of managerial decision-making in which the president's personal agenda appeared to his critics to have overridden his institutional public law responsibilities. The decision taken by President Clinton to restructure the administration of environmental policy illustrates the significance of the dichotomy. The proposal to abolish the CEQ and to move the administration of NEPA to a cabinet-level Department of Environmental Protection while creating an Office of Environmental Policy in the White House may have been consistent with the Clinton-Gore "reinvention of government," but overlooked the statutory status of the CEQ.[35] The philosophic assumption underlying this action appears to be that the functions of administrative management which the EOP was intended to assist should devolve upon the cabinet-level agencies, thus freeing the president for a role primarily of policy formulation and persuasion.

The reasons for placing central managerial agencies in the EOP were set out in the Report of the President's Committee on Administrative Management

(1937). Not the least of these was interdepartmental rivalry, competition, and noncooperation. Conflicts between the Corps of Engineers and the Bureau of Reclamation, between the National Park Service and the Forest Service, and between separate armed services were public knowledge. Observers close to the Washington scene also noted a parallel tendency among departments and interagency committees to accommodate complementary interests by compromises that protected each other's projects, programs, and budgets but not necessarily in consideration of a broader, longer-range public interest.

It appears that neither the Congress nor the courts can directly compel the president to enforce a particular interpretation of the law, as through a writ of mandamus. Indirectly the Congress might influence presidential action. It does possess powers (e.g. appropriation, confirmation, investigation) to persuade presidents to take NEPA more seriously. But popular apathy on nonspecific issues of principle, and the well-organized pressures of groups whose economic interests conflict with environmental protection, diminish the prospect of supportive congressional oversight of NEPA. Nevertheless, such oversight hearings as have been held have resulted in an affirmation of NEPA and the CEQ.

It is uncertain whether altering or amending the text of NEPA would in itself result in the Act's enhanced effectiveness, all other things being unchanged. When problems of policy implementation arise, there is a tendency characteristically (but not exclusively) American to seek technical solutions. The real difficulties, however, often lie elsewhere—usually in values and perceptions which technical remedies cannot fix. Even so, the implementation of NEPA and the integrative role of the CEQ cannot realistically be separated from the constitutional responsibilities of the institutional presidency. Indecision over the administration of the National Environmental Policy Act leads to the suggestion that the status and significance of the Executive Office of the President needs reexamination.

CONCLUSION

NEPA is potentially a powerful statute, well-integrated, internally consistent, and flexible, although not entirely clear on some points of law. The *extent* to which NEPA has directly influenced national policy may be debatable. That it has made a significant difference in the United States and has influenced governments abroad is not debatable. NEPA was not a sudden inspiration, nor was it put over on an unsuspecting Congress and the public by an environmental lobby. Its purpose was never the writing of impact statements, but this action-forcing procedure has been a great inducement to ecological rationality in Federal actions which traditionally had largely ignored environmental consequences.[36] No technical fix or administrative reorganization will achieve the NEPA's intent. To implement NEPA as intended requires a president committed to its objectives and who uses his appointive, budgetary, and leadership powers to this end.

The argument that the president cannot realistically be expected to support policies and agencies laid upon him by Congress misstates the issue. Laws are enacted by the Congress and the president. The Constitution requires that the president take care that the laws are faithfully executed. As with the Crown in Great Britain, the presidency is more than the personal incumbent. The constitutional duties of the president prescribed in Article II of the Constitution preclude lawful neglect of a statutory agency because its functions do not serve the president's personal agenda. But the Congress, and especially the Senate, need to use more effectively its confirmation and oversight responsibilities to take care that national policies are not neglected. For it is the duty not only of the courts, but equally of the president and the Congress "to see that important legislative purposes, heralded in the halls of Congress, are not lost or misdirected in the vast hallways of the federal bureaucracy.[37]

But legislative purposes may change with voting majorities (even by one vote) in successive Congresses. The printed record of the genesis of NEPA should make clear the intentions of the architects of NEPA, its congressional sponsors, and committee staff. Nevertheless, many critics of NEPA appear to have interpreted it from subjective premises without inquiry into the legislative history of the Act or into the assumptions and expectations of the persons responsible for its language and content. These critics have missed the implications of NEPA's broad and basic principles and goals. From one perspective NEPA is seen as the capstone of national environmental policy; more importantly, it should be viewed as a foundation for the future.

3

Environmental Impact Assessment

WHAT IS NEEDED IN RESTRUCTURING THE GOVERNMENTAL SIDE OF
THIS PROBLEM IS TO LEGISLATIVELY CREATE THOSE SITUATIONS
THAT WILL BRING ABOUT AN ACTION-FORCING PROCEDURE THE DE-
PARTMENTS MUST COMPLY WITH. OTHERWISE, THESE LOFTY DECLA-
RATIONS ARE NOTHING MORE THAN THAT.

—STATEMENT BY SENATOR HENRY M. JACKSON
HEARING ON S.1075, APRIL 16, 1969

Impact assessment as a process and technique appeared during the latter half of the 20th century in response to consequences, unforeseen and unwanted, of rapidly expanding technological innovation and economic development. Several forms of analysis and assessment emerged, including environmental, socioeconomic, technological, and comparative risk assessment, and extended cost-benefit analysis. Of these, environmental impact assessment (EIA) gained prominence, being integral to the National Environmental Policy Act of 1969.[1] The direct purpose of NEPA Section 102(2)(c) was to force agency attention to the substantive Section 101 provisions of the Act. To comprehend fully the implications of the impact assessment requirement, all of the Section, especially (d), (e), (f), (g), and (h) should be read in addition to the *Regulations* of the CEQ for implementing the provisions of the Act.[2]

The assessment and the resulting impact statement (EIS) have implications for NEPA that extend beyond the documents to the administration of the Act and to the coordination of Federal environment-affecting programs generally. Beyond its purpose in NEPA, the EIS initiated a process which has achieved worldwide significance and has implications for future public and private policy-making having major or lasting impact upon the environment. The term "assessment" (in EIA) has two meanings in relation to NEPA: (1) a specific exploratory process to determine whether a full EIS is required and (2) a general term, synonym for analysis and evaluation. Both meanings are used here, distinguished by context.

The strategy of EIA was to correct the tendency of Federal agencies toward single-minded pursuit of development objectives, with inadequate information and little attention concerning side effects or unintended consequences. If a national policy for the environment were to be declared and implemented, reform of Federal agency practices was a place to begin. By the 1960s a broad range of environment-impacting activities throughout the country required some form of Federal participation or permission. Without directly legislating for the private sector, the Federal government might influence or limit its environment-affecting activities through requirements for licenses, permits, subsidies, leases, loans, and grants. The intent was not to curb the Federal contribution to the nation's economic growth, but to take care that its actions did not result in costly and avoidable environmental harm.

With regard to the management of the public lands, the Congress faced a growing diversity of demands, many of which were incompatible with the traditional dominant policy of resource development. New environmental values in ecologic and historic preservation, outdoor recreation, national parks and monuments, wilderness areas, wildlife refuges, and Native American religious sites were asserted, competing with the hitherto dominant uses of timbering, mining, grazing, and farming. Faced with incompatible demands upon the public domain, the Congress passed the Multiple Use—Sustained Yield Act of 1960. This legislation, enacted largely on behalf of resource development interests to prevent their exclusion from protected areas, provided no criteria for deciding what uses should be preferred where demands were incompatible. NEPA, however, provides an informed alternative to traditional political conflict. Section 101(b)(4) declares an intent "to preserve important historic, cultural, and natural aspects of our national heritage, and maintain, wherever possible, an environment which supports diversity, and variety of individual choice." Over the total public domain multiple uses may be compatible in some areas with environmental quality and NEPA values—but not in others. NEPA mandates, and in principle provides, criteria for informed choice among alternatives.

The initial purpose of impact assessment in NEPA was to force the Federal agencies to identify and consider the environmental consequences of their plans, programs, and decisions. The ultimate objective was to bring agency policy into conformity with the values declared in the preamble and Section 101(b) of NEPA—its substantive provisions. Although the environmental impact assessment (EIA) and statement (EIS) did not in any case mandate a particular agency decision, the process would force the agencies to discover and disclose the environmental effects of their proposals, thereby opening ill-conceived projects to challenge.

Subsection (v) of Section 102(2)(c) requires that "Copies of such [impact] statement and the comments and views of the appropriate Federal, State, and local agencies, which are authorized to develop and enforce environmental standards, shall be made available to the President, the Council on

Environmental Quality and to the public as provided by Section 552 of Title 5, United States Code [Freedom of Information Act]." These formal procedures, summarized as "the NEPA Process," became the essence of the Act for many commentators, while in reality it was the beginning of a process involving much more than "paperwork." The instrumental objective of impact assessment was a better informed, coordinative, and more rational Federal public administration.

PROCESS OVER PURPOSE

No generalization is without exceptions, and it therefore seems fair to say that Americans have an obsession for procedure over substance in matters of law. Whether it is the NEPA Process, the "peace process" in the Middle East, or in the courts' "due process of law" or numerous strictures on civil rights and criminal justice, *process* is often the governing consideration. There are historical explanations for this emphasis on process, but they can easily obscure the intent of the law for which process presumably has been invoked. NEPA has been criticized as concerned primarily with the production of documents—i.e. the NEPA Process. In fact there are at least five types of documents that may be required, depending on the circumstances. They are:

(1) Notice of Intent to prepare an EIS (NOI)

(2) An EIS draft, final, and supplementary

(3) Record of Decision (ROD)

(4) Environmental Assessment (EA), for actions neither categorically excluded nor subject to an EIS, or to determine whether a full EIS is required

(5) Finding of no significant impact (FONSI)

Obviously not all of these documents are needed in every case. It is the gathering and analysis of relevant information that leads toward fulfilling NEPA's purpose. Ridiculing impact statement writing has been popular with antienvironmentalists—denigrating environmental legislation in general and NEPA in particular. Critics single out the alleged defects of the NEPA Process: excessive costs—delays in project implementation—misuse of science—and ideological bias—these complaints illustrated from worst case scenarios. Seldom do the critics explore or explain the real causes of their criticisms—private ambitions frustrated by environmental protection—or critics blaming the statute rather than the administrators and agencies responsible for its implementation. The detractors appear to be oblivious of impact assessment as a learning process. Overlooked are the provisions in Section 102(2)(c) and (d) intended to obtain coordination and integration of major projects or programs impacting upon the environment. Although these provisions, detailed as follows, do not force policy integration, they do provide procedures to facilitate it. Section 102(2)(c)(v) decrees that:

> Prior to 102(2)(c)(v) making any detailed statement the responsible Federal official shall consult with and obtain the comments of any Federal agency which has jurisdiction by law or special expertise with respect to any environmental impact involved. Copies of such statement and the comments and views of the appropriate Federal, State, and local agencies which are authorized to develop and enforce environmental standards, shall be made available to the President, the Council on Environmental Quality and to the public as provided by section 552 of title 5, United States Code, and shall accompany the proposal through the existing agency review processes;
>
> (d) Any detailed statement under subparagraph (c) after January 1, 1970, for any major Federal action funded under a program of grants to States shall not be deemed to be legally insufficient solely by reason of having been prepared by a State agency or official, if:
>
> (i) the State agency or official has statewide jurisdiction and has the responsibility for such action,
>
> (ii) the responsible Federal official furnishes guidance and participates in such preparation,
>
> (iii) the responsible Federal official independently evaluates such statement prior to its approval and adoption, and
>
> (iv) after January 1, 1976, the responsible Federal official provides early notification to, and solicits the views of, any other State or any Federal land management entity of any action or any alternative thereto which may have significant impacts upon such State or affected Federal land management entity and, if there is any disagreement on such impacts, prepares a written assessment of such impacts and views for incorporation into such detailed statement.
>
> The procedures in this paragraph shall not relieve the Federal official of his responsibilities for the scope, objectivity, and content of the entire statement or of any other responsibility under this Act; and further, the subparagraph does not affect the legal sufficiency of statements prepared by State agencies with less than statewide jurisdiction.

The NEPA Process is more than writing and reviewing impact statements. It provides means for improving the substance and the economy, efficiency, and effectiveness of the public administration of environmental policies and projects. It has the capacity of revealing where Federal agencies and State and local governments might be pursuing cross-purposes or duplicative agendas.

Excepting the indefensible costs that some agencies have loaded onto impact statements, the NEPA Process, fully and objectively administered, could avoid much greater expense in public projects than does the cost of analyzing and assessing environmental impacts.

Environmental impact assessment cannot be understood by reference to Section 102(2)(c) alone. Since 1978 *Regulations* having the force and effect of law have been issued by the CEQ, their purpose being to guide, direct, correct, and assist the agencies in fulfilling their responsibilities under Section 102(2)(c). Responsibility for observing the NEPA intent and procedures rests with the agencies. The CEQ *Regulations* were developed in consultation with the agencies, drawing upon experience with previous guidelines. On December 12, 1977, with presidential approval, the CEQ issued for agency review official regulations to replace the former guidelines for implementing NEPA and the EIA procedures. This action led to significant improvements in the focus and content of impact statements consistent with recommendations by the Commission on Federal Paperwork (February 25, 1977) by the General Accounting Office (May 18, 1972, and August 9, 1977) and with analysis by the CEQ (March, 1976) of six years' experience with the EIS in seventy Federal agencies. Consistent with the CEQ *Regulations*, the agencies were free to develop supplementary regulations appropriate to their own particular missions. NEPA did not provide a model for the form and content of impact statements. A period of trial and error, of experiment and experience was necessary.

MISCONSTRUING THE EIS

In comparison with other statutes, NEPA, in its EIS information-forcing aspects, has been generally effective. An undocumented survey by the CEQ and Department of State found that NEPA has been emulated abroad in at least 80 countries—more than any other U.S. statute. "Little NEPAs" have been enacted in as many as 16 states, including Puerto Rico and the District of Columbia, that have EIA requirements, and provide a model of an analytic procedure for policy development which many municipalities and some private corporations have adopted.[3] Then why should the EIS be regarded by some critics as controversial? There are several reasons that help to explain why the NEPA Process has overshadowed the NEPA Purpose.

The most apparent reason is an incomplete, foreshortened interpretation of the NEPA Process by lawyers and judges as confined to the preparation of documents. The coordinative and economizing potential of impact assessment has commonly been overlooked. A second reason is the convenience of the EIS as a target for attack upon the environmental movement. Some critics profess concern for environmental protection but allege that the public would be better served by private choice in the market place, common-law remedies for individual injuries, and self-discipline by the agencies under their organic statutes and public scrutiny without NEPA superimposed.

Two additional reasons for controversy have resulted from the "imposition" of NEPA procedures and principles upon the customary behavior of the Federal bureaucracies. First, because NEPA, in effect, amended the basic missions and organic laws of all Federal agencies, there has been intraagency resentment against this external imposition of new rules to live by. The environmental impact statement in particular aroused scornful indignation among some older officials who pursued their missions like blinkered horses. But many younger agency personnel welcomed NEPA procedures as a more rational and defensible way of program- and project-planning and decision-making.

A second bureaucratic objection was the opening of agency expertise to question. Once a project authorization was received from Congress, the agencies had customarily felt free to plan dams, highways, airports, drainage projects, and other environment-shaping activities with little, if any, public interference. The agencies were seldom obliged to tell the public (or other agencies) anything about their plans and were not accustomed to being questioned by persons without official standing. It had been customary in many agencies to delay public hearings until the bulldozers were ready to roll and it was too late to alter plans or stop the project. The full-disclosure provision of NEPA, which supplemented the Freedom of Information Act, was an affront to bureaucratic autonomy and expertise. NEPA produced a new approach to public information which questioned and sometimes contradicted the attitude that the agency always "knows best."

Some agency personnel, importuned by clients, saw NEPA as complicating, encumbering, and delaying their missions. EIS paperwork was alleged to slow progress and drive up costs. No accounting was made of the much greater costs that could be incurred by projects that were ecologically and economically flawed, that imposed unforeseen environmental damage, or required expensive continuing monitoring or mitigation. Some agencies may have sought to conceal the true full costs of public works by off-loading some of the unavoidable expenses of project-planning onto EIS procedures, thus making it appear that environmental impact analysis was an expensive imposed add-on and presenting a deceptive impression of agency budgetary frugality.

In addition to professional bureaucratic conservatism, there are beliefs and biases among some Americans incompatible in principle with environmental impact assessment as a mandatory process. At least four viewpoints may be identified. *First,* there is the opinion that regard for the environment (i.e. love of nature) is a subjective value — sentimental, impractical, and anti-people. A *second* belief is that public environmental protection (especially impact analysis) tends to cost more than it is worth — that it burdens the economy and is counterproductive to jobs, earnings, private property, economic growth, and "progress." *Third* is the attitude of individualistic libertarians who argue that the benefits of environmental quality (e.g. national parks and wilderness areas) ought to be bought and paid for by those who feel the need for them; the public should not be asked to bear costs that reflect the values of only a selective group of Americans.

Section 102(2)(b) of NEPA, requiring that presently unquantified amenities and values be given appropriate consideration in decision-making, has been dismissed by some critics as unmanageable in a nation of cultural diversity. This leads to the *fourth* objection, that values which can't be measured and are in any case subjective, can't be rationally implemented. The cumulative effect of these contentions has spread the belief that NEPA's EIS action-forcing procedure imposes unnecessary costly and inequitable burdens on the economy and obstructs "progress" (undefined). But complaints about the impact statement requirement have diminished as experience with impact analysis has accumulated, and the process has become professionalized. To the extent that improved techniques of impact analysis have enlarged the roles of science, nonquantifiable values, and foresight in agency planning and decision-making, the EIS has become an effective instrument for environmental and economic quality and sustainability. But professionalization of the assessment process, in many ways desirable, does entail a risk of becoming an end in itself.

Separate from, but reinforcing the objectives of the EIS provision, is the mandate of Section 102(2)(a) to "utilize a systematic, interdisciplinary approach which will insure the integrated use of the natural and social sciences and the environmental design arts." To ascertain whether Section 102(2)(a) and the unquantified values mandated (Section 102(2)(b)) do, in fact, characterize agency decisions, a "desk audit" review of agency planning, procedures, and their outcomes would be necessary. This would be consistent with CEQ oversight functions under Title II, Section 204(3) of NEPA. But without clear evidence of presidential support for NEPA, these action-forcing provisions risk being evaded or finessed.

The impact statement provides information (at least by implication) about what may happen and by implication about what should or should not be done where Federal action affects the quality of the environment. Section 101(2)(c) requires the agencies to identify alternatives to environmentally impacting proposals, and Section 101(b) declares principles and goals that should guide agency policy-planning. The plausible implication is that in the absence of compelling arguments to the contrary, the alternative closest to NEPA objectives should prevail. But NEPA does not compel an agency to adopt the most environmentally friendly alternative. Although the CEQ *Regulation* 40 CFR 1502.2(d) links impact assessment with the 101(b) values, the provision appears to lack strength to guarantee observance.

The report of a CEQ survey of agency *Consideration of Alternatives in the NEPA Process,* revealed a considerable variation in practice.[4] Of twenty-eight agencies that responded to a questionnaire, twenty indicated that the goals and objectives of NEPA were referred to in the environmental documentation for projects under discussion. Two other agencies indicated that although NEPA was not specifically mentioned in impact statements its goals were nevertheless being implemented.

A weakness in achieving the NEPA objective is the tendency in some agencies to adopt a preferred proposal and plan of action before alternatives are considered. Agency personnel thus have a vested interest in the initial proposal as the preferred decision. The impact assessment was intended to be informative, cautionary, and (potentially) corrective. But narrowly interpreted, it has risked making more acceptable an action that should not be undertaken at all. The analytic process required by Section 102 is essential to responsible decisions that affect the environment but alone is insufficient to realize the full measure of the NEPA intent. Unfortunately the impact statement as mandated in Section 102(2)(c) of the statute was not explicitly linked to Section 101(b), thus enabling the Supreme Court to interpret the Act as essentially procedural. The Court majority has given a narrow interpretation of NEPA and has consistently reversed decisions of lower courts that have upheld the substantive intent of the congressional declaration of environmental policy (Section 101(a) and (b)).[5] Some lower courts have agreed that the substantive provisions of NEPA establish responsibilities that cannot be neglected with impunity.

SCIENCE AND IMPACT ASSESSMENT

An intent of NEPA was to draw upon science as a source of information and a corrective for public policies impacting upon the environment. Science has been invoked and employed in many public programs and projects. But these uses of science have often been narrowly and selectively focused on particular agency objectives. Moreover, science characteristically reports probabilities rather than absolute certainties and is thus inconsistent with legal questions requiring unequivocal yes or no answers. Interdisciplinary science approaches to Federal legislation required by Section 102(2)(a) have been exceptional, as have been legislative uses of the social sciences and environmental design arts other than engineering.

NEPA, however, required a systematic integrated interdisciplinary use of all sciences that could reveal the probable effects of agency action that significantly impacted the environment and thereby broadened the informational base of environmental policy and enlarged the uses of science in agency-planning and decision-making. This expanded recourse to science was viewed with skepticism by some administrators and scientists who argued that science was not yet adequate to answer many environmental policy questions. Some scientists argued that politicians and bureaucrats should stay away from science-related issues that only scientists could understand. As environmental considerations were injected into policy-making, decision processes necessarily became more complex and administrative procedures were extended to issues heretofore unrecognized or avoided. Moreover, in the affairs of government, political influence and popular opinion count for more than science. Some scientists objected that impact analysis would produce "interdisciplinary mish-mash" and argued that political influences would result in "bad science," an allegation readily adopted by antienvironmentalists.

Present-day science alone cannot answer all questions relevant to the environmental consequences of all proposed actions. There are almost always matters of uncertainty and risks in assuming certainty where potentially critical factors remain unknown.[6] Moreover, a one-time assessment may not be a reliable indicator of environmental trends or consequences. Monitoring of change, revisiting predictions, and consideration of cumulative effects of environmental impacts are necessary attributes of a reliable EIA process.[7] Moreover the content of scientific information may change over time. A reliable environmental impact assessment can seldom be a one-time only event. The rational response to uncertainty, cumulative effects, and the inevitability of change is adaptive environmental management.[8] Flexibility, being guarded against abuse is a concomitant of effective environmental decision-making. The EIS was not intended to be a scientific document even when utilizing science to the fullest extent. More than science must be considered in an adequate environmental impact analysis. As previously noted (Section 102(2)(b)) Federal agencies are authorized and directed to "identify and develop methods and procedures in consultation with the CEQ which will ensure that presently unquantified environmental amenities and values may be given appropriate consideration in decision-making along with economic and technical considerations." And the admonition to include the social sciences in agency-planning and decision-making (Section 102(2)(a)) could bring considerations of equity, ethics, and environmental justice into the decision process and could enlarge the basis for mediation when values conflict.

Where science is applicable and generally adequate to the analysis, it should not be assumed to always yield definitive results. The purpose of Section 102(2)(a) is to introduce a systematic use of science as a corrective to selective narrowly conceived proposals that fail to reveal all of the ascertainable effects of their implementation. But science as practiced today is not holistic—most scientific research is focused on selective dimensions of the subject under investigation. There are many sciences, and among them are gaps in knowledge and unresolved contradictions in their assumptions and interpretations. The inclusion of the social sciences in impact analysis may enlarge its informative value but adds to its complexities and exposes its uncertainties. In summary, science is essential to impact analysis but it has its limitations and is only part of the process.

Identification of a probable environmental impact is generally easier to ascertain than is an evaluation of its significance. When social, economic, and ecological consequences of environmental impacts are considered, it is not exceptional to find that not all people—or indeed all elements in an ecosystem—are equally affected or affected in the same way. Science may not be able to resolve all anomalies in impact assessments, but it may help to identify the salient facts that should be considered in policy choice.

Perhaps the best use of science in impact analysis is the testing of assumptions underlying programs or project proposals. Science is not necessarily indicative of all foreseeable consequences but it contributes to informed decision-making when it reveals the extent to which assumptions are supported by verifiable evidence. If its assumptions can be falsified or revealed as selectively biased, the scientific basis claimed for a proposition becomes questionable. But the assumptions underlying public policy decisions are not always demonstrably right or wrong. They often express beliefs regarding values, ethics, equities, or economies that fall beyond the reach of science and are often the opinions that motivate political decision makers. Science affects the environmental politics when its methods or findings arouse public concern, for example, apprehension over present contamination of air, water, food, and radioactive radiation; less so when future impacts are conjectured, as with climate change, stratospheric ozone depletion and multiplication of human populations.

The drafters of NEPA recognized that the existing state of science was inadequate to resolve numerous problems relating to the environment. Valid impact assessment requires reliable science, therefore some of the objectives of the earlier Ecological Research and Surveys Bill were written into Title II of NEPA. Responsibility for these research provisions has been largely transferred to the Environmental Protection Agency. The major research role envisioned for the CEQ was to monitor, stimulate, sponsor, and assist advancement in environmental science. It was not to do research, but to become a catalyst with resources to enable it to work with the National Science Foundation, the National Research Council, universities, and the research offices of the executive agencies and nongovernmental organizations in addressing critical environmental problems. To accomplish this task requires appropriate funding and a clear signal of congressional or presidential approval, neither of which the CEQ has received.

To the extent that scientific methods and findings become more reliable instruments of prognosis, science may have correspondingly greater influence in public policies—but influence does not necessarily translate into decisions; it may also extend and intensify political polarization. Among objectors to environmentalism, and skeptics questioning the validity of science, are persons whose motives and objectives are self-serving and/or ideological. In our society, a traditional role of science in relation to political policy has been to serve—not to question. Thus, the provision of Section 102(2)(c) requiring agencies to show that alternatives to environmentally impacting proposals have been considered has led to controversy over the objectivity of scientific evidence, as in the global climate-change issue in which a few scientists contend that no problem exists. As the weight of scientific evidence and consensus among scientists increases, the influence of science on environmental policy has also increased. Even so, a politically appreciable number of Americans have mixed feelings about the "truthfulness" of science, many preferring their "common sense" opinions or theological convictions to scientific findings.[9] More threatening to science in environmental policy is the distortion and dissimulation of scientific information in virulent antienvironmental rhetoric. A theme common to the antienvironmental advocates is their defense of "sound science" against the allegedly biased pseudoscience of environmentalism.[10]

The charge that environmental policy is based on flawed or biased science continues to be made by a few well-publicized scientist contrarians but most often by organizations or individuals opposed to "environmentalism" in principle. Individuals associated with so-called conservative foundations and "think tanks" such as the Pacific Legal Foundation, the Mountain States Legal Foundation, the Heritage Foundation, the American Enterprise Institute, the Cato Institute, and the Claremont Institute have attacked "environmentalism" and the credibility of environmental science and environmental education, arguing that "sound science" discounts environmental apprehensions and alarms. Science has in some instances been misinterpreted and misapplied, but no more often in environmental issues than in other areas of policy. The weight of scientific evidence supports concern for the consequences of human impact upon the environment.[11]

A PERSONAL RETROSPECTIVE

Compelling ideas occur under many different circumstances in the minds of many different people. The admonition "to look before you leap" is as old as any proverb, but especially in a world of rapidly expanding new technologies and developments, ascertaining the probable outcomes of action may not be easy and forecasts may not be certain—but they are safer than unrestrained ignorance. The concept of analytic procedures and guidelines for planners and decisionmakers is not new. As early as 1930, the Design and Industries Association of Great Britain published *Cautionary Guides* to illustrate good and bad environmental development in urban areas. In 1960 the U.S. Public Health Service published an *Environmental Health Planning Guide,* a checklist-procedures handbook. More than checklists but less than present-day systematic impact analysis, such guides often served to inform the public as well as to assist public officials.

Concern in the 1960s over worsening environmental conditions stimulated search for ways to prevent environmental harm resulting from unanticipated effects of underexamined action. Concern for the quality and sustainability of the environmental life-support system led to the exploration of means to identify risks, prevent inadvertent damage, and utilize the best available knowledge in planning and decision-making affecting the environment. There was recognition of the need for anticipating the consequences of proposed action, but less certainty regarding how this need could be fulfilled. My contribution to the developing concept of impact analysis was hardly unique, but my role as consultant to Senator Henry Jackson and the Senate Committee on Interior and Insular Affairs provided the opportunity to introduce the impact assessment and statement concept into the drafting of the National Environmental Policy Act. Controversy over the EIS is rooted in both misinformation and lack of information, so a brief account of my personal involvement with the environmental impact assessment idea is recounted to illustrate how concepts may evolve, and that the substantive and procedural aspects of NEPA had a common ancestor.

The occasion for my introducing the EIS requirement occurred in 1969 when I was consultant to the Senate Committee on Interior and Insular Affairs to assist in developing concepts for environmental policy legislation. My concern for better environmental decision-making, however, had arisen a decade earlier. Although I possessed a strong and long-standing interest in natural history and ecology, my professional life at the time concerned the study of public policy and administration in a political context. I understood that statements of policy could be used either to induce action, deflect criticism, or to conceal inaction. But if action were intended, policies needed to be formulated in terms that could be acted upon. This is essential when persons who must execute a policy may not understand it, may resist it, or may lack the means to give it effect. And when the officials responsible for administration of a policy oppose it or misunderstand its purpose, statutory language may be needed to induce compliance. Without action-forcing provisions, policy statements may be mostly hortatory—admonitory without means to action. In 1968 in a background paper for the Senate Interior Committee entitled *A National Policy for the Environment,* I stated my belief that "Effective policy is not merely a statement of things hoped for; it is a coherent, reasoned statement of goals and principles supported by evidence and formulated in language that enables those responsible for implementation to fulfill its intent."

I concluded that for effective operational policy two approaches were required. The first was a clear statement of the policy, expressed through declarations, resolutions, statutes, or guidelines. The second was the means to action, a process or mechanism to assure, so far as possible, that the intended action would occur. My first effort to find a way to join these two aspects in a single policy instrument was made in July 1964. In an unpublished paper entitled "Making Environmental Concepts Operational," I developed in ten points the following chain of reasoning leading to what I then called "a checklist of criteria for environmental planning":

(1) Man's manipulation of the physical aspects of his environment is proceeding at an accelerating rate.

(2) Pressure on environments generated by increasing populations, rising demands upon national resources, and rapidly expanding technologies indicate the probability of radical and far-reaching environmental changes in the years ahead.

(3) Environmental and ecological science have not grown at a pace commensurate either with human demands upon the environment or with the technological means of pursuing these demands.

(4) The individuals and organizations that plan and execute policies affecting the environment cannot, in the absence of informed assistance, be expected to appreciate ecological relationships or to understand the implications of environmental change.

(5) On the basis of statistical probability and historical experience, a large number of ecological errors, ranging from the inconvenient to the catastrophic, can be predicted in rough proportion to the increasing tempo of environmental change.

(6) Although some of these errors will be unavoidable, others need not occur if action is guided by existing knowledge. However, in the absence of far more widespread and practical methods of environmental decision-making than we have today, many of these mistakes *will* occur *even* when the knowledge to avoid them is actually available.

(7) Human societies need not—indeed cannot—afford to incur an unnecessarily high cost in ecological errors, some of which could easily be disastrous for all mankind.

(8) If the number and severity of these errors are to be reduced, rapid, far-reaching systematic improvement of ecological and environmental decision-making is necessary.

(9) The normal processes of education alone are too slow and too abstract to bring the perceptions, values, and understandings of people as rapidly

as need be into consistency with valid scientific knowledge of environmental and ecological relationships.

(10) Some instrumental means are therefore needed to improve the quality
of decision-making on environmental and ecological matters, and which
can be successfully applied under conditions wherein ecological sophis-
tication is minimal.

I concluded that although it would be unrealistic to think that a panacea
or prescription can be devised that will *ensure* careful and far-sighted environmental decision-making, under existing circumstances, a "make do" device, although imperfect, might be a great improvement in situations where
there were no guidelines whatever for environment-affecting decisions. A
checklist of factors or considerations relevant to decisions impacting upon
environments might therefore be of great utility in improving the quality of
decisions by alerting planners and administrators to the environmental implications of their actions. Linkage between substantive policy and administrative procedure was emphasized in the assertion that introduction of a
checklist into the regular administrative procedure of government should be
preceded by high-level consideration of the position of the government regarding the principles that ought to guide environmental decisions.

Referring to the substance of the checklist, I noted that "At the very least,
it should identify and, in some measure, interpret the principal factors that
should be considered in environmental decisions." These factors were substantially those which Federal administrators are now required to address
in the environmental impact statement: the probable environmental consequences of and alternatives to the proposed action, the relationship between
short-term effects and long-term costs or benefits, and effect upon future
opportunities (e.g. irreversible and irretrievable commitments).

I did not attempt to construct an environmental policy checklist, but believed that it should contain both principles to follow and questions to answer
so that it would be useful "in analyzing a problem involving environmental
change," and could be "a guiding factor in reaching practical decisions." But
the idea was not well-received by some of the critics to whom it was exposed.
Economists thought "environment" was an unmanageable concept (things in
general); most political scientists found it "uninteresting," and some ecologists were skeptical—the environment was too complex for science-illiterate
officials to understand. In the opinion of some scientists, such an analytical
tool in the hands of nonscientists would lead to ineffectual—or worse—to
misguided conclusions. A little knowledge being a dangerous thing, it would
be unwise to encourage public officials to assess the environmental consequences of their actions. Such assessment, if feasible (which many doubted),
should only be undertaken by scientists whose findings might then be turned
over to the public authorities for their consideration.

These negative reactions did not persuade me that the idea was without value but they caused me to consider other ways of making environmental concepts operational. Two years later in an article in *BioScience* I made briefest mention of the checklist idea but did suggest "the drawing up of a balance sheet of ecological accounts by which the probable true costs and benefits of alternative environmental decisions might be compared."[12]

The checklist concept has a continuing utility. In 1987 the American Bar Association Section of Natural Resources Law published as Monograph Series No. 5 *Checklists for Preparing National Environmental Policy Act Documents* for use "by agency environmental staff, other agency staff, and agency contractors as a reminder of minimum requirements" (and of categorical exclusions from NEPA).[13] The U.S. Department of Energy Office of NEPA Oversight developed an Environmental Assessment Checklist (1994) to aid in preparing and reviewing DOE environmental impact assessments, and application of the device is being explored in the Economic Commission for Europe. The checklist, alone, is no substitute for the NEPA impact analysis, but is a practical tool for impact assessment. The CEQ included a section on checklists in its 1997 handbook on *Considering Cumulative Effects under the National Environmental Policy Act*. The technique adds to the probability that all things relevant to the EIS are included and irrelevant data left out. An additional approach toward EIS improvement was undertaken by a Department of Energy Environmental Process Improvement Team which in January 1994 issued a detailed report covering agency experience, recommending ways to deal with implementation problems, including a draft checklist for reviewing environmental assessment documents. Among other agencies producing NEPA compliance handbooks are the National Park Service (looseleaf since 1983) and the Bureau of Reclamation (1990).

In 1968, in a memorandum to Russell E. Train and a report to the Citizens Advisory Committee on Recreation and Natural Beauty,[14] I emphasized the dual need "to obtain adoption of a clear national commitment to environmental quality as a public responsibility; and, second, to make this commitment operational and effective by appropriate institutional support." In the report to the Citizens Advisory Committee, I pointed out that there was no specific action-forcing provision in my paper on *A National Policy for the Environment*, or in the *Congressional White Paper on a National Policy for the Environment*, prepared by the Congressional Research Service.[15] But the focus of these reports was on the substance of a declaration of national environmental policy. We did not then have a policy and hence offered no specific provisions to make anything happen. Yet the need for action-forcing was recognized. I observed that

> In this sense [the reports] are like shopping lists without money. They are useful as summaries of what ought to be done, but to become fully developed policy statements, the meat must have some muscle. The objectives of envi-

ronmental policy must be provided with means to bring about their realization. Unless positive requirements reinforce policy objectives, those objectives
may be little more than moralizing precepts—and no more effective.[16]

An opportunity to obtain application of this concept of policy implementation came unexpectedly and rapidly after 1968. Through arrangements between Senator Henry M. Jackson, Chairman of the Senate Committee for Interior and Insular Affairs, and Russell E. Train, then president of the Conservation
Foundation, I joined the staff of the Committee as a consulting member on the
drafting of legislation for a national environmental policy. My initial involvement with the NEPA came about not so much because of my views on action-
forcing legislation but as a consequence of published writings beginning in
1963 with an article entitled "Environment: A New Focus for Public Policy."[17]
Although the first versions of S.1075 did not contain the EIS provision, means
to make the declaratory provisions of the Bill operational were under discussion with committee staff members William J. Van Ness and Daniel A. Dreyfus
in particular, and with Wallace D. Bowman and Richard A. Carpenter of the
Congressional Research Service of the Library of Congress.

Although there were inputs from the Congressional Research Service and
from scientific and nongovernmental sources, S.1075 that emerged was largely
the work of Senator Jackson and the staff of the Senate Interior Committee,
with inputs from Senator Edmund Muskie. A House version sponsored by
Representative John Dingell paralleled the Senate version in intent. NEPA was
not the product of environmental lobbyists, nor was it put together hurriedly
without consultation with the agencies.

Among the dozens of environmental policy bills introduced into the 90th
and 91st Congresses, none provided means to obtain agency compliance.
Until the addition of the EIS requirement to S.1075 none provided means for
ensuring that their provisions would receive official attention or would be
likely to change the behavior of Federal agencies or the nation. Senator
Jackson and the Committee staff wanted an act that would make a difference—that would ensure responsiveness of the Federal agencies to the new
environmental priorities which public opinion appeared to demand. Following the suggestion of William J. Van Ness, it was agreed that I would introduce the idea of an action-forcing provision in testimony before the Committee at a hearing on April 16, 1969. At this hearing, which preceded the
definitive drafting of the NEPA, I urged that "a statement of policy by the
Congress should at least consider measures to require the Federal agencies,
in submitting proposals, to contain within the proposals an evaluation of the
effect of these proposals upon the state of the environment."[18]

The foregoing history of the EIS has been recounted as a personal nar-
rative for two reasons. First, to establish for the record that the inclusion of
the EIS in the NEPA was not an unanticipated last-minute addition as a few
critics have alleged. Second, to demonstrate that it was the intent of the

drafters that the EIS embodied in Section 102(2)(c) of NEPA should compel agency attention and conformity to the preceding sections of the Act. Its purpose was not the preparation of documents.

DEFINING THE EIS PROCESS

Detailed language for the EIS requirement of Section 102(2)(c) was worked out by William J. Van Ness and Daniel A. Dreyfus in consultation with me and others closely associated with the development of the Act. In retrospect, it appears curious that the EIS provision occasioned no debate and almost no external objection or endorsement. The Federal agencies at first showed little interest in the legislation, possibly failing to perceive the implications of the EIS. The popular environmental organizations did not initially see the EIS as a tool that they could turn against the agencies, although they gave general support to the legislation. Potential effects of the Act were, however, foreseen by the editors of the weekly newsmagazine *Time*.

In its issue of August 1, 1969, *Time* introduced a new section, "Environment," in which it predicted that if the Jackson Bill became law, its effects might be felt by "every imaginable special interest—airlines, highway builders, mining companies, real estate developers," and it would open "all Federal policies to challenge."[19] But even this strong and prophetic assessment in a widely read publication aroused no marked reaction. There was unmistakable public demand for national legislation for the environment and it might be logically assumed that those who willed the end also willed the means to make that end effective. There would have been little point in scheduling public hearings on the EIS when its effects had not been demonstrated in action, and action was what the vocal public was demanding.

The impact statement requirement did not appear in the early versions of the legislation because the primary concern at that time was to formulate a national environmental policy and a council (the CEQ) to oversee its implementation. Action-forcing was not introduced until there was a policy to be enforced. There was no intention to slip in a potentially controversial provision at the "eleventh hour." Such a maneuver could have jeopardized passage of the bill.

The intent to make the Act enforceable was present in the early stages. As previously recounted, the idea of impact identification had been developing over several years, but the particular device to ensure official action had not been readily apparent. The revised bill that emerged in the summer of 1969 from the Senate Interior Committee drafters contained the EIS provision and became one of the more innovative pieces of legislation enacted by Congress. Its very novelty was one of its safeguards and the political time for its adoption was right. If the EIS requirement had been introduced in Congress in 1996, it would certainly have encountered some vigorous and highly vocal opposition. In 1969 few had the imagination to foresee how the EIS might be used, and the effect that it would have upon future program-planning and administration in the Federal agencies and upon applied ecology and the economy.

The drafters of the EIS provision had to reckon with two highly independent variables—the president and the courts. Although his oath of office commits the president to faithful execution of the laws, he is largely left to his own interpretation of his responsibilities.[20] President Nixon in 1969 had initially opposed enactment of S.1075; his commitment to legislation, which he had not wanted, was at best conjectural. And the position of the courts on a variety of critical issues could not be foreseen; among them would be the applicability of the EIS requirement retroactively to unfinished projects initiated before NEPA was enacted, to the ability of aggrieved groups to achieve standing, and especially to the scope and importance of issues to which the EIS requirement applied. The retroactivity issue related primarily to the necessity for preparing impact statements for projects long since approved by the Federal government—or well on the way to completion.[21] The scope of NEPA and the EIS was often defined by a perception that the "environment" meant "nature" and more specifically "pollution"—and did not apply to sociological, psychological, or economic effects. Another area that required definition was the applicability of the EIS procedure to U.S. actions occurring beyond the territorial limits of the country. Consideration of this question will be deferred to chapters 5 and 6.

The retroactivity question was resolved early in the history of the Act (1972) in the so-called *Gillham Dam* case *(EDF v. Corps of Engineers)*.[22] The U.S. Court of Appeals for the Eighth Circuit made two important interpretations of the NEPA, both affecting the subsequent history of the EIS. The Court, in effect, held not only that previously authorized and ongoing projects might require impact statements, but also that Section 101 of the NEPA created judicially enforceable rights. The Court declared its obligation to review the EIS to ascertain an agency's good faith and objectivity in applying Section 101 standards to its planning or review procedures. The purpose of Section 102 would therefore logically be the implementation of Section 101, which was what the drafters of the NEPA intended.

Although this ruling reinforced NEPA, it also created a dilemma for agencies. The choice was whether to reject or to revise old projects that were incompatible with Section 101. To revise old projects in the light of the new environmental principles might prove impossible in some instances, costly and time-consuming in many others. The Corps of Engineers, for example, had a multibillion dollar backlog of authorized projects, many of them near and dear to the hearts of incumbent congressmen. An honest application of Section 101 directives, and of realistic cost-benefit analysis, would result in impact statements that would in effect "damn" many projects. To request deauthorization of environmentally "bad" projects was considered to be impolitic—better to let them lie dormant than to stir up trouble in Congress. Agency staff and congressional sponsors were often deeply committed to the projects and were not in tune with the new environmental priorities. The "pork barrel" was, and is, a perennial source of political nourishment for congressmen.

The expedient way out of this inconvenience was to regard the EIS as strictly procedural. If there was no link between Sections 101 and 102, the agency had merely to show that it had considered each of the five points required by Section 102(2)(c) on the "detailed" environmental impact statement. Section 102, standing alone, does *not* require that an agency select the least environmentally damaging alternative and it does *not* require that the EIS show that the decision of the agency conforms to the principles declared in Section 101. That Section 102 and the EIS were intended to implement Section 101 may be implicit in the logical construction of the statute and in its legislative history, but unfortunately it is neither sufficiently explicit in its text nor forceful enough in implementation of the CEQ regulations. In consequence, the Supreme Court and some agencies have asserted or assumed the separability of the sections, thus opening the way to narrowing the application of the EIS.

PROBLEMS OF IMPLEMENTATION

Preparation of an environmental impact statement or assessment, often called "the NEPA Process," has been vulnerable to several risks: (1) to the inadequacy of reliable scientific information; (2) to misuse by litigants to stop or delay projects having little to do with the purpose or principles of NEPA; and (3) to an information overload, running up costs and overwhelming the public and the courts with data of dubious relevance to NEPA intent. These risks have been and are being addressed. In January 1997 the CEQ released a report—*The National Environmental Policy Act: A Study of Its Effectiveness after Twenty-Five Years.* Because of its concern with effective implementation, the study focused on the NEPA Process and its relationship to agency decision-making and interagency coordination. The uses of science and the overloading of extraneous information on impact statements are subject to correction by the CEQ. The improper use of NEPA to block the enforcement of Federal policies only remotely related to the environment is a matter primarily for the judiciary. Manufacturing corporations have invoked the EIS to prevent enforcement of regulations which they oppose.[23]

If NEPA is to be effective, oversight of compliance with Section 102(2)(c), as free as possible from partisan agendas and independent of agency influence is needed. The CEQ was established to provide this independent oversight which is shared with the Environmental Protection Agency. A

NEPA oversight and monitoring office in a cabinet level department of the environment could hardly avoid resistance from coequal departments, and the risk of "political" considerations might be greater in a nonstatutory White House office. The Environmental Protection Agency reviews impact statements in the first instance, but interagency controversy is submitted for resolution to the CEQ.[24]

A greater risk to achieving NEPA objectives has been a too-frequent failure to integrate NEPA policy into agency planning and decision-making in a timely manner. The CEQ and several agencies have addressed the integration problem (see chapter 4) but these efforts could be assisted significantly if the OMB and the GAO were to exercise appropriate surveillance over decisions in which NEPA principles are involved. The effectiveness of the EIS as a means toward integration of policy and procedure within and between agencies has not been helped by the overuse of external consultants in preparation of impact statements. Under some circumstances, consultants independent of any Federal agency might be able to facilitate cooperative and integrative relationships. But this is not a function that they are ordinarily employed to perform. In a critique sympathetic to NEPA, the editor of the journal *New Engineer* provided the following interpretation of the problems of consultants in impact analysis:

> Although the law makes clear that the various federal agencies themselves are to author the environmental impact statements, congress has never given the agencies the money to carry out that task from scratch. As a result the courts, in a number of decisions that may each have had merit individually, have allowed private corporations and other vested interests to file their own impact reports—usually using private consultants hired for the purpose. Needless to say, a consultant is under great pressure from his client and from other industrial firms that might profit by the construction of a new facility to suppress or gloss over unfavorable data. (Most reports seem to be devoid of outright lies, although unnecessarily wordy to discourage close agency reading. The record for size, 50 pounds, goes to the assessment prepared for the Alaska gas pipeline.)[25]

The statement is correct, but it does not explain the more important causes of EIS abuses. Funding for environmental protection has always been a problem—never a purpose popular in the White House or with the Congress. The failure of the Congress to make timely budgetary provisions for learning how to undertake environmental impact analysis may account for improprieties in the early application of Section 102(2)(c) but is debatable as the basic cause of mismanagement of the NEPA Process. It seems probable that well over half of EISs originate outside the government, submitted by private applicants for grants and permits. This practice bypasses the Act's intent to reorient and reeducate agency planners and decisionmakers. The budgetary implications of the EIS were considered during the drafting of the statute. In the judgment of the congressional sponsors, the Act required a reordering of agency priorities, and this objective was to be accomplished through a reallocation of funds within existing agency budgets. This new task of environmental impact assessment would not necessarily make a case for *additional* appropriations *if* savings from the elimination of environmentally unjustifiable projects could be applied to cover such new costs as might arise where novel or exceptionally difficult environmental problems were encountered. But Congress seldom allows agencies to shift funds appropriated for one purpose to another.

To implement NEPA effectively, additional funds would have doubtless been helpful, especially in the early years. The need then was not only to provide for a one-time review of previously authorized and currently proposed projects, but also to reorient the technical and administrative staff who must translate the new priorities into action and to review the validity of the environmental assessments. In considering the implementation of my unpublished checklist proposal in 1964, I noted that

> people must not only be trained to understand and apply the criteria in actual decision situations, but they must be given the opportunity to do so. Thus the practical utility of the checklist depends, *first,* upon the readiness of governments to accept the idea in principle and to support its application in practice and, *second,* upon the successful orientation and training of the planning and administrative corps who constitute the central policy-deciding elements.

There is a significant, although indistinct, line between training to write impact statements and educating people in the substantive purposes of NEPA. The functions are logically complementary; both are needed for adequate implementation of the Act. But for several readily comprehensible reasons agency concern from the beginning focused directly on impact statement writing.

First, an impact assessment or statement was mandatory, enforceable by law, whereas failure to implement Section 101 could not easily be challenged, being a matter of agency judgment, perspective, and weighing of values. The impact statement was soon seized upon by environmental groups to attack agency projects and programs and, conversely, the process was ridiculed by advocates of agency proposals and by opponents of "environmentalism." Agencies were vulnerable to judicial rulings on the need for, or adequacy of, the EIS. It therefore followed that for many agencies NEPA was synonymous with Section 102(2)(c). Such training or indoctrination as the agency provided was largely for the purpose of understanding guidelines issued by the agency and the CEQ and in meeting the tests of adequacy laid down by the courts.

A second reason for focus on the action-forcing procedural aspect of the impact statement was agencies' incapacity—actual or alleged—to interpret or implement the provisions of Section 101. A broad new dimension had been added to agency policy considerations. In effect, a broad range of agency authorizations and mandates had been amended. But the agencies had to cope with these brave new policies with the same old people—often narrowly trained to administer narrowly focused agency missions, also often subject to micromanagement by committees of Congress. Also in many agencies, a new type of personnel was needed. Prior to 1970, ecologists were negligible factors in the employment needs of most agencies. But the NEPA created an expanding market for environmental and, especially, ecological expertise. Given the politics of budget and personnel it was easier to recruit temporary experts and consultants than to recruit permanent staff.

For reasons previously noted, agencies often found it preferable to contract for competence in environmental analysis rather than to develop it within their regular structures. Sometimes there were legitimate reasons for specialist outreach. By hiring temporary environmental impact consultants, the agencies could seek the particular kind of expertise which a specific agency policy required—no agency could assemble all of the specialized skills that environmental impact analysis might require. It was recognized by the drafters of NEPA that agencies might need assistance from other agencies or external consultants. Actual involvement of the agency in the process was the essential requirement. Moreover, contracting for personal services avoided long-term financial commitments and manpower ceilings. And it might be easier to disavow (or to discard) impact statements prepared by external applicants or experts than by regular agency staff.

A consequence of these considerations was the sudden rise of a new growth industry—impact statement writing. "Instant ecologists" set up shop, and consulting firms were formed to assist the agencies to meet the procedural requirements of the new law.[26] Environmental consultants were not often employed to assist agencies to review or revise their priorities or to reorient or reeducate their personnel. Too often an agency bought an EIS just as it would procure any other service or facility—for example, an insurance policy. From an agency perspective, the test of effectiveness of an EIS was survival of the agency project or program under judicial review. In the most crass case, the responsible agency representative would say to the environmental consultant: "Here is our project; your job is to give us an EIS that will get it by the courts." Although particular consultants may have produced honest and adequate impact statements, the practice without agency participation does not meet the purpose of the action-forcing provision and it opens the door to misapplication of the law's intent.

Charges that impact statements are excessive in length, that they rely on "bad science," and are too often irrelevant in detail should be directed against the politics of administration. The NEPA imposes no burden that, in the public interest, ought not be borne. The costs that it entails should be more than offset by the savings it makes possible through sparing the public the unnecessary burden of economically and ecologically unwise projects, with their overhead and maintenance charges continuing into an indefinite future in addition to the loss of environmental quality. And, of course, there is more to the impact statement provision than the preparation of documents. Section 102 of NEPA not only provides for public disclosure of agency intentions; it also requires and facilitates cooperation and coordination between Federal agencies and State governments. It provides as process for policy integration and coordination that was previously missing in Federal public administration.

IMPLICATIONS FOR THE FUTURE

In 1969 no one could foresee how the courts, the Congress, and the president would respond to the implementation of NEPA or the EIS. There was sufficient uncertainty to persuade Senator Edmund Muskie that a "back up" provision for review of impact statements should be provided. Accordingly, Section 309 of the Clean Air Act (PL 91-604-84 Stat. 1676), which he sponsored, authorized review of environmental impact statements by the Environmental Protection Agency as well as by the CEQ.[27] Section 309 of the Clean Air Act states:

> (a) The Administrator shall review and comment in writing on the environmental impact of any matter relating to duties and responsibilities granted pursuant to this Act or other provisions of the authority of the Administrator, contained in any (1) legislation proposed by any Federal department or agency, (2) newly authorized Federal projects for construction and any major Federal agency action (other than a project for construction) to which Section 102(2)(c) of Public Law 91-190 applies, and (3) proposed regulations published by any department or agency of the Federal government. Such written comment shall be made public at the conclusion of any such review.

> (b) In the event the Administrator determines that any such legislation, action, or regulation is unsatisfactory from the standpoint of public health or welfare or environmental quality, he shall publish his determination and the matter shall be referred to the Council on Environmental Quality.

Imperative to the full effectiveness of NEPA is the ability of the CEQ to review the adequacy of impact statements and to remand questionable or inadequate statements to agencies for reconsideration or upgrading. This overview function has been a reason for a three member council as contrasted to the single administration preference of recent presidents. Advocates of environmentally questionable projects and defenders of agency autonomy object that in exercising the overview authority would in effect become the environmental court.[28] Short of this, however, the CEQ could be given "ombudsman" functions which might be invoked through complaints regarding agency implementation of the NEPA, especially as indicated by disputed environmental impact statement procedures. The CEQ may already possess statutory authority sufficient for this function in Section 204(3), declaring it "a duty and function of the Council to review and appraise the various programs and activities of the Federal government in light of the policy set forth in Title I of this Act for the purpose of determining the extent to which such programs and activities are contributing to the achievement of such policy, and to make recommendations to the president with respect thereto."

This role for the CEQ might be enlarged with enactment of the proposed Institute for Environmental Conflict Resolution, established by Public Law 105-156 (signed by President Clinton on February 11, 1998). Impact assessment should be an important contribution to mediation efforts in conflict resolution. Discovery and agreement regarding the facts in controversy is a necessary first step toward rationally defining the issues and assessing probable results of alternative resolutions. Not all environmental conflicts can be reconciled, nor can government alone resolve all controversies. NEPA recognizes a cooperative role for the Federal government in association with State and local government and concerned public and private organizations—"to create conditions under which man and nature can exist in productive harmony, and fulfill the social, economic, and other requirements for present and future generations of Americans."

Impact assessment may not only provide a common informational base for mediation, but may also contribute to the environmental education of the participants. The internationalizing of environmental policy through impact assessment will be treated at greater length in chapter 5. That the EIS has significant implications for international relations in the future seems evident by events since 1977 when Senator Claiborne Pell proposed that an international environmental impact statement requirement be adopted by international treaty. An EIS would be required for any major national project, action, or continuing activity which might be expected to have a significant adverse effect on the physical environment or environmental concerns of other nations or on the global commons. In 1991 a *Convention on Environmental Impact Assessment in a Transboundary Context* was signed in Finland by 30 nations including the United States, and impact assessment was strongly recommended in Agenda 21, adopted by the 1992 United Nations Conference on Environment and Development. The European Union has issued directives to member states, and the UN Economic Commission for Europe has issued a series of reports on environmental impact assessment.[29] There can be little doubt that the NEPA Process, initiated in the United States, has had global influence and implications for future international relations.

To fully implement the functions of the CEQ specified under Title II of NEPA would need presidential support and congressional funding beyond what it has received thus far. But I am led to the conclusion that with these reinforcements NEPA would be adequate to its purpose as it now stands. For its alleged deficiencies and, in particular, the misuses of the EIS, remedies lie in adequate interpretation and visible support by the president, the EPA, the courts, and the CEQ, and in the response of the agencies. A CEQ 1997 team project on *Rediscovering and Implementing the National Environmental Policy Act* revealed a marked increase in agency support for NEPA. Unfortunately the Congress denied funding for this project and it was necessary to discontinue the effort. In the House of Representatives, where appropriations bills originate, the Republican leadership in the 104th and 105th congresses has been hostile to environmental legislation. Regarding a direct attack on NEPA as impolitic, the leadership has sought to render the Act ineffective through exemptions and financial restriction. The project offered an opportunity for further internalizing and integrating the administration of NEPA. It appears that NEPA is nevertheless gradually being internalized throughout the Federal system. This may not always be true of political appointees heading the agencies, as was evident in the environmentally unsympathetic Reagan and Bush administrations.

I conclude, therefore, that there is little wrong with the administration of NEPA or the EIS that could not be largely remedied within the present language and with an interpretation of the law in conformity with its intent. There are possibilities for textual clarification that although perhaps desirable are not essential. The ready remedy for the misuse or nonuse of the NEPA lies in persuading the responsible officials of the United States to act in accord with what the Act declares. This would appear to be a presidential responsibility. No less, and perhaps more, important would be the election of a Congress committed to protection of the environment. Although environmental quality appears to be a core value among a majority of Americans, it may not be their foremost policy concern on election day. Beyond NEPA, however, there remains the possibility that environmental policy in the United States cannot achieve its declared objectives unless affirmed in the fundamental law of the nation — the Constitution of the United States. Although not a present prospect, it would be presumptuous to believe that it will never become a possibility.

4

Integrating Environmental Policy

A DILEMMA CONFRONTS MANY AGENCIES OF THE FEDERAL
GOVERNMENT:

—HOW TO ACCOMMODATE ENVIRONMENTAL QUALITY OBJECTIVES,
AS DEVELOPED IN DOZENS OF STATUTES;

—WHILE AT THE SAME TIME EFFECTIVELY CARRYING OUT THE
AGENCY'S PRIMARY MISSION;

—WHEN THAT MISSION, IN MANY RESPECTS, MAY BE AT ODDS
WITH THOSE OBJECTIVES.

THE NATIONAL ENVIRONMENTAL POLICY ACT RESOLVES THE DI-
LEMMA BY MEANS OF AN UMBRELLA POLICY THAT *INTEGRATES* PUR-
POSES AND OBJECTIVES AND PROVIDES FOR CHOICE WHERE AGENCY
MISSIONS AND ENVIRONMENTAL QUALITY MAY CONFLICT.

—FROM A PRELIMINARY REVIEW DRAFT OF THE 21ST ANNUAL RE-
PORT OF THE COUNCIL ON ENVIRONMENTAL QUALITY (1990)

Why is integration of environmental policies within and between
Federal agencies a major objective of NEPA?[1] Integration of policy is not an
end in itself. Its purpose is to prevent or correct counteractive and wastefully
competitive programs and projects and to sharpen and strengthen the focus
of constructive public efforts. How was NEPA intended to promote this
objective? The fact that many of the threats to the quality of the American
environment could be traced to unintended effects of conflicting Federal
policies and programs was a logical reason for NEPA's focus on the interrelating activities of the Federal agencies. Integration of Federal policy affecting the environment is implicit in Section 2 of NEPA, to "encourage productive and enjoyable harmony between man and his environment," in Section
101(b), to "coordinate Federal plans, functions, programs, and resources,"
and in Section 102(2)(a), to "utilize a systematic, interdisciplinary approach
which will insure the integrated use of the natural and social sciences and
the environmental design arts in planning and decision-making which may
have an impact on man's environment."

Congress has characteristically enacted legislation in response to particular demands with little consideration of interactive effects or inadvertent economic or environmental consequences. In a pluralistic democratic society each interest group or local constituency pushes its agenda, with competitive indifference to the values of the others. A consequence has been conflicting priorities in a government that has often worked at cross-purposes, resulting in interagency conflict and waste of effort and public money.

In a less complex economy with less government involvement in the lives and activities of people, integration of interrelating government programs was not an issue. The political response to conflicting environmental policies for the public lands was either to establish a presidential-level coordination facility such as would have been provided in Senator James Murray's Resources and Conservation Act of 1959–60 or to establish a policy for negotiating conflicting claims as in the Multiple Use—Sustained Yield Act of 1960 (generally accounted a failure). Especially in multi-agency departments, such as Interior and Agriculture, political power and program autonomy was legislatively based in the bureaus. Integration of related inter and intra-agency programs affecting the environment had neither mandate nor means until NEPA took effect in 1970. Agency intransigence has historically been reinforced by bureaucratic and professional commitment to narrowly defined missions and politically influential client relationships. Many officials in the natural resources agencies have been indoctrinated in specialized professional schools of agriculture, forestry, mining, wildlife management, and engineering. Mission commitment, often single-purpose, is reinforced from a viewpoint that "the expert knows what's best." Requirements that complicate or qualify the focused pursuit of mission objectives are almost certain to be resisted by agency personnel. Where there were counterproductive and mutually defeating tendencies in competing agency missions, environmental quality was almost always a loser.

A key to understanding the problems of integration and rationalization of environmental policy may be found in policies governing the uses of land and coincidently its waters, minerals, soils, and living resources. Land in public ownership, and in various forms of private ownership, is subject to State and local controls where there is a legally recognized public interest. Virtually all environmental problems arise ultimately from uses of the land, including those manifest in air, water, climate change, ecosystem integrity, wildlife, public safety, transportation, and urbanization, among others. Senator Jackson saw land use policy as a logical step toward implementing NEPA objectives. In 1970 he proposed a National Land Use Policy Act (S.3354), legislation intended to persuade the States to make rational and informed decisions regarding the uses of environmentally sensitive areas. The Act was not the intrusion on private property rights or a Federal "land grab" claimed by its opponents and most of the news media. For a short time land use policy became an active public issue adopted by the League of Women Voters, associations for urban and regional planning, landscape protection, and preservation of farmland. But the very concept of land use policy aroused vigorous opposition.

Far from being an intrusion on States' rights, the National Land Use Policy Act would have protected the States and the Federal treasury from duplicating, competing, and mutually defeating Federal projects. Environmental impact assessment should, but did not always, reveal the need for integrating Federal public works planning. NEPA did not address this problem directly, but remedial action was implicit in the NEPA Process. Section 102(2)(c) of NEPA requires Federal agencies to "study, develop, and describe appropriate alternatives to recommended courses of action in any proposal which involves unresolved conflicts concerning alternative uses of available resources."

In preparation for a Senate hearing on a National Land Use Policy Act on March 24, 1970, a set of transparent overlay maps was prepared by Interior Committee staff which graphically revealed the places where Federal projects were in conflict. The locations were numerous. Especially notable were the Florida Everglades. The objectives of five Federal agencies were in conflict: the National Park Service, Department of Agriculture, Corps of Engineers, Federal Aviation Administration, and the Federal Highway Administration. Unfortunately for coherence and consistency in environmental policy, national land use legislation was prevented from reaching the floor of the House of Representatives although it passed in the Senate and was endorsed by the president. Senator Jackson reintroduced the bill in 1971, and in 1973 as the National Land Use Planning and Assistance Act, but thereafter abandoned the effort in the face of orchestrated highly emotional opposition. Land speculators, real estate developers, the building trades, private property owners, and natural resources industries had made the disagreeable discovery that environmental policy was not just for cleanup and prevention of pollution. NEPA had been enacted with no significant opposition, but the land use legislation stimulated an antienvironmental movement which extended to all Federal policies regulating uses, emissions, and disposal of hazardous industrial products, limiting the uses and abuses of private ownership of land and natural resources, and fixing responsibility for cleanup of contaminated sites. Antienvironmentalists have complained about complexities and incoherence in Federal environmental laws but have not been supportive of efforts to reconcile and integrate existing legislation. Improvements in environmental administration might only strengthen policies which they would like to see repealed.

NEPA does not directly affect private interests. But to prevent Federal agencies from undertaking or assisting unnecessarily damaging activities beyond the Federal establishment, it was necessary to redefine the responsibilities of the agencies and to redirect and reconcile agency priorities. And because of the customary single-purpose objectives of various agency projects and programs, an effort was needed to introduce and integrate environmental values into agency priorities. A declaration of national policy alone would not accomplish this. But Senator Jackson observed that a "declaration of a national policy could, however, provide a new organizing concept by which governmental functions could be weighed and evaluated in the light of better perceived and better understood national needs and goals."[2]

The responsibility of Federal agencies to build environmental values into their missions is explicit in NEPA—but adherence at the performance level is another matter. Integration of environmental values is required, but how it may best be accomplished has been problematic. The task is neither simple nor straightforward. The National Environmental Policy Act and *Regulations* issued by the Council on Environmental Quality under Executive Order 11991 of May 25, 1977, contain specific instructions toward integration. But the integrative task requires more than adherence to administrative, legal, and technical uniformities. NEPA and the CEQ *Regulations* require adaptation to the needs and circumstances of particular missions and programs. Policy integration, once regarded as a counterproductive imposition on agency missions, is increasingly being seen as an opportunity for more effective and sustainable programs. The integration of policies affords opportunities for interagency collaboration in planning and decision-making which were formerly unavailable, unrecognized, or politically risky. Statutory mandates formerly treated as inflexible by Federal agencies, the courts, and Congress have gained adaptability to additional objectives and values. Paradoxically, integration may narrow some agency options and enlarge others. Policy integration requires a process of agency-wide learning and reorientation that leads to more coherent and broader-based public administration and effective public service. But micromanagement of favored special programs by Congressional committees remains a chronic obstruction to the rational execution of public policy and law.

AN ADMINISTRATIVE FUNCTION

Federal agencies today face the task of integrating environmental values into a broad range of both previously established and presently anticipated programs and procedures. Despite obstructive attitudes in some agencies and Congress, the integration required by NEPA is also being pushed by demands for more effective and efficient management along with the growing opinion that damage to the environment is no longer an unavoidable price to be paid for desirable and necessary public objectives. The task of building environmental considerations into agency programs begins with legislation and administrative policy that permits or encourages flexibility and collaboration within and between agencies where interrelating purposes may be served. Identifying the needs and means toward integrative relationships is a task of public administration in which executive leadership oversees the implementation of public policy. Legislative responsibility is also involved because without authority to redefine existing programs, administrative coordination among agency subdivisions, and interagency collaboration is unlikely to occur—and because of the multifaceted character of most environmental impacts, interagency coordination is often a prerequisite for effective environmental management.

The ad hoc structuring of the Federal government presents a difficulty for programmatic integration. Client-responsive congressmen are protective of the separate identity of their personally sponsored programs. In a 1968 article on *Environmental Policy and the Congress,* Senator Jackson observed that "our governmental structure in the Executive Branch and even in the committee system of the Congress, while adequately designed for many specific objectives, is not easily adapted to the multifaceted needs of an overall environmental policy."[3] In the Senate hearing on bill S.1075, April 16, 1969, he suggested a general requirement that would be applicable to all agencies that have responsibilities affecting the environment rather than trying to go through agency by agency. Section 105 of NEPA implemented this idea, declaring that "the policies and goals set forth in the Act are supplementary to those set forth in existing authorizations of Federal agencies."

To test, evaluate, and where necessary redesign agency programs is a task of both legislation and public administration. The Congress and the courts can initiate policies and mandate programs but they cannot administer them. On occasion Congress has attempted to micromanage policy, notably in relation to resource issues. Peremptory and inflexible commands by the Congress have sometimes tied the hands of managers of the public lands and forced environmentally bad decisions. The courts deal with specific cases and controversies although their decisions may have broader implications. They may mandate action in conformity with their interpretations of the law, but the ad hoc history of environmental legislation has bequeathed a body of law that is not always clear or consistent. A 1995 Panel of the National Academy of Public Administration recommended that "Congress should begin a process to a truly integrated approach to environmental problems."[4]

Without the direction, support, or consent of top political authority, the lower levels of an agency cannot responsibly alter or modify policies or programs. Initiative for integrating environmental policies into ongoing programs is thus a responsibility of leadership within each administrative agency, and follow-through may be diffused throughout the agency under the guidance of its managerial personnel. Overall management policies may be initiated or adopted by the president and overseen by the Office of Management and Budget (OMB). Specific program management and the actual integration of policy with performance is most effectively undertaken at the agency levels where action occurs but may be subject to interposing directives laid down by the Congress or the courts.

Executive leadership, while essential, is alone insufficient to attain program integration throughout an agency or throughout the Federal government. Leadership is needed at all organizational levels. Persons closest to the performance of program functions are in position to see the problems and opportunities of program integration where it ought to occur. But lower-level program administrators may not welcome outside interposition in management of their missions. Program integration implies more than the harmonization of policies and practices. It may also require the elimination of redundant or conflicting practices.

Once a reoriented agency policy is firm and comprehensible, agency personnel at all levels should be enabled to contribute to or accommodate to its implementation. If the people who carry on agency missions in the office and the field do not understand or accept the integration of environmental values into their duties and objectives, NEPA's integrative task will not be accomplished. An organization learns through its people, and so the basic task of integrating environmental values into agency programs is a process of social learning guided by interpretation of the National Environmental Policy Act and its implementing *Regulations*. The integrative process requires reconciliation between NEPA and other statutes affecting environment and natural resources as, for example, with the Federal Land Policy and Management Act (FLPMA, 1976), the National Forest Management Act (NFMA, 1976), and with the antipollution legislation administered by the NEPA.

CONGRESSIONAL INTENT

Administrative responsibility for building environmental values into agency policies, plans, and programs has been mandated, in effect, by NEPA. Unfortunately, the legislative purpose as declared in the Act has not been seriously pursued at the highest administrative level. Administrative performance has not been consistently monitored by Congress but has been periodically reviewed by the General Accounting Office. Because the principal means of interpreting the NEPA has been through judicial review of agency conformity with the required impact statement (Section 102(2)(c)), this provision has been widely interpreted as the essential purpose of the Act. In fact, as has been noted, the impact statement was intended to force agency compliance with the substantive provisions of the Act declared in Section 101(b). A major purpose of the Act was to integrate environmental values into Federal policies and programs—and the impact statement was conceived as one means to that end.

That Congress intended more in NEPA than impact analysis is evident not only in its text but in its legislative history. A proposed draft Joint Resolution on a National Policy for the Environment appended to a special report of the Senate Committee on Interior and Insular Affairs on July 11, 1968, anticipated an intent incorporated a year later in NEPA. The following paragraph indicates the responsibility of Federal agencies for incorporating environmental values into the interpretation and administration of "the policies, programs and public laws of the United States":

> It is the intent of the Congress that policies, programs, and public laws of the United States be interpreted and administered in a manner protective of the total needs of man in the environment. To this end, the Congress proposes that appropriate legislation be adopted and, where necessary, that administrative arrangements be established to make effective the following objectives of national policy for the environment:
>
> (1) To arrest the deterioration of the environment.
>
> (2) To restore and revitalize damaged areas of our Nation so that they may once again be productive of economic wealth and spiritual satisfaction.
>
> (3) To find alternatives and procedures which will minimize and prevent future hazards in the use of environment-shaping technologies — old and new.
>
> (4) To provide direction and, if necessary, new institutions and new technologies designed to optimize man-environment relationships and to minimize future costs in the management of the environment.[5]

Elaborating on the four objectives declared in the draft resolution of 1968, six substantive principles of environmental policy were specified in NEPA (Section 10(b)), and additional provisions have been stated in the Clean Air Act, the Water Quality Amendments, and the Endangered Species Act. These statutes, among others, provide the goals and standards against which the environmental impacts of administrative action can be measured. The environmental values implicit in NEPA principles were intended to characterize all Federal programs. Enumerated in Section 101(b) they are specified as follows:

> In order to carry out the policy set forth in this Act, it is the continuing responsibility of the Federal Government to use all practicable means, consistent with other essential considerations of national policy, to improve and coordinate Federal plans, functions, programs, and resources to the end that the Nation may
>
> (1) fulfill the responsibilities of each generation as trustees of the environment for succeeding generations;
>
> (2) assure for all Americans safe, healthful, productive, and aesthetically and culturally pleasing surroundings;

(3) attain the widest range of beneficial uses of the environment without degradation, risk to health or safety, or other undesirable and unintended consequences;

(4) preserve important historic, cultural, and natural aspects of our national heritage, and maintain, wherever possible, an environment which supports diversity and variety of individual choice;

(5) achieve a balance between population and resource use which will permit high standards of living and a wide sharing of life's amenities; and

(6) enhance the quality of renewable resources and approach the maximum attainable recycling of depletable resources.

It is important to the integration of NEPA into agency missions, that administrative personnel understand those principles against which agency conformity with NEPA should be measured. Impact analysis and assessment without reference to policy may provide information but fail to establish relevance to NEPA principles. Regardless of the validity or reliability of its reported factual findings, an environmental impact statement will fall short of its integrative potential if it fails to consider the longer-term sustainability of the policy or program assessed. Although efforts to improve the technical quality of impact assessment are commendable, there is always need to guard against the triumph of technique over purpose—a risk endemic to professionalized expertise in and out of government.

AGENCY RESPONSIBILITY

Integration of environmental values into all Federal programs having major environmental impacts is required by NEPA. The Act specifies goals of environmental policy and also contains action-forcing provisions intended to introduce environmental information and standards into planning and decision-making. Supplementing and interpreting provisions of NEPA are the *Regulations* issued by the Council on Environmental Quality under Executive Order No. 11991 of May 25, 1977. Application of the NEPA goals is further elaborated and specified by regulations or directives adopted at the departmental level. In addition, departments must take account of environmental statutes administered by other agencies, along with judicial interpretations of NEPA. Too often the legislative intent of NEPA is evaded in efforts to protect previous agency mission preferences. Pro-forma procedure under Section 102(2)(c) is undertaken as evidence of NEPA compliance. Effective policy integration may not occur, but the preferred policy of the agency may avoid judicial reversal.

The language of NEPA in Sections 101 and 102 is mandatory and unequivocal. Section 102 is logically intended to bring agency policy into compliance with the substantive provisions declared in Section 101. Means and procedures toward NEPA implementation are specified in Sections 102(2)(a), (b), and (c). Pursuant to the purpose of the Act, they instruct agency action toward incorporating environmental values into all programs affecting the environment. These instructions are as follows:

> Sec. 102. The Congress authorizes and directs that, to the fullest extent possible: (1) the policies, regulations, and public laws of the United States shall be interpreted and administered in accordance with the policies set forth in this Act, and (2) all agencies of the Federal Government shall:
>
> (a) utilize a systematic, interdisciplinary approach which will insure the integrated use of the natural and social sciences and the environmental design arts in planning and in decisionmaking which may have an impact on man's environment;
>
> (b) identify and develop methods and procedures in consultation with the Council on Environmental Quality established by title II of this Act, which will insure that presently unquantified environmental amenities and values may be given appropriate consideration in decisionmaking along with economic and technical considerations;
>
> (c) include in every recommendation or report on proposals for legislation and other major Federal actions significantly affecting the quality of the human environment, a detailed statement by the responsible official on:
>
> (i) the environmental impact of the proposed action,
>
> (ii) any adverse environmental effects which cannot be avoided should the proposal be implemented,
>
> (iii) alternatives to the proposed action,
>
> (iv) the relationship between local short-term uses of man's environment and the maintenance and enhancement of long-term productivity, and
>
> (v) any irreversible and irretrievable commitments of resources which would be involved in the proposed action should it be implemented.

The foregoing provisions together with other directives in NEPA clearly indicate the intent that environmental values be incorporated in the policies, plans, and programs of Federal agencies. In 1972, the Eighth Circuit Court of Appeals in the *Gillham Dam* case interpreted the intent of Congress, that NEPA procedures apply to all programs and projects impacting upon the environment, including those previously authorized or underway (i.e. *Environmental Defense Fund v. Corps of Engineers*, 470 F. 2d 289, 1972). In this case the agency was required to prepare an adequate impact statement regardless of the degree of completion of the project or of the funds expended on it.

The remaining subsections of 102(2) are significant for environmental policy and program integration between Federal agencies and State and local governments. These provisions require the lead or principal agency preparing an environmental impact statement or assessment to consult with any other Federal land management agency or State or local entity that may be affected by the proposal. Subsection 102(2)(d) deals principally with coordinating NEPA policies and procedures with the States. Its provisions assist the integration of environmental policy nationwide. For example, Subsection 102(2)(d)(iv) requires that "the responsible Federal official provides early notification to, and solicits the views of, any other State or any Federal land management entity of any action or any alternative thereto which may have significant impacts upon such State or affected Federal land management entity and, if there is any disagreement on such impacts, prepares a written assessment of such impacts and views for incorporation into such detailed statement" (i.e. Subsection 102(2)(c)). As noted in chapter 3, the environmental impact assessment process provides an informing and, so far as possible, a factual basis for program integration within and between Federal agencies and with State and local governments.

In addition to subsection (e), previously cited, other subsections of 102(2) NEPA require that all agencies of the Federal government shall:

> (d) Recognize the worldwide and long-range character of environmental problems and, where consistent with the foreign policy of the United States, lend appropriate support to initiatives, resolutions, and programs designed to maximize international cooperation in anticipating and preventing a decline in the quality of mankind's world environment;

> (e) Make available to States, counties, municipalities, institutions, and individuals, advice and information useful in restoring, maintaining, and enhancing the quality of the environment;

> (f) Initiate and utilize ecological information in the planning and development of resource-oriented projects.

And, as previously noted, Section 105 declares that "the policies and goals set forth in this Act are supplementary to those set forth in existing authorizations of Federal agencies." Thus NEPA amends all other Federal statutes and programs having major impacts upon the environment but it does not change their substantive statutory missions.

INTEGRATIVE STRATEGIES

Several forms of policy analysis—assessment of environmental impacts, risks, technological effects, and costs and benefits—may be used to ascertain the probable consequences of a policy or program over and beyond its ostensible objectives, and could reveal where integration was needed. But the applicability of these analytic techniques to policy integration depends upon their ability to discover the range and effects of the probable consequences of an agency proposal. NEPA and departmental policies provide standards for comparing agency practice with declared principles. As the 1990 *Environmental Quality: The Twenty-First Annual Report of the Council on Environmental Quality* observed, "The NEPA Process [impact analysis] can be understood only in the context of a statutory scheme and program to which it applies." Policy integration to be effective must also be pervasive and systematic throughout the agencies. In practice integrative strategies must be issue-specific in focus, and there are rules to assist an orderly integrative procedure.

Regulations issued by the CEQ for the implementation of NEPA provide guidance for integrating environmental values and principles into programs, notably in Section 1505.1, Agency Decisionmaking, and Section 1507.3, Agency Procedures. These sections emphasize the importance of agency review of policies and programs for implementing procedures under NEPA Section 102(2) to achieve the substantive objectives of Sections 101 and 102(1). To satisfy CEQ *Regulation* 1505.1, agency procedures require designation of the major points of decision in programs affecting the environment, and require that relevant environmental documents become a part of the Record of Decision which should specify the alternatives considered and should be made available to the public. Section 1507.3 specifies the format and coverage of agency regulations and states that "Agencies are encouraged to publish explanatory guidance" for applying the *Regulations* and agency procedures, thus acting "to ensure full compliance with the purposes and provisions of the Act." With the *Regulations* and their own procedures in view, agencies should be able to develop policies, plans, proposals and programs that are consistent with NEPA principles, thus advancing an integrative approach to environmental policies throughout the Executive branch.

Two major strategies for program coordination and integration are "scoping" and "tiering." If integration has not previously occurred earlier in agency planning, it may be assisted by the process of "scoping" (*Regulations,* 1501.7, 1508.25). The purpose of "scoping" a proposal is to ascertain its full dimensions and implications and to avoid duplication or conflict among projects and programs. An outline for scoping procedures is provided by Figure 5-2, "Planning for Integration of Environmental Laws," in Appendix B of the twenty-first annual environmental quality report of the CEQ. The scoping process is a logical concomitant to the provisions of NEPA Section 102(2)(c)(v) which require that the agency initiating a proposal (i.e. the responsible Federal official) "consult with and obtain the comments of any Federal agency which has jurisdiction by law or any special expertise with respect to any environmental impact involved."

For any major Federal program there may be as many as a dozen different environment-related statutes of which account must be taken. The scope of a proposal or program will often exceed the mission of any single agency, and, as has been noted, Section 105 of NEPA amends the basic statutes of all Federal agencies, establishing NEPA objectives common to them all. Integration of environmental provisions into the programs of any agency will frequently require interactive cooperation with the relevant offices and administrators of other agencies. This is a significant departure from the exclusiveness and noncommunication that formerly tended to characterize many interagency relationships in areas of parallel or overlapping jurisdiction (e.g. between the Corps of Engineers and Bureau of Reclamation).

"Tiering" is described in Section 1502.20 of the *Regulations* and provides for the building of one environmental assessment onto another, thereby facilitating the integration of related provisions into a coherent whole. The process of "tiering" (like a layered cake) may also contribute to program integration especially where State and local agencies have undertaken environmental assessments or when a project is integral to a more comprehensive program.

It follows that the principal mechanism for integrative action in any agency should be its own environmental regulations and procedures required by and consistent with general regulations as issued by the CEQ. If departmental regulations do not offer adequate guidance toward this objective, revision or expansion of those regulations may be necessary. This necessity may be ascertained by a review of agency performance in the administration of NEPA. Performance reviews by the CEQ have found substantial variations in agency implementation of NEPA. Some agencies have not taken the mandate of Sections 1505.1 and 1507.3 seriously, and Executive Order 11991 provides no sanctions to back up CEQ *Regulations*. Criticisms of agency performance by the General Accounting Office have little influence where there are no penalties.

The effectiveness of agency regulations should be of concern to the Office of Management and Budget. Early in the drafting of NEPA a proposal was made that the OMB be charged with certain oversight responsibilities for agency program conformance with NEPA. In the course of the April 16, 1969, hearing on S.1075 Senator Jackson suggested that "maybe the Bureau of the Budget could be given the authority to deal with this problem in a broad discretionary way in which the agencies would be required both in quasi-judicial proceedings and in legislative comments to the Congress to meet certain environmental conditions."[6] This suggestion, however, did not obtain congressional support. And since its establishment the management functions intended for OMB have been steadily displaced by its fiscal-budgetary oversight. Moreover, there has been reason at times to question OMB support for NEPA and the CEQ.

INTEGRATION IN ACTION

For policy integration to be attained throughout the Federal service it is necessary to know where it is needed as well as how, in particular circumstances, it may best be accomplished. In September 1996 a National Workshop on Environmental Monitoring and Research was convened by the Office of Science and Technology Policy (OSTP). The resulting report proposed "a national framework for integrating environmental systems and resources." Although the findings of the effort would be essentially scientific, OSTP director John H. Gibbons observed that "integration of our environmental monitoring and research networks will also provide the knowledge base required for selecting management approaches that ensure ecosystem and resource sustainability."[7]

The process and difficulties of integrating environmental values declared in NEPA into agency plans and programs may be illustrated by experience under the military Base Closure and Defense Authorization Amendments and Realignment Act of 1988. The statute requires that before a military base can be transferred to other ownership it must be free from environmental hazards. The disposition of bases must be integrated with statutes administered by the EPA (e.g. the Toxic Substances Control Act), the Comprehensive Environmental Response Compensation and Liability Act of 1980 (CERCLA or Superfund), and with the Superfund Amendments and Reauthorization Act of 1986 (SARA) and the Resource Conservation and Recovery Act (RCRA), which includes the Federal Facilities Compliance Act. Account must also be taken of the protective provisions of the Endangered Species Act of 1973, administered by the Fish and Wildlife Service. In addition to base closure issues, the DoD as third largest Federal land holder unavoidably interacts with other Federal land management agencies (e.g. Bureau of Land Management and Forest Service), considered at the conclusion of this chapter.

Reconciling interrelating statutory requirements may be difficult, but failure to do so may invite administrative frustration, interagency conflict, loss of public confidence, and possible litigation. The principal strategy for implementing the Endangered Species Act (ESA) is habitat preservation or restoration. Section 2(b) of the ESA declares that its purpose is "to provide a means whereby the ecosystems upon which endangered species and threatened species depend may be conserved." But the Act does not provide adequate means for resolving conflicts over property rights. Conflicting demands for future uses of the areas to be released by base closures involve more political than scientific considerations. Impact assessment should employ integrated interdisciplinary analysis as required by NEPA Section 102(2)(a) but it cannot resolve the conflicts among values inherent in the transfer of a base to other ownership.

Policy integration through conflict resolution is often difficult to attain. For example, military base closure and realignment proposals may be integrated with ESA and NEPA requirements by timely surveys and assessments of the environmental properties of the bases. Recourse to scientific opinion, considerations of environmental hazards from previous base uses, and evaluation of alternative future uses contribute to the integrative analysis needed for conformity to NEPA. The Nature Conservancy and State Heritage Programs have the capacity of providing ecological information, which for some bases has already been provided.

More numerous are the activities of nonmilitary agencies affecting cultural and natural resources. Environmental impact assessment and the scoping process provide information needed for integrated management planning. Section 102(2)(h) requires the agencies to "initiate and utilize ecological information in the planning and development of resource-oriented projects." Effective integration requires that this data be available at the beginning of the planning process—a consideration emphasized by the CEQ under *Regulation* 1502.5. Problems involving nonquantifiable values will require informed resolution. Section 102(2)(b) requires that "presently unquantified environmental amenities and values may be given appropriate consideration along with economic and technical considerations" and Section 101(b)(4) declares the responsibility of the Federal government to "preserve important natural aspects of our national heritage, and maintain wherever possible an environment which supports diversity and variety of individual choice."

NEPA does not provide criteria for applying these provisions. To implement Section 102(2)(b), *Regulation* 1506.8 requires the agencies to "identify and develop methods and procedures in consultation with the CEQ"—but this objective has not been easily accomplished. There are obvious uncertainties over what environmental amenities and values should be considered and how such considerations should be weighted and integrated into the decision process. Criteria might be obtained from analytic studies provided for in the national Historic Preservation Act (16 U.S.C. 470 et seq.), in the Wild and Scenic Rivers Act (16 U.S.C. 1271 et seq.), and the Wilderness Act (16 U.S.C. 1131 et seq.), and by nongovernmental organizations such as the Nature Conservancy and the National Trust for Historic Preservation. Consideration of unquantified values perhaps can be best met through an interdisciplinary study team which includes persons able to deal with cultural, aesthetic, and evaluative considerations. The National Park Service in particular is custodian of a great variety of legally protected sites. The NPS maintains a National Center on Cultural Resources, Stewardship, and Partnership Programs and an Archaeology and Ethnology Division.

Environmental impact assessment can provide grounds for arriving at a clarification of issues or for resolution of policy differences and should enable an agency to counter a charge of arbitrary or capricious decision-making.[8] Preparing an EIS should assist an agency in more effectively integrating environmental values into its own proposals and programs. This advantage and the learning experience may be lost when an agency contracts with consulting firms to do the thinking and analysis which it was intended that the agency itself undertake. As noted, the scoping and tiering processes are intended to reveal the interrelationships which policy decisions must take into account and reconcile. Information regarding the effects of agency policies and practices on environmental values—cultural and natural—is a prerequisite for developing integrative strategies. Without this information it is difficult to know where integrative efforts are most needed or what changes in policy and procedure they may require.

Rhetorical policy statements and directives are necessary but alone are insufficient to integrate environmental values where, in practice, they have never been seriously considered. Workshops or seminars, where face-to-face discussions and exchange of experience can occur, are among the better ways to obtain understanding and compliance throughout an agency. Experts from outside the government or from other agencies may facilitate problem identification and resolution, provided that they are sufficiently informed regarding agency history and its current clientele, policies and relationships. It is difficult to apply a cost-benefit evaluation to efforts of this kind. But damage to morale and the monetary costs of conflict, litigation, and loss of public confidence could far outweigh the time and money expended to help people do a better job. A report on *The National Environmental Policy Act in DoD* (Department of Defense Report PL 909 R1, June 1990) recommended that "The subject of NEPA should be introduced in the curricula of the appropriate Service schools and training courses." Of broader significance and indicative of a contemporary trend, a NEPA Reinvention Workshop of agency compliance officers was sponsored by the CEQ at the White House Conference Center on June 19, 1997. But follow-up from this effort was "vetoed" by an environmentally unfriendly Congress.

OBSTACLES TO INTEGRATION

To appreciate the difficulty of coordinating policy and performance in the expanding national state in the 20th century, a historical retrospective is revealing. From the three departments of State, Treasury, and War, and the Attorney General in George Washington's administration to the fourteen cabinet-level departments (and at least eighty independent or semi-independent agencies today), the Federal government has grown to a size and complexity that in the ordinary sense of the word appears "unmanageable." Over the years the Federal "structure" has been created ad hoc by the Congress. Each agency has its own basic authorization, mission, clientele, and congressional

oversight. The task of integrating environmental policy throughout this inchoate structure is indeed formidable.

Efforts have been made to bring coherence and rationality into the Executive Branch, notably by the first and second Hoover Commissions (1947-
49 and 1953-55)[9] and by the Ash Council during the Nixon administration.
Proposals have been made to consolidate the various natural resources and
environmental programs in a single cabinet-level department. These proposals have been vetoed by client groups and existing departments (e.g. Agriculture, Defense, Interior) and opposed by congressional committees jealous
of their oversight authorities.

Interagency integration is also opposed philosophically by persons who
agree with Thomas Jefferson that "it is not by the consolidation or concen-
tration of powers, but by their distribution, that good government is ef-
fected."[10] Jefferson was addressing a constitutional question, but to persons
who see government as the enemy of personal liberties, "healthy competition" among autonomous agencies is advantageous to freedom. This viewpoint is congenial to those persons and organizations hostile in principle to
the environmental movement and to NEPA.

Article II, Section 1 of the Constitution declares that "the executive power
shall be vested in a president of the United States," but the substance of
executive power is not defined. The president is commander-in-chief of the
armed forces, but it is not clear how far he is manager-in-chief of the civilian
agencies. This authority may be implicit in the president's specified powers
and especially in Article II, Section 3 that "he shall take care that the laws
be faithfully executed," but Congress may impose its own conditions on the
administrative process.[11]

As previously noted, the ambiguity of Article II has permitted two different interpretations of presidential responsibility. The dual concept of the
presidency described in chapter 2 and its effect upon the Executive Office of
the President and hence on the functions and status of the CEQ in relation
to policy coordination require restatement here. One interpretation sees the
presidential role as primarily political—persuasive in leadership, policy formulation, and personal in style (and as some critics would say) the national
preacher in his "bully pulpit." The other interpretation views the presidential
office as institutional—an essential function being to oversee the performance of the agencies of the Executive Branch—the presidential incumbent
being the national chief executive officer. The distinction has implications
for NEPA, the CEQ, and agency-wide integration of NEPA principles.

The personal-political presidency pushes managerial responsibilities
downward to the cabinet level. The advent of television has exaggerated the
personal political role of the president as head of state, the self-appointed
mentor, chief national and international moralizer, with symbolic "photo op"

appearances at public events resembling functions of British royalty more than the traditional posture of American presidents. The extent to which personal style displaces the managerial role of the presidency varies with the incumbent president, but with variations it has been a dominant presidential tendency since the administration of John F. Kennedy.

A consequence of this tendency, important to the administration of NEPA and the integration of environmental policy, has been the misconception and operational disintegration of the Executive Office of the President as the central managerial and coordinative institution of the Federal government. The concept of the EOP was developed in 1936 by Franklin D. Roosevelt's Committee on Administrative Management chaired by Louis Brownlow, a long-time adviser to presidents.[12] The EOP was intended to assist the president in his managerial functions. The offices comprising the EOP were to be concerned with broad and fundamental areas of executive responsibilities—in the words of one committee member—with budget, personnel, and planning. The Brownlow Committee also invented the White House staff, but its present size and functions have come to exceed the committee recommendations.

As observed in chapter 2, the distinction between the White House staff and the Executive Office of the President have been largely lost. The White House staff was intended to provide personal political assistance to the president but not to engage in policy-making. The EOP is not White House staff, and the intended functions of its agencies require a degree of independence from political party pressure. The EOP was intended to assist and supplement the president's executive responsibilities and the effectiveness of its agencies depend upon presidential recognition and support. The agencies in the EOP have been created by Congress, and their officers have been subject to senatorial confirmation. This suggests that their responsibilities are not exclusively to the president. The EOP as the central managerial agency was intended to assist, oversee, and coordinate the execution of national policies as required under Article II, Section 3 of the Constitution.[13] Confusing the EOP with the White House staff by the news media and successive presidential administrations has deflected the purpose for which the EOP was created—and exemplifies the decline of the institutional presidency.[14]

The effective administration of NEPA depends on a degree of visible presidential support, which it seldom has received. Integration of NEPA principles throughout the Federal agencies has been hampered by the Supreme Court's narrow interpretation of the Act and of the purpose of the Environmental Impact Statement. The general indifference of the Congress along with inattention of successive presidents has also been responsible for the slow pace of integrating NEPA principles into agency performance and interagency programs.

A logical organizational response to NEPA has sometimes turned out to be an obstacle. The practice in many agencies was to add an environmental assessment office or function to the preexisting organizational structure. In principle, this could assist the integration of NEPA into agency policy. Very often, however, the principal responsibility of this office was to keep the agency out of trouble for noncompliance with NEPA. Few environmental officers had the authority, responsibility, or opportunity to promote environmental policy integration in programs administered by other and higher divisions of the agency. Without agency commitment to NEPA this add-on disjunctive structuring of environmental office, isolated from the power centers of the agency, has rarely been able to advance the objective of program integration. Obstacles have been less in structure than in political-administrative indifference and bureaucratic resistance. However, the NEPA Reinvention Workshop sponsored by the CEQ of June 19, 1997, provided numerous examples of positive innovative implementations of NEPA within Federal agencies.[15]

As mentioned earlier, the scope and progression of impacts often has exceeded the expertise of agency personnel, necessitating the employment of outside experts. Rather than employ additional personnel some agencies (as noted) have preferred to require clients or to contract with private consulting firms to prepare environmental impact statements—a dubious way to achieve the essentials of program integration. Even though agency personnel review a consultant's draft environmental statement, the consultants—not the agency personnel—did the analysis and thinking that went into the EIS. Furthermore, the consultants are unlikely to be asked to consider or to appreciate the need for interagency program integration. Although integration of NEPA principles into practice often requires cooperation among Federal agencies, program integration must occur within each agency and in the minds and perceptions of its leadership. Expert consultants may be necessary and valuable adjuncts to the application of NEPA to agency programs—but the relationship should be one of advice—not a substitute for an agency's learning at first hand how its mission may impact upon the environment. Participation by agency personnel in assessing the impact of its plans and programs on the environment is an indispensable aspect of institutional learning.

The employment of professional expertise in environmental impact analysis within an agency may improve the quality and reliability of impact statements, but it also carries a risk in separating the experts from the rest of the agency personnel. A common source of obstruction to holistic integrative policies is a tendency toward occupational specialization. In many ways the motivation for this tendency is constructive—even essential—but under some circumstances it may create difficulties for communication and coordination. Much of our environmental protection and antipollution legislation is incremental, addressing specific categories of problems with insufficient consideration of related issues upon which the ultimate resolution of a categorical problem may depend. Ridding an area of toxic wastes or of unexploded ammunition frequently encounters this type of difficulty—a tangle of complex related problems may require sorting out in the course of developing optimal integrative strategies.

Early environmental protection laws and regulations addressed specific physical entities—air, water, soil, radiation, and toxic substances, without sufficient regard for their interactive relationships. Regulations bounded by specific substances or phenomenon in the environment still pose potential barriers to integrating environmental programs. But there is growing recognition that pollutants, pathogens, particulates, and many forms of life move from one medium to another (e.g. to air, water, soil, and biota), and require multimedia strategies for prevention, protection, or controls. Action, however, may entail initial economic, technological and even political costs. In the private sector the loss of some jobs and retraining for new production methods may be necessary. In the long run, however, prevention is less costly and certainly more effective than is control. But human beings live in the present where up-front costs of prevention are incurred—not in the long run when benefits are realized by others.

The need for an integrative approach to environmental policies and programs was recognized with the establishment of the EPA. By bringing under one roof the various environmental protection programs previously administered by separate agencies, a first step was taken toward interagency integration of interrelated environmental programs. Successive amendments to the clean air and water quality legislation have enlarged EPA's scope and effectiveness. The scoping and tiering provisions implementing NEPA have broadened the base for coordination to include all agencies or programs having relevance to any major Federal program or proposal impacting upon the environment. But the statutory bases for most programs have remained categorical. This is partly explained by our tendency to control the externalizing of pollutants into the environment rather than taking the more drastic step of internalizing their production in closed systems—or phasing out their manufacture or distribution.

One of the principal obstacles to program integration has been the way in which environmental issues have ordinarily been addressed in Congress. Policy decisions requiring legislation must pass through various congressional committees and subcommittees where competition, preemption, compromise, accommodation, and status maintenance are more often the practice than the exception. This has been a factor in rejection of proposals for a Joint House-Senate Committee on the Environment. Congress, moreover, is not bound in its actions to conform to requirements laid down for the executive agencies. It is not required to assess the environmental impact of its proposals nor the consistency of its actions with NEPA, whereas the agencies are required to review their legislative proposals in accordance with CEQ

Regulation 1505.8. Administrative agencies may be faced with the task of making coherent policy out of legislative provisions which may be mutually inconsistent or even contradictory.

A final source of possible barriers to environmental program integration may be found in the prevailing practices of judicial review. Insofar as agencies are not found to be in flagrant violation of NEPA procedures (notably as specified in Section 102(2)(c) the courts, with few exceptions, have allowed them substantial discretion in their compliance with NEPA. As the law stands today, integration of environmental principles into agency policies, plans, programs, and procedures is unlikely to be affected by judicial action. Agencies have been relatively free to determine the extent of their own compliance. Judicial deference to agency policy and common-law principles may act as a barrier to citizen lawsuits to force compliance with NEPA.

Judicial interpretations of the Constitution, however, may act as barriers to integrative policy. The "taking" clause in the Fifth Amendment has been interpreted in ways that find governmental regulation of land use, or exercise of the power of eminent domain, to be in certain cases "unconstitutional" and sufficiently costly to discourage government action. For example, there is a growing consensus that the best way to assist the survival of endangered species would be through the protection of ecosystems and species habitat. Ecosystem protection might (more often than not) require integration of policy and management of land under various public jurisdictions (e.g. Federal, State, and local agencies) and private ownership. In many instances, however, this would require government purchase of privately owned land, or restriction on those uses which might jeopardize the endangered species but which also might be interpreted by the courts as a "regulatory taking" requiring "just compensation." Protection of endangered species or ecosystems is not a value that the Constitution of the United States recognizes. There is some opinion (possibly growing) that an amendment to the Constitution may be necessary to place environmental protection on a level equal with economic and civil rights. An amendment could conceivably have the effect of reinforcing NEPA integration with other policies—especially where economic considerations must be taken into account.

AGENCY OPTIONS AND OPPORTUNITIES

During the early years of its implementation NEPA faced substantial agency indifference, resistance, and evasion. Its principles were neither recognized nor considered relevant to many agency missions and practices adopted in the years before the environmental movement emerged. NEPA altered agency missions by amending the statutory bases of customary assumptions and operating practices and by requiring observance of new substantive and procedural mandates. The action-forcing provisions of NEPA were intended to overcome institutional inertia and the persistence of pre-NEPA environmental indifference.

The substantive provisions of NEPA and of other environmental statutes provide opportunities for decisions previously unavailable to agencies. In particular, the big material-resources management agencies now have an option of declining politically privileged, poorly conceived, or wasteful projects. The option to say "no" to misapplied political influence is an opportunity that many public officials have not always enjoyed. In some cases, NEPA might protect the declared mission of an agency against its perversion by misguided or aggrandizing interests. Stability of agency staffing and budgeting would be served by policies that were protective against arbitrary or capricious political importunities. This would offer some protection from vendettas by congressmen disgruntled by agency unwillingness to pursue environmentally damaging projects urged by politically influential constituents.

The NEPA process has affected projects more often than programs because enforcement has been left primarily to the courts, which rule on specific cases and controversies more often than directly on general policies and programs. Nevertheless, policies and programs may be altered—even reversed—in consequence of rulings on collateral or procedural issues, such as incidental infringement of constitutional protection for property or civil rights. Agency programs sometimes have been left in a state of ambiguity, with the future course of program implementation uncertain. Such circumstances damage the reputation of the agency and its program administrators, and tend to diminish public confidence in agency leadership. A way to lessen such reverses is through making environmental decisions in conformity with the provisions of NEPA. Instead of leaving the interpretation of NEPA to litigation through the courts, the leadership of the agencies and the president could take a positive approach to the implementation of NEPA. Rather than regarding NEPA as external to their missions and responsibilities, agency administrators might regard the Act, as intended, integral to the agency mission and its authorizing legislation—as some are now doing—and as Section 105 makes explicit. However, if White House support is perceived as ambiguous, agencies are more likely to choose inaction over initiative—status quo over innovation.

The president as chief executive officer is the constitutional coordinator of Federal programs except when, as sometimes happens, the Congress interposes barriers on presidential action—usually at the behest of politically influential constituents. NEPA, however, provides a mandate to build environmental considerations into agency policies, plans, programs and projects—indeed it requires this action. In theory, it should seldom be necessary to wait for presidential orders or OMB approval to undertake positive implementation. In practice, White House inattention and budgetary constraints have sharply limited the oversight capabilities of the CEQ and diminished the opportunities for pressure on the agencies to honor the NEPA intent. Nevertheless some agencies have taken initiatives that, in effect, implement NEPA's principles.[16]

For example, within the Department of Defense (DoD) attitudes toward NEPA have been mixed, but since 1991, DoD has undertaken the Legacy Resource Management Program for the identification, protection, and enhancement of natural and cultural resources.[17] DoD is custodian of 25 million acres of land, the third largest Federal land management agency. Nearly all environmental problems originate on the land and policy integration between as well as within the land management agencies is necessary for realization of the NEPA mandate. Environmental responsibilities of the DoD on military bases abroad are discussed in chapter 5. Program integration is an integral objective of Legacy. Its projects are separate and apart from actions required under NEPA or the Endangered Species Act, but it parallels NEPA objectives. Its key themes are the need to (1) Protect and enhance significant resources, (2) Integrate biological, cultural, and geophysical resource management, (3) Manage resources for the long term, (4) Train DoD personnel about stewardship responsibility, (5) Develop partnership mechanisms, and (6) Provide public information and access programs. If fully implemented, Legacy could be a major contributory factor and model in the integration of environmental values into Federal programs.

Stewardship of the public lands of the United States—one third of the nation is divided among five land-management agencies—the DoD, Bureau of Land Management, Forest Service, National Park Service, and Fish and Wildlife Service. The recent Federal policy of ecosystem management on the public lands requires for its implementation an interagency integration of environmental planning and programs. NEPA has been found to be "a powerful collaborative planning process."[18] The degree of difficulty in integrating any new policy with an existing program depends upon the compatibility of the old program with the new policy. Some "pre-environment" policies of Congress and some agency programs can be harmonized with environmental values only through statutory change and the always difficult redirection of agency priorities and client relationships. An example (and there are others) is the 1872 Mining Act which persists despite its unjustifiable economic and environmental costs. This Act has been a source of repeated conflict over protection of national parks and monuments. The difficulty of realizing the NEPA mandate is greater when the integration of policy must alter established programs in contrast to integration at the initial stages of conceptualization and planning.

Officials whose perspective is narrowly fixed on particular goals or policies reinforced by congressional allies often find difficulty in modifying or redirecting their priorities. Fully effective program integration begins with the conceptualization or reformulation of policies and programs for consistency—or at least not inconsistency with environmental objectives. This may require reconsideration of agency assumptions and goals. Unless NEPA goals are up front in the minds of agency leadership, effective integration of environmental values into traditional agency programs is unlikely to occur. Agency leadership need not be conversant in all cases as to how this integration can be accomplished. But it alone can send out the signals which enable persons closer to the operative programs to undertake integrative initiatives.

For example, a directive from agency heads reinforcing Sections 102(2)(a) and (b) of NEPA followed up by "workshops" within agency divisions might provide impetus and direction toward achieving operational integration. In addition, agency programs and procedures could be reviewed for consistency with the six aspects of national environmental policy declared in Section 101(b) of NEPA. These substantive provisions of NEPA, too often dismissed as unenforceable rhetoric, may also be understood as valid jurisprudence—"soft law" in the philosophic sense of the principles which, in the public interest, the Federal government should observe in action. They are as explicit and ascertainable as are many criteria applied to economic development or to social justice. Environmental values expressed in NEPA have no explicit constitutional referent, and the courts have left their implementation largely to the direction of the administrative agencies. Thus administrators have a relatively free hand in shaping substantive policies and principles for consistency with NEPA mandates unless countermanded by the Congress, the White House, or OMB. It is therefore important to integrate these principles into the ethos and practices of the agencies. A question remains concerning the extent to which NEPA provides an incentive and opportunity for a thorough review, clarification, rationalization, and consolidation of environmental legislation. Ad hoc legislating by successive Congresses has resulted in a vast mass of statutes, declarations, and resolutions—interpreted, modified, or confirmed by the courts and supplemented by Executive Orders of the President. Is there a need for, or a practical advantage in, integrating the essential and interrelating provisions of environmental legislation? Would a systematic, cross-referenced code of law facilitate administration and reduce uncertainty and litigation? The U.S. Code of statutes indexes the laws but does not reconcile or integrate them.

The National Academy of Public Administration (NAPA) has published two reports on this subject and reaches two somewhat different conclusions on the best way to integrate environmental legislation administered by the EPA.[19] The question of feasibility appears to be open. The collateral questions on how such an effort might be organized and what it would cost would certainly be raised. A Congress willing to appropriate millions of dollars for military hardware that the Department of Defense has not requested should have no monetary problem with a rectification of law which promised future economies. The issue is not about funding but over priorities. The 1995 Panel report from NAPA concluded that "until Congress reforms itself and its systems the promise of a fully integrated environmental program will not be met."[20]

There can be little doubt that the clarification, simplification, and integration of U.S. environmental law would serve the public interest, advancing the principal purpose of NEPA. Action to this end, as has been noted, has been recommended by panels of the National Academy of Public Administration and by the National Science and Technology Council. Given the growth of environmental issues and problems, the volume of environmental law seems certain to increase. Its substantive codification and reconciliation would seem to be a priority consistent with the NEPA agenda. The codification task should be undertaken by an independent commission composed of persons of unquestionable dedication and competence. The obvious deterrent today is ideological hostility in the Congress. A strategy analogous to selective military base closures would be necessary — an up or down vote on commission recommendations free from "a special interest" exception interposed by members of Congress. The effort should not afford a subterfuge for weakening or misdirecting the nation's environmental laws. The CEQ could initiate a codification effort if there were presidential support and congressional funding. It would be a very large task, and will not lessen with the passage of time.

5

International Environmental Policy

IN MY VIEW, THE INTENTION OF THE NATIONAL ENVIRONMENTAL
POLICY ACT AND THE ENVIRONMENTAL IMPACT STATEMENT WAS TO
APPLY TO MAJOR FEDERAL ACTIONS WHEREVER THEY IMPACT
WITHIN THE UNITED STATES OR OUTSIDE.

—SENATOR EDMUND MUSKIE, *HEARINGS ON EXPORT-IMPORT
BANK AMENDMENTS*, JULY 11, 1978, P. 220.

If world trends and forecasts are reliable, the environmental policies
of the United States in coming decades seem certain to be affected (and already
are) by developments beyond its national borders. Therefore this chapter and
the one following address the policies of the United States in relation to transnational environmental issues.[1] Chapter 5 deals with issues between sovereign
nations—bilateral and multilateral. Chapter 6 deals with multinational regional
environmental issues and planetary issues affecting all or most nations that are
beyond the control of separate national governments—"common spaces" (e.g.
atmosphere, oceans, and outer space). Distinctions are not always clear between bilateral or—country to country—agreements entered into by the United
States, and multilateral cooperation among all or most states on global environmental issues. Relations between two or several countries are commonly
described as foreign affairs. Negotiations between the United States and other
countries on issues in the common spaces are, from an American perspective,
also foreign affairs. But the area of the Earth and extraterrestrial space beyond
the jurisdiction of particular states are called "the global commons," and involve issues unique to their circumstances, e.g. stratospheric ozone depletion,
global climate change, and contamination of the oceans. They constitute a new
and expanding dimension in environmental policy.

The scope and substance of national foreign policy reflect changes in
beliefs, values, and economies which have been occurring in industrialized
countries during the past quarter-century. Issues once regarded as strictly
within a nation's internal affairs (e.g. civil rights, labor policies, status of
women, drug traffic, and the environment) have now become potential

subjects of international inquiry and negotiation. They involve present and future activities of United States agencies at home and abroad. NEPA, properly interpreted, could guide reconciliation between domestic environmental, economic, and political values and priorities, along with international concerns and commitments.

NEPA by law is supplementary to the missions and mandates of all U.S. Federal agencies. The most celebrated (or, to some, troublesome) provision of NEPA is the requirement of an environmental impact statement addressing any major effect on the environment of proposed legislation or administrative action. According to Nicholas C. Yost, who was general counsel to the CEQ under President Carter, NEPA-like legislation "has now been adopted in the national laws of more than 83 countries," making NEPA probably "the most imitated U.S. law in history."[2]

The latter third of the twentieth century has seen the rapid "globalization" of economic activities, and communications, of military "peacekeeping," mass migrations of people, and of environmental impacts and concerns. The establishment of the United Nations and of numerous specialized agencies with international missions, along with the growth of national foreign aid programs, has resulted in an expanding and diversifying international law and policy infrastructure. Paralleling this development has been the growth of multinational corporate enterprise, worldwide instantaneous electronic communication, and complicated international monetary and trade transactions. These developments have been influenced by continuing advances in environment-related science and technology, accelerating international movement of natural resources and manufactured products and the explosive growth of human populations. The cumulative effects of these developments have been changing the face of the Earth and the substance of international law.[3] The consequences are largely uncertain, but they are sure to be profound.

One consequence for national law and policy has been the emergence of popular environmental protection movements. In many countries, nongovernmental organizations (NGOs) have arisen, many of which have both national and international concerns. In both domestic and international policy, environmental NGOs have become political factors of which government agencies and policymakers are beginning to take account.[4] While NGOs are usually perceived as having voluntary citizen membership, a large and growing group of nongovernmental organizations are multinational business corporations, many of which have profound and often deleterious effects upon natural environments. Some business organizations, however, have committed to an environmental conscience, largely under the rubric of "sustainable development."[5] In not all, but in many nations today, governments are under pressure to protect the environment, natural resources, and the "national cultural patrimony." In many countries (France, for example), the cultural patrimony—including cultivated landscapes, historic artifacts (e.g. buildings, monuments, special places), and communities are regarded as values integral to the environment.[6] These values have generated country policies which the United States government and American business firms must take into account in the planning and administration of its international activities. In its globe-encircling programs, the United States in its own interest must recognize emergent national and international environmentalism in relation to its own environmental and economic policies, population issues, and national security. In the world as a total system, few domestic policies remain unaffected by external trends, and therefore it makes sense to use the NEPA declaration of national policy for guidance in U.S. actions affecting environmental affairs abroad and at home (e.g. in actions relating to international trade).

FEDERAL LAWS AND FOREIGN RELATIONS

In the United States and other countries, domestic policies and practices are found increasingly to have international implications. For example, international transactions in economic affairs and in science-based technologies applied to energy production, agriculture, communication, transportation, forestry, manufacturing, and mining have implications for American economic and environmental policies even though there may be no direct Federal action abroad. Investment by foreign firms in the United States, notably in mining, has generated controversy over contractual rights, local economic growth, and American environmental laws and policies. Activities of Federal agencies with environmental effects abroad are not confined to activities carried on within the territory of foreign nations or global commons but also include Federal actions within the United States which indirectly but demonstrably impact upon the economies and environments of foreign nations. The "war" on drugs, transnational business investment, and regulations affecting international trade, transportation, communication, agriculture, and wildlife are among numerous examples. The implementation of NEPA on U.S. actions abroad in no way intrudes upon the right of a foreign government to initiate or undertake an action impacting upon its territorial environment. But the United States is not obligated to assist another nation in activities having environmental or civil rights effects contrary to the policies or laws of the United States. New findings through science may trigger new obligations under domestic and international policy law and, increasingly, under multinational global policies.

Discovery of chemical (CFC) threats to the stratospheric ozone layer is a case in point. U.S. adherence to the international ozone treaty affects domestic legislation and policy.[7] Although vague as to implementation, the treaty on Global Climate Change, to which the United States became a signatory at the 1992 United Nations Conference on Environment and Development, may lead to policy obligations and conflicts in the future.[8] Transboundary pollution of air and water has become a common feature of international negotiation, yet for largely economic reasons, the United States as of 1997 was unwilling to accept a firm timetable for implementing the Global Climate Change Treaty and has signed but not ratified the Biodiversity Treaty. The U.S. has rejected European and Japanese timetables for reduction of greenhouse gas emissions. The American position is seen abroad as largely symbolic, promising to get serious about emission controls in the 21st century, but not in our time.

Chemical contaminants in the North American Great Lakes from airborne deposition (e.g. DDT and PCBs) have been traced to heavy use of herbicides and pesticides in Central America. Similarly the acidification of lakes in Scandinavia appears to have been caused by fallout of sulphur dioxide from industrial gases generated in Germany and the United Kingdom. Increased flooding in Bengal and Bangladesh has been attributed to deforestation in the mountains of Nepal. Damage to fruit trees in the U.S. was traced to the atmospheric drift of airborne fumes from copper smelters in British Columbia, Canada, leading to the Trail Smelter Arbitration of 1935.

Federal agencies in the United States operate under authority of their own statutory legislation and rules which they interpret as defining their missions. However their mandates are also subject to interpretation by other authorities—notably by the president, White House staff, the Federal courts, and by the Office of Management and Budget. Moreover, in pursuit of its own agenda, an agency is obligated to conform to numerous statutory laws applicable to all Federal agencies (e.g. the Administrative Procedures Act of 1946, the Government in the Sunshine Act of 1976, and NEPA, as interpreted by the courts). These laws, covering a broad range of procedural, personnel, financial, environmental, and security issues may complicate the actual administration of environment-affecting activities of Federal agencies within the United States and abroad. U.S. military bases excluded, direct impacts on overseas environments have been largely indirect—as through participation in NATO, OECD, the World Bank, associated international development banks, and international projects abroad for which the U.S. has contributed significant funding.

A special class of laws affecting Federal action abroad comprises the international conventions (or treaties) which the U.S. has ratified.[9] These treaties may have the force of law.[10] Executive Agreements with other nations may also guide agency action under the authority of the president over international relations, but they should be distinguished from Executive Orders ostensibly binding on Federal agencies wherever they may be operating. President Carter's Executive Order 12114 (1979) declares that the focus of environmental harm "is on its geographical location and not on the location of the action" (presumably action by the responsible official in Washington)—a distinction that seems to contradict a logical reading of NEPA Section

101(2)(c). But actions taken in the U.S. and resulting effects abroad may not be politically separable. Thus the Marine Mammal Protection Act, under which the sale in the United States of tuna caught with purse seines (causing death of dolphins) was prohibited, led to controversy with Mexico and the General Agreement on Tariffs and Trade (now World Trade Organization) to which the U.S. adheres by treaty. The tuna embargo also led to the House of Representatives Committee on Ways and Means declaring opposition to any North American Free Trade Agreement which would invalidate the policy on imported tuna. The action of the embargo took place within the United States, but the impact of the action fell on the nationals of another country.[11]

NEPA is applicable where the action taken is by a responsible Federal official (e.g. in Washington) not where the resulting event would occur. It is the official action that is subject to U.S. law. Nevertheless, confused interpretations of President Carter's Executive Order 12114, and State Department reservations regarding the application of NEPA to matters covered by U.S. treaties as presumably intruding upon the sovereignty of other nations have left uncertain the status of U.S. environmental law in relation to foreign affairs.

In addition to NEPA, Federal agencies' administration of their statutory missions may be modified by two additional and complicating factors. *First*, for activities in foreign countries, there are those general U.S. laws and regulations to which agencies are expected to conform. But conservative courts have generally held that the activities of Federal agencies abroad are not bound by U.S. statutory law except where Congress has specifically imposed conditions (as in the "Foley doctrine").[12] But there are also nonlegal political and economic considerations that restrict or promote actions by agencies having impacts abroad. And, of course, presidential control over foreign relations ultimately determines what U.S. representatives may officially do.

Second, ambiguities in the application of United States legislation through administrative action are inherent in the American practice of judicial review. Although the Federal courts tend to defer to the substance of decisions in and appropriate to the Executive branch, they nevertheless may affirm or reverse agency action on constitutional and procedural grounds. The courts may also place difficulties in the way of citizen action to challenge the lawfulness or propriety of agency action abroad, and they have tightened the rules for standing, apparently to discourage class-action lawsuits within the territory of the United States.[13]

Legislative ambiguities and judicial uncertainties complicate the administration of Federal programs abroad, but do not necessarily prevent the attainment of their objectives. The activities of Federal agencies in foreign jurisdictions must take account not only of the official policies of the host countries, but may also (and increasingly), take cognizance of popular attitudes, traditions, political movements and trends within those countries which have been increasingly concerned with environmental conditions.

Federal policy may also need to consider the concern of American citizens over the negative environmental policies or dereliction of foreign governments. Environmental organizations in the United States have actively opposed destruction of tropical rain forests (especially in Latin America), have activated the tuna-dolphin controversy, and protested against the joint Mexican-Japanese proposal to build the world's largest salt factory in the San Ignacio lagoon of Baja California (the birthing area for the Grey Whales). Some of the opposition to the North American Free Trade Agreement (NAFTA) reflected a fear that the Agreement would override environmental protective legislation. In response to concerns over the effect of NAFTA on the environment, and to reduce opposition in the U.S. Congress, the trinational North American Commission for Environmental Cooperation (NACEC) was established in 1994. As of 1997 it was not clear how NEPA might be involved in its deliberations.[14]

RELEVANCE OF NEPA TO ACTIONS ABROAD

There have been three viewpoints on how NEPA should be interpreted regarding its applicability to the actions of United States agencies overseas. *One* is the focus of the decision (e.g. in Washington, D.C.); *two* is the place of action (beyond U.S. territorial jurisdiction); and *three* is the effect of the proposed action (presumably but not exclusively its environmental effects), which might have sociological as well as political implications (e.g. as in a proposed highway across the Darien region in Panama). In actual circumstances these viewpoints may not be separable. Controversy and indecision have arisen where no clear or firm doctrine governs agency actions.

Differences of opinion on this matter derive from differing interpretations of congressional intent. There has been a persistent, but I believe erroneous, argument that NEPA does not apply beyond the U.S. territorial limits. President Carter's Executive Order 12114 (presently to be considered) has confused rather than clarified the issue.[15] A straightforward reading of the text of NEPA and statements of its chief sponsor, Senator Henry M. Jackson, and of Senator Edmund Muskie, would seem to leave no doubt regarding its applicability to Federal decisions having significant environmental effects anywhere. Section 102 of NEPA states, "the Congress authorizes and directs that, to the fullest extent possible: (1) the policies, regulations, and public laws of the United States shall be interpreted and administered in accordance with the policies set forth in this Act. . . ." Among the purposes of NEPA (Section 2) is "to promote efforts which will prevent or eliminate damage to the environment and the biosphere" and (Section 102(2)(f)) "Recognize the worldwide and long-range character of environmental problems and, where consistent with the foreign policy of the United States, lend appropriate support to initiatives, resolutions, and programs designed to maximize international cooperation in anticipating and preventing a decline in the quality of man's world environment."

These statements of policy are intended to guide and direct the actions of the Congress and Federal agencies in relation to the world at large. They would seem to be criteria for determining the kinds of action that the United States should take, or refrain from taking, in relation to the environment in other countries and in cooperation with international organizations. They have no direct bearing upon what other nations may do. But successive Congresses may determine what Federal agencies may or may not do in relation to foreign states.

The impact of NEPA is clearly on Federal agencies—not upon foreign governments. Section 102(2)(a) requires all agencies of the Federal government to "Utilize a systematic, interdisciplinary approach which will insure the integrated use of the natural and social sciences and the environmental design arts in planning and decisionmaking which may have an impact on man's environment." "Man's environment" surely extends beyond the United States. The focus of NEPA is on action by United States agencies and not on projects or action proposed by foreign governments. For the Congress to require the Federal agencies to inform themselves and the public on the environmental impacts of their actions wherever they occur is hardly "environmental imperialism."

Objection to the application of NEPA to U.S. action in foreign countries has been focused on the geographic location of the activity proposed rather than on the process of Federal decision-making. Conservative opinion in agencies with major overseas activities opposed the "onerous task" of preparing impact statements and argued that for American officials to investigate the environmental impact of U.S. projects in foreign countries constituted interference in their internal affairs. In fact, agency opposition to the application of NEPA to projects in foreign countries appears to have been motivated primarily by (1) a desire to avoid the inconvenience of impact assessment and (2) to avoid embarrassment in relations with foreign governments.

Possibly the most detailed and emphatic rejection of the applicability of NEPA outside United States territory was a memorandum of June 21, 1978, prepared by the Office of the General Counsel, Department of Defense entitled "The Application of the National Environmental Policy Act to Major Federal Actions Outside the United States." To critique and evaluate in detail the arguments advanced in this memorandum would require a length at least as great as its 123 pages. Its thesis, however, may be summarized in five general propositions:

(1) *Congressional intent* that NEPA applies to actions that have impacts outside the United States cannot be derived from the language of the statute.

(2) *The legislative history* of NEPA demonstrates that Congress did not intend extra-territorial application of the environmental impact statement requirement.

(3) *The courts* have not decided whether the environmental impact statement requirement applies to Federal actions outside the United States, and no clear inference can be drawn with respect to how that question might be decided in the future.

(4) *Administrative action* since enactment of NEPA has been based on an interpretation that rejected the applicability of Section 102(2)(c) outside the United States.

(5) *Important policy considerations* support an interpretation that Section 102(2)(f) of NEPA does not apply to Federal actions outside the United States.

The arguments advanced under the foregoing headings may be superficially plausible to one unfamiliar with the history of the Act or of the obligations of nations under international law, and who are naïvely susceptible to legalistic distortions of clear prose. The memorandum rests upon several assumptions that are not made explicit and which misconstrue both the purpose of NEPA and the EIS, and their relationship to American foreign policy. It should be noted, however, that this memorandum was merely advisory and presumably had no official significance. It should not necessarily be taken as an expression of Department of Defense policy. Its argument, however, provides a convenient text for considering how NEPA affects Federal responsibility for its environment-affecting activities abroad. The question, in principle, is to what extent and under what conditions Federal officials are exempt from laws of the United States when the object and locale of their action is situated within the jurisdiction of a foreign state.

1. Congressional Intent. For example, Proposition 1 appears to assume that Congress intended NEPA to apply only to actions having impacts within the United States. A straightforward reading of the Act and the previously cited comments of Senators Jackson and Muskie could lead to an opposite conclusion. Section 102 of NEPA—regarded by its drafters as an action-forcing provision—was intended to reform and reorient the planning and decision-making activities of the Federal agencies. Nothing in the Act defines or restricts the places where the substantive action or impacts occur—its directive is to the Federal decisionmakers. Section 101 specifies the environmental considerations and values that the responsible Federal official (or agency) should take into account. These principles apply largely to the United States as they should; Congress legislates only for the United States, but this does not preclude consideration of actions by Federal officials affecting the environment abroad. Section 101 declares the policies that Congress has established for the United States. Would not a rejection of their relevance to the United States' actions in foreign states resemble diplomatic schizophrenia? The contention that environmental priorities and values should govern policy in the United States only and not in relation to plans or decisions governing Federal action in other countries fails to recognize the implications of such reasoning—establishing a higher standard for official action in the United States than in action affecting foreign countries.

No mention was made of NEPA's applicability to projects planned for overseas because such distinction would have been irrelevant to the declared intent of the Act, which was to redirect United States policy and action through procedural reform. The argument that if Congress had intended NEPA to apply to decisions affecting Federal activities overseas it would have said so is less persuasive than is the counterargument that Congress made no exception in its mandate and instructions because none was intended. The intent that the United States, consistent with foreign policy, lend support to initiatives, resolutions, and programs designed to maximize international cooperation in anticipating and preventing a decline in mankind's world environment would seem to preclude its participation in environmentally damaging projects.

2. *Legislative History.* The argument that legislative history demonstrates a congressional intent that the impact statement requirement have no extraterritorial application misconstrues the fundamental purpose of NEPA. Clearly, NEPA was national legislation governing planning and decision-making in Federal agencies. Policy decisions are made or authorized within the United States, and in no way infringe on the right of other countries to determine their own policies. Those countries are free—within constraints of international law—to proceed with whatever projects they please, regardless of environmental impacts or United States policies. NEPA was conceived and enacted because there were policies, decisions, and derelictions of Federal agencies which contributed to the declining quality of the American environment—and by extension through foreign policies to the rest of the world. Foreign nations are hardly entitled to expect American technical or financial aid for projects inconsistent with American law and policy.

NEPA operational directives apply to United States Federal agencies—not directly to the environment per se. Their purpose is to redirect the decision processes of Federal agencies to conform to the principles and values enumerated in Section 101 which apply to the American nation and its people and to decisions taken in Washington, or wherever Federal decisions are made which could have significant environmental impacts.

Obviously the Congress cannot legislate for other nations. But it can and has specified criteria for decision-making by Federal agencies and does so in a number of policy areas affecting the United States' activities abroad (e.g. human rights, the drug trade, race and sex discrimination). The question of the extraterritorial application of the EIS requirement (or of other subsections of Section 102) never arose in Congress because the purpose of the Act was to reform the decision processes of the Federal agencies in relation to environmental impacts. There is no extraterritorial application of the EIS—the application is to actions by Federal agencies having a major environmental impact anywhere. NEPA thus precludes a double standard of policy for the Federal agencies—one for United States territory and another governing Federal activities in other countries.

Members of Congress most intimately involved in the enactment of NEPA have declared that the Act was intended to apply to extraterritorial actions and impacts. A 1971 House of Representatives report on Administration of the National Environmental Policy Act stated that "the history of the Act makes it quite clear that the global effects of environmental decisions are inevitably a part of the decisionmaking process and must be considered in that context."[16] And in 1978, testifying in a hearing on a bill to exempt certain activities of the Export-Import Bank from NEPA, Senator Edmund Muskie declared that "In my view, the intention of the National Environmental Policy Act and the environmental impact statement was to apply to major Federal actions wherever they impact within the United States or outside.[17] The CEQ has consistently supported this interpretation.

3. The Courts. Opinions of courts and lawyers regarding the applicability and intent of NEPA have varied, and no fully definitive or generally accepted legal interpretation has been made. The Foley doctrine, previously cited, would require an explicit statement of intent by Congress for a statute of the United States to have applicability beyond the nation's jurisdiction. But NEPA applies to action by Federal officials without reference to where the object of that action occurs. NEPA requires an assessment of the environmental impact of a proposed action by the responsible official without regard to the location of the action or its impacts. In any case, the environmental impact statement does not determine the decision regarding the action proposed. Hence the Foley doctrine (that the laws of the United States are inapplicable beyond U.S. territory unless Congress specifies extraterritorial application) would appear to be irrelevant to the application of NEPA in relation to actions taken in the United States by Federal officials respecting proposals for actions abroad.

Adjudication in the Federal courts has provided no conclusive ruling regarding NEPA's overseas applicability. But because the courts have generally deferred to the Executive agencies on substantive environmental issues, there have been calls for amending NEPA to insure its applicability to decisions of Federal agencies without excepting decisions affecting actions overseas. There have also been proposals to amend the Constitution to more authoritatively define the responsibilities of the government in relation to the environment and to offset misconceived and ideological biases too often evident in justices of the Supreme Court. The constitutional question is discussed at length in chapter 7.

4. Administrative Action and 5. Policy Considerations. The opinion in some Federal agencies that NEPA does not apply to their overseas activities reflects their objection to NEPA as an imposition upon their missions—especially to the inconvenient prospect of assessing and reporting on the insufficiently considered environmental impact of their proposals. Many agency personnel initially regarded Section 102(2)(c) as a nuisance and obstruction. Today there is less reluctance to honor the requirement, but in no case is the opinion of agency staff or counsel alone determinative or definitive of departmental obligations under NEPA (e.g. the 1978 DoD memorandum).

The DoD memorandum argues the point that to require the application of NEPA to actions in foreign countries could seriously compromise the exclusive authority of the president in international relations. Does that authority extend to disregarding the laws of the United States? Moreover, the memorandum alleged that assessment of the environmental impacts of the United States' actions overseas could infringe upon the sovereign rights of other countries, constituting an "environmental imperialism." Meeting the stipulations of Section 102(2)(c) could require a foreign country seeking American financial or technical assistance to furnish information that might be unavailable and could be regarded in the foreign country as an intrusion into its domestic affairs, especially if investigation by American personnel on foreign territory were contemplated. But if there is a reason to suspect that Federal activities abroad might entail adverse environmental effects and the Federal agencies are precluded from ascertaining their probability or extent, what reasons compel the American citizen and taxpayer to support projects abroad that would not be permitted in the United States? Reasons of national security have been alleged to justify (often covert) activities abroad by the Central Intelligence Agency and the U.S. Army and have been severely criticized in both Congress and the press as illegal and contrary to democratic values. The Title I Declaration of NEPA contains the qualification "consistent with other considerations of national policy"—but does this provide a loophole in the law? The answer doubtless depends upon circumstances.

The principal difficulty with the "environmental imperialism" argument is that there are other statutory provisions governing the policies and decisions of Federal agencies abroad that are accepted and observed. While some argue that the only appropriate means for applying United States environmental policy abroad is negotiation under the exclusive foreign relations authority of the president rather than application of NEPA provisions, this approach falls short of political reality. Politically, the president is not free to negotiate agreements abroad that are contrary to the Constitution and statutes of the United States. Emergency agreements not expressly forbidden might be given a de facto short-term legality. But the president, for reasons of politics as well as law, could hardly legalize drug traffic with a particular foreign nation, nor approve arms shipments forbidden by Congress. The United States did not refrain from applying its civil rights precepts to its actions respecting the former racial laws of South Africa.

It should again be emphasized that NEPA is intended to direct the way in which Federal agencies make plans and decisions affecting the human environment. It does not mandate particular decisions, either at home or abroad, although it specifies (Section 101) substantive policies applicable within the territorial jurisdiction of the United States, and relevant wherever Federal programs are undertaken. NEPA thus mandates the consideration that should govern Federal action anywhere, including activities on foreign soil, but does not directly determine where or what Federal action is undertaken. Other statutes and treaties may more directly trigger Federal action — for example, in response to international environmental commitments or emergencies.

The negotiating latitude of the president in foreign affairs may be narrowed by the laws and policies of other countries, by decisions taken by the United Nations, and especially by influential interests in the United States. Growth toward a common approach to environmental policies is indicated by the Goals and Principles of Environmental Impact Assessment formulated by the United Nations Environment Programme (UNEP) and the recommendations of Agenda 21 of the United Nations Conference on Environment and Development.[18] The Convention on Environmental Impact Assessment in a Transboundary Context sponsored by the Economic Commission for Europe and signed in February 25, 1991, at Espoo, Finland, while not in effect as of 1997, may nevertheless presage the future. The nongovernmental International Association for Impact Assessment (IAIA) is professionalizing the art and science of impact analysis in a truly international context.

The growth of environmental movements and the adoption of impact statement requirements by other countries may presently render moot the question of the application of NEPA to U.S. government activities in foreign countries. Federal agency assistance in assessing the impact of projects in which the U.S. is a participant may be required by the host country. The frequent references to impact assessment in UNCED's Agenda 21 in conjunction with substantive environment-development objectives, notably those adopted by the U.N. Commission on Sustainable Development, the European Economic Commission, and the European Union, in effect place NEPA principles on the agenda of world affairs. Agenda 21 recommendations were not spontaneous political rhetoric, but were the product of many months of serious international negotiation. The pace of change is uncertain, but the direction seems more certain. The coercive effects of environmental change, predictable for the years ahead, seem certain to push nations toward cooperative action to arrest the deterioration of the biosphere regardless of theories of sovereignty and traditional views of national self-interest. The argument that NEPA is applicable only to actions occurring within the United States is neither consistent with the spirit of the Act nor with the way the world appears to be moving.

EXECUTIVE ORDER 12114

On January 4, 1979, President Carter issued Executive Order 12114 on *Environmental Effects Abroad of Major Federal Actions*,[19] which was intended to clarify and reinforce the obligations of Federal agencies in relation to their activities overseas that had significant environmental effects. It supplements NEPA, perhaps unnecessarily, but does not depend upon NEPA for its validity. It might be argued that it weakens the effectiveness of NEPA if it is taken to imply that NEPA per se has no effect on actions abroad. The Order is lengthy and detailed, with eight clauses of exemptions and provisions for an indefinite number of categorical exclusions pertaining to "foreign policy and national security sensibilities."[20] The purpose, scope, and agency procedures in the EO 12114 are as follows:

> 1-1 *Purpose and Scope.* The purpose of this Executive Order is to enable responsible officials of Federal agencies having ultimate responsibility for authorizing and approving actions encompassed by this Order to be informed of pertinent environmental considerations of national policy, in making decisions regarding such actions. While based on independent authority, this Order furthers the purpose of the National Environmental Policy Act and the Marine Protection Research and Sanctuaries Act and the Deepwater Port Act consistent with the foreign policy and national security policy of the United States, and represents the United States government's exclusive and complete determination of the procedural and other actions to be taken by Federal agencies to further the purpose of the National Environmental Policy Act with respect to the environment outside the United States, its territories and possessions.

> 2-1 *Agency Procedures.* Every Federal agency taking major Federal actions encompassed hereby and not exempted here from having significant effects on the environment outside the geographical borders of the United States and its territories and possessions shall within eight months after the effective date of this Order have in effect procedures to implement this Order. Agencies shall consult with the Department of State and the Council on Environmental Quality concerning such procedures prior to placing them in effect.

Eight years later, in 1987, the CEQ surveyed the Executive agencies to ascertain compliance with Executive Order 12114. More than 60 agencies were queried. The responses appeared to reflect a wide range of agency compliance. Of course the extent and substance of Federal overseas activities affecting the environment vary greatly among the agencies.

Survey returns revealed that eight years after the Executive Order was issued, many of the agencies queried reported no action taken—some declaring that none of their activities were covered by the Order or that they had no environmental effect. Among officials responsible for American projects abroad there was widespread opinion that the Order lacked clarity and would benefit from supplementary guidance from the CEQ. Agencies reported as actually applying EO 12114 included the Defense Logistics Agency, Defense Nuclear Agency, Joint Chiefs of Staff-Pacific Command, Army, State Department, and Coast Guard—agencies particularly responsible to the constitutional authority of the president.

Meanwhile in the Congress, legislation was introduced to extend, or in effect to confirm, the application of Section 102(2)(c) of NEPA to extraterritorial actions and impacts. This legislation was opposed by the president (i.e. White House staff) who, although "firmly committed to ensuring that the environmental impacts of Federal extraterritorial activities are properly considered," contended NEPA should not be extended to include extraterritorial actions and that an Executive Order was the proper vehicle for this purpose.[21] This opinion assumes that NEPA has no extraterritorial applicability—an opinion shared by conservative courts but not by all members of Congress. Legislation to resolve these differences in the interpretation of NEPA has not yet been enacted. An amendment to NEPA may not be needed, but clarification and reinforcement of the extraterritorial environmental obligations of Federal agencies is becoming a practical necessity with the growth of organized environmental concern around the world.

The relationship between EO 12114 and NEPA remains largely unclarified. Efforts to give extraterritorial effect to other environmental statutes have generally not been successful. In the case of Lujan v. Defenders of Wildlife, the Supreme Court reversed a judgment of a Federal Court of Appeals which ordered the Secretary of the Interior to restore a rule initially issued to implement Section 7(a)(2) of the Endangered Species Act of 1973 by extending its coverage to actions taken by the United States government in foreign nations.[22] A coalition of environmental organizations challenged a revised rule limiting the geographical scope of the section to United States territory and the high seas. The Supreme Court reversed the appellate court on the (common law) grounds that the plaintiffs lacked standing to sue, being unable to show that they had personally suffered procedural injury.

The implication of court decisions on the overseas applicability of EO 12114, NEPA, and the Endangered Species Act is that the practical state of the law is ambiguous. The law as interpreted frequently appears to contradict the law as written. For almost any legislative act, it is easy to find among members of Congress conflicting interpretations of intent. This may be regarded as an inevitable characteristic of democratic politics. It may also be regarded as an American tendency to regard the judiciary as the final if not the sole interpreter of statutory law and the Constitution.[23] For whatever reason, a succession of presidents since 1970, with the uncertain exception of Jimmy Carter, have abstained from the interpretation and systematic implementation of NEPA, leaving that task largely to the courts. The principal advocate of environmental policy in the Executive Office has been the Council on Environmental Quality, which has played a positive although often handicapped role in clarifying and advancing NEPA objectives. Nevertheless a Controller General's report in 1981 (CED-81-86) found that the "CEQ has been successful in carrying out its responsibilities."

U.S. OVERSEAS BASING

Among the more apparent and continuing environmental impacts of Federal agencies on foreign soil have been those associated with overseas military basing. Since World War II, a far-flung system of U.S. military installations has been established abroad. Only recently have there been indications of some retraction of this system and a realignment of operations both geographically and technologically. Public attention has focused on base closures in the United States but little public attention has thus far been given to bases abroad (which are in no congressman's electoral district). Few Americans know how many overseas bases there are, where they are located and why, and what activities they support.

That there could be international environmental problems associated with these bases has not generally been foreseen. But base closure and realignment issues in continental United States have involved interagency and intergovernmental (i.e. State-local) questions. NEPA applies and is a force for cooperative and integrative environmental policy, especially as it relates to land-use decisions. Also involved are concerns including issues of health and safety, ecological integrity, costs of remediation, socioeconomic impacts, and legal responsibility. It would be logical to surmise that such issues might now arise overseas in countries where environmental expectations and responsibilities have hitherto been less focused than they are becoming in the United States—but have been rising with the spread of environmental awareness and the generally diminishing threat of foreign military aggression. The Department of Defense has adopted procedures to inform officials of pertinent environmental considerations when authorizing or approving certain major actions that could do significant harm to the environment of a foreign nation, or to protected global resources.[24] Nonetheless these procedures do not appear to have always been effective in preventing environmental harm on and around American military installations abroad.[25] Moreover it appears unclear whether the reservation in Section 101(b) of NEPA "consistent with other considerations of national policy" affects the application of NEPA to U.S. bases on foreign soil, established under agreements with foreign governments. President Carter's Executive Order 12114 is presumed to apply, but its relationship to NEPA remains ambiguous.

There is, of course, a host country responsibility to protect its territory and citizens from adverse environmental impacts. Yet foreign governments, for reasons often unrelated to environmental concerns, seem reluctant to make issues of the environmental impacts of base operations. Until recently, there has been little information readily accessible to the public on base-related environmental issues. On particular issues arising in areas of United States territorial jurisdiction, environmental organizations have sometimes challenged military action (as in Puerto Rico and Hawaii). These instances have mostly involved combat training or ordinance testing by shelling or bombing. But a 1990 study on overseas bases, sponsored by the Department of Defense and undertaken by the reputedly conservative Hudson Institute, made no mention of environmental issues or their possible effect on the future of basing.[26]

The environmental impacts of basing abroad have received belated attention from the news media. On June 18, 1990, a staff writer for the *Los Angeles Times* reported that "U.S. Military Leaves Toxic Trail Overseas" and "Pollution Hot Spots Taint Water Sources." According to an internal memorandum obtained by the *Times* and prepared by a senior Pentagon environmental official who visited bases in West Germany in 1988, hazardous waste contamination is "an emerging political issue" and "a serious budget problem." Thus far the German government has not made a public issue of base contamination, but Green Party investigators have described the extent of the contamination on the American bases as "shocking." The German government has been faced with the more pressing costs of clean-up of the massive contamination left by Red Army forces in the former German Democratic Republic. Will foreign governments be willing to indefinitely assume such costs for American bases abroad when the Congress has required the defense agencies to sanitize their bases in the United States before they can be transferred to other custody?

Responsibility for the environmental impacts of base operations is complicated by jurisdictional arrangements. The legal status of each base on foreign soil is presumably determined by an agreement negotiated between the United States and the host country. Other than NEPA and EO 12114, there appears to have been no general criteria for determining the environmental obligations of command and control authorities throughout the basing system. There are, however, at least three different opinions regarding the environmental obligations of basing operations. The *first* is to observe the environmental laws and regulations of the United States; *second* is to apply the laws of the host country; and *third* is to enforce whichever is the stricter of the two. In practice it appears that none of these options is consistently exercised. On October 23, 1978, President Carter issued Executive Order 12088—Federal Compliance with Pollution Control Standards that might be regarded as a negation of any role for NEPA in environmental protection in bases abroad. However, chapter 20 of Agenda 21 adopted by the United Nations Conference on Environment and Development (UNCED) declared that "Governments should ascertain that their military establishments conform to their nationally applicable environmental norms in the treatment and disposal of hazardous wastes," and recommends the use of technology assessment 20.13(g), environmental auditing 20.13(i), and environmental impact statement 20.19(d) in analysis and correction of site contamination.

INFLUENCE OF INTERNATIONAL AGREEMENTS

A factor in increasing significance for environment-affecting activities of Federal agencies abroad is the growing matrix of treaties and other agreements which the government of the United States is obligated to observe. The complexity of international relations has been growing rapidly and the line between foreign and domestic policy is becoming blurred. Federal policies intended solely for domestic purposes may affect economic and environmental conditions abroad. Laws intended to give advantage to American agricultural, mining, timber, and textile interests may affect land use and natural resources development not only in the U.S. but also in other countries. And supplementing the North American Free Trade Agreement (NAFTA) by the North American Commission for Environmental Cooperation (NACEC), headquartered in Montreal, could affect the environmental responsibilities of U.S. Federal agencies abroad, in relation to the domestic policies of Canada and Mexico.[27]

To forecast future developments regarding American environmental activities abroad is an exercise in uncertainties. Several factors could influence future policy. *First* is the weight and salience of public opinion in the United States along with the positions taken by the president and Congress—and these may not be harmonious. *Second* is the greatly enlarged and global expansion of international economic activities which has had direct and indirect environmental impacts, has led to demands for protective national and international action, and may have unforeseen conterintuitive consequences in the future. Examples are the contaminating effects of atmospheric deposition in the United States, Canada, and Scandinavia from emissions beyond their boundaries. Other examples are the explosive spread of so-called exotic species (including pathogens)—intentional or accidental—into countries where they were previously unknown, and the psychological effects of the exposure in poor countries to the affluent life styles of the Western world which they cannot realistically emulate. An international response has been the 1979 Convention on Long-Range Transboundary Air Pollution and the 1988 and 1991 protocols. *Third* is the acceleration of mass migration of human "refugees" from socioecologically "bankrupt" countries into North America and Western Europe. This movement of people will not diminish the problems of the poor countries and will add to social and environmental problems of the receiving countries. Vice President Gore has called for a "Global Marshall Plan" modelled after the cooperative efforts to restore post-world war Europe.[28] There are persuasive arguments for such an effort. But before it could be initiated there must first be a receptivity and initiative at the level of national governments, especially in the United States.

The more apparent of the environmental impacts result from activities in the nongovernmental private sector; for example, in agriculture, deforestation by burning, and national and multinational industrial emissions. For many of these activities, governments, including the United States, have domestic regulatory responsibilities. For some exports and imports there are legislative and administrative controls. In the United States these appear to have been established in an ad hoc manner, responsive to certain domestic pressures. In many countries the relationships between private and public enterprise overseas is closer and more transparent than in the United States—in Japan for example.

For many countries, however, environmental deterioration is the consequence of long-standing behaviors that have almost literally ground the environment down to bare rock or created man-made deserts—Haiti and sub-Sahara Africa are cases in point. Historical attrition of environmental quality and sustainability has been documented in North Africa, Western Asia, and Northern China. Many tropical countries are rapidly harvesting their forests, extinguishing wildlife and preparing a future of environmental and human impoverishment.

The United States Agency for International Development (USAID) has carried on an environmental information and assistance program. Its Environmental Education and Communication Project (Green COM), initiated in 1993, has assisted communication of environmentally sound policies and practices in at least thirteen developing countries. USAID's publication *Strategies for Sustainable Development* (March 1994) contains a constructive statement of policy for environmental protection. The publication declares its consistency with Agenda 21 of UNCED, but does not mention NEPA, with which it is also consistent. Considering State Department opposition to the application of NEPA abroad, this omission may reflect discretion regarding the relevance of NEPA to foreign affairs. Nevertheless the USAID program is thoroughly in accord with NEPA's Section 102(2)(f): "to lend support to initiatives, resolutions and programs designed to maximize international cooperation in anticipating and preventing a decline in the quality of mankind's world environment."

There is a growing recognition of the responsibility of agencies to consider the environmental effects abroad of their regulatory action or inaction over exports and imports. The departments of Agriculture, Commerce, Treasury, and the Export-Import Bank have been reluctant to take any action that would restrict or burden international commerce in commodities or technologies. The chemical and pharmaceutical industries have effectively lobbied Congress to reject the enactment of restrictive export measures. Federal import restrictions under the Endangered Species Act and the Marine Mammal Protection Act have been criticized as nontariff barriers to international commerce. Policies governing foreign trade are paradoxical. International treaties and other agreements have been progressively narrowing the scope of unrestricted "free trade." Nevertheless the Bush and Clinton presidencies pushed "free trade" as a national priority. But developments during recent decades (e.g. concerns over biodiversity and toxic materials) may be changing the validity of the assessment.

The strength of the environmental commitment in the White House and on Capitol Hill will surely be a factor in future U.S. operations abroad. In view of emerging trends and allowing for inevitable collision and contradiction, it seems safe to predict a greater (even though reluctant) future attention to international environmental issues. In the long run, international conferences and actions by the United Nations may influence the United States' policy. The international transport of hazardous waste and chemical biocides have become issues to which NEPA might be assumed to apply so far as U.S. actions were involved. In fact U.S. policies have not been consistent with NEPA.[29]

On December 17, 1979, the United Nations General Assembly adopted Resolution 31/173 urging members to exchange information on hazardous chemicals including pharmaceuticals that were banned in their countries and to discourage their export. President Carter subsequently created an interagency Hazardous Substances Export Task Force to develop guidelines for the export of hazardous products. After many compromises, the substance of the Task Force report was given a brief legal status in Executive Order 12264 (January 15, 1981), Federal Policy Regarding the Export of Banned or Significantly Restricted Substances. This Executive Order was promptly revoked by President Reagan on February 17, 1981, by EO 12290, Federal Exports and Excessive Regulations. President Reagan alleged that Carter's Order imposed American values on choice in other countries and was harmful to U.S. business at home and abroad.

Efforts in Congress to restrict the export of hazardous substances have not thus far succeeded. Hearings in the House of Representatives, July 11–13, 1978, on export of banned substances came to nothing. In 1980 and 1981 Representative Michael Barnes of Maryland introduced legislation to force exporters to obtain a government license before shipping hazardous products abroad. Hearings were held in the House, but no legislation resulted.[30] The Department of State and the EPA recognized the risk to foreign relations in the export of domestically banned materials. But Congress was more concerned to protect jobs and profitability in American industry. Nevertheless, public awareness of the issue has been growing with evidence that pesticides and herbicides dumped abroad circle back in food imports and in atmosphere deposition.[31] Activities of the U.S. Trade Representative are in some cases intended to protect American exports from environment-related restrictions in foreign countries. Environmental aspects of public health may be affected, as in former efforts by the United States Trade Representative to push the sale of American-made cigarettes abroad.

For some years there have been proposals in the United States and abroad to formalize and make operational national-international responsibilities for environmental protection. On March 31, 1977, Senator Claiborne Pell introduced a bill (S. Res 49) expressing "the sense of the Senate that the United States government should seek the agreement of other governments to a proposed treaty requiring the preparation of an international environmental impact statement for any major project, action, or continuing activity which may reasonably be expected to have a significant adverse effect on the physical environment or environmental interests of another nation or a global commons area." In 1978 Senator Pell's resolution was adopted by the Senate but no further action was taken.

In 1987, ten years after Senator Pell's proposal and at the request of the UNEP Governing Council, a report on *Goals and Principles of Environmental Impact Assessment* was issued by a UNEP Working Group. If generally adopted, the recommendations of this document would, in effect, universalize NEPA principles and procedures—thus largely obviating the American debate over the extraterritorial relevance of NEPA. In 1982, the House of Representatives took up the idea of an international environmental impact statement in its review of the decade following the 1972 United Nations Conference on the Human Environment.[32] Transboundary environmental impacts are become subjects of national agreement at regional levels as well. The Commission of the European Union has issued directives to member states on environmental impact assessment, and as previously noted, an environmental cooperation agreement has paralleled the North American Free Trade Agreement (NAFTA) among Canada, the United States, and Mexico. Furthermore, the 1991 Convention on Environmental Impact Assessment in a Transboundary Context sponsored by the Economic Commission for Europe was signed by 30 nations at Espoo, Finland, including the United States.[33] As of early 1998, however, the treaty had not received sufficient ratifications to put it into force. Interagency disagreements, State Department reservations, and objections by sovereignty-jealous senators have obstructed

U.S. ratification. A similar obligation in the form of an "agreement"—not a treaty—has been adopted by the North American Commission for Environmental Cooperation, but how it may relate to NEPA is not yet clear. The UN Economic Commission for Europe has issued a series of comparative studies on environmental impact assessment in various countries.

PROSPECTS AND UNCERTAINTIES

The performance of Federal agencies abroad will continue to be influenced by our national policies for defense and economic development. National objectives and options have changed with changes of circumstance which now involve the whole Earth. It is uncertain how many of the present international missions and programs of Federal agencies, unmodified, will be appropriate for the 21st century. For the United States prudential strategies—adaptable to various contingencies—may be summarized by the words *information, access, foresight,* and *flexibility*. Such openness entails risks for traditional policy preferences. But in the emergent information era, exclusiveness, secrecy, and disinformation may be increasingly difficult to pursue. It will be in the national interest to know as much as may be significant regarding the environmental consequences of Federal activities abroad. It would also be in the national interest to keep informed regarding the environmental laws and trends in other countries. This kind of information, while available, has not been readily accessible to most people but is now becoming more so through the networking activities of NGOs, the World Wide Web, and the growth of environmental publications and information services.[34]

Functional as well as geographic boundaries are blurring as transboundary transactions of all types are growing in volume and complexity. It is increasingly difficult to separate economic and environmental impacts anywhere. In international affairs—economic, environmental, and political—the world has undergone more fundamental change in the course of the late 20th century than in any previous period of comparable length. It has not been, nor will it be, easy for peoples or governments to make the transition from the assumptions of the 19th century to the necessities of the 21st century. Critical to this transition will be each country's realistic reassessment of its national interests and responsibilities abroad. The international activities of national governments and commercial enterprises may need more than unmonitored voluntary compliance with international standards. Since 1992, however, the International Organization for Standardization (ISO—Geneva, Switzerland) has developed a series of voluntary environmental management standards (ISO 14,000) that might otherwise become a function of governmental and international regulation.[35]

For implementing the international cooperative provisions of NEPA there are practical reasons for agencies to keep informed regarding the relevant actions of other countries and international organizations—public and nongovernmental. Actual practices do not always correspond to official reports by their governments. Principal sources of official information have been international organizations such as UNEP, UNESCO, FAO, the World Bank, and OECD, among others. Nongovernmental organizations and institutes, for example, the World Conservation Union (IUCN), the World Resources Institute, the International Institute for Environment and Development, and Worldwatch, are more reliable sources of information and evaluation. Networks of NGOs have been formalized, but most have had only a short-term success. Funding has been a problem and the component organizations have been primarily concerned with their own financial futures. Official information on environmental questions is usually based on statistical data compiled by economists in a nation's capital. The validity of the reporting depends upon what data was collected, what was omitted, and how the information was obtained and interpreted. Some environmental information may be regarded by governments as politically "sensitive." Official reports tend to inform on those nations which provide the government with a favorable image. There is less information on "ground truth"—on actual conditions throughout the country and on how environmental policies and laws are actually administered.

The Organization for Economic Cooperation and Development (OECD) and the United States Agency for International Development (USAID) have surveyed environmental circumstances abroad. This information is important for U.S. foreign aid activities and for consistency with NEPA. A case in point was the projected American assistance in constructing a section of the Pan American Highway across the Darien isthmus in Panama. The project was found to be harmful to the resident native people and the natural environment. NEPA was invoked as a major reason to prevent the U.S. from moving forward with the highway construction.[36]

Today there are relatively few reliable systematic assessments of the effectiveness of national environmental policies or of the way in which they are administered by national governments and intergovernmental organizations. Down-to-earth evaluations are expensive and may be obstructed by public authorities. Some on the ground reviews of environmental policies and programs (e.g. tropical deforestation, wildlife protection) are made by nongovernmental organizations. Yet for international treaty observance, reliance must usually be placed on reporting by individual governments. Too often independent inquiry shows these reports to be unreliable. No nation is likely to report that it evades or neglects its treaty obligations.

A 1992 report by the U.S. General Accounting Office (GAO) declared that international environmental agreements are not well monitored. In summarizing its findings the GAO noted that

Recognizing the seriousness of environmental problems, a number of international environmental experts have proposed measures to strengthen international oversight as well as parties' capacity to comply with agreements. For example, some have suggested that environmental agreements be modeled after other types of international agreements that provide for monitoring and review, such as those governing labor and human rights. Some agreements also include financing mechanisms to aid developing countries in complying. In any case, efforts to strengthen monitoring and countries' capacity to comply will require both the approval and financial support of parties.[37]

In 1987, Vice President Victor H. Martinez of Argentina proposed to the juridical committee of the Organization of American States, the establishment of a system to monitor conformity to environmental treaties in the Americas.[38] In the past, government representatives have sometimes found it expedient to sign an environmental treaty or declaration with no expectation of its implementation. In the future it seems possible that negligent performance or premeditated evasion will be less easily accomplished than in the past. The necessity for all nations to cope with mounting problems of population, pollution, resource depletion, impoverishment, and prospects for climate change will almost certainly result in further modification of the international order even though its form is not yet in view.

Prospects for Federal activities abroad having environmental impacts are for more involvement, more complexity, greater transparency, and critical attention to evaluating results. Government agencies are less likely to be able to have an alibi or ignore the environmental impacts of their activities. Tunnel vision characterizing single-purpose programs will be progressively less acceptable. Coordination of multifocused efforts will present problems of organization, administration, and conceptual synthesis (e.g. harmonization of diverse efforts). For the United States government, and presumably for its international activities, the National Environmental Policy Act directs that environmental and economic policies be administered in accordance with coordinative and harmonizing principles.

In most sociopolitical respects the state of the world is severely fragmented. But there is also a growing recognition of the necessity for environmental cooperation in the interest of all people and nations. Unfriendly nations, working together to enhance the prospects for mutual survival, may lead to an international politics of antagonistic cooperation. Thus an important area of international policy beyond rhetoric may emerge in which there is a coincidence between national interest and the interest of mutual survival. For the United States this development is advanced by NEPA's admonition (Section 102(2)(f)), "to maximize international cooperation in anticipating and preventing a decline in the quality of mankind's world environment."

SOME CONCLUSIONS

The sudden end of the Cold War and the emergence of a politically significant international environmental movement has been followed by challenges which American policymakers had not anticipated. For both developments, adjustments in foreign policy have become necessary and these inevitably affect Federal activities in foreign countries and in the global commons. Military and technical assistance programs abroad have been or are being restructured and redirected. Many of the assumptions upon which American foreign policy has been based historically are no longer generally credible, and the task of replacing them with policies more responsive to present realities will require time even though policy change is already overdue. A report by the Secretariat of the General Agreement on Tariffs and Trade (GATT—now the World Trade Organization) declared that "it is no longer possible for a country to create an appropriate environmental policy on its own."

An important area for policy realignment is among economic development, national security, rights of people and property, and environmental protection. In many countries environmental reconstruction could improve the quality of life and economy. NEPA would legitimize American assistance in such efforts. The United States Department of Defense has engineering and surveillance capabilities that are probably unmatched. War is not the only strategy of national security. Promoting conditions of international stability could reduce inducements to armed conflict. Armies may be more than fighting machines, as the civil works of the Roman legions demonstrated 2000 years ago. The arming of "developing countries" to fight communism and insurrection often yielded unintended results (e.g. civil wars within newly liberated states, and Americans being attacked with their own weapons fallen into unfriendly hands).

Can we deduce from the foregoing discussion some directions of foreign policy that the United States might take in coping with environment-related problems during the 21st century? Focusing our observations on the environment-affecting activities of Federal agencies abroad, the following actions deserve serious consideration:

First. Reconciliation between environmental statutes and executive orders, foreign aid and trade missions, and economic and defense policies having environmental implications. Are U.S. policies counteractive? This inquiry might be undertaken by the CEA, the CEQ, and the GAO, jointly or by each. For the nation to play a constructive role in the years ahead, ambiguous and contradictory interpretations of the law should be replaced by a restatement of policy and law on those issues in which health, welfare, equity, and quality of life are critical. Sustainability in the sense of protection and renewability of the biosphere should be a guiding principle. Among the purposes declared in NEPA are "efforts which will prevent or eliminate damage to the environment and biosphere."

Second. The president could undertake to administer the National Environmental Policy Act in preference to leaving its interpretation almost wholly to the courts. This initiative would require use of the Council on Environmental Quality as intended — truly advisory to the president and fulfilling the Title II mandates.

Third. NEPA should be regarded as fully applicable wherever a major Federal action affecting the environment is contemplated. In any event, enactment of NEPA-like laws in foreign countries may soon necessitate U.S. accommodation to impact assessments adopted by other states or by international agreement.

Fourth. The Federal government should consider further partial peacetime redeployment of its military capabilities to environmental reconstruction in the United States, and as requested in foreign countries.

Fifth. A capability to identify and evaluate significant trends in population, natural resources, environment, and the economic future should be provided. This would be in part an assessment of interactive national and world trends. It could draw upon and correlate comparable assessments by private and international sources. Being anticipatory, it could guide priorities and criteria for foreign assistance and contribute to an integrative approach to multiple activities of the Federal agencies in foreign nations.

Sixth. The Congress should establish or authorize a facility to consider the recommendations of UNCED Agenda 21 and their implications for U.S. policies, recognizing that domestic and foreign activities may be distinguished, but may no longer be wholly separated. A revitalized CEQ could be designated as the lead agency in such effort, but foreign aid and economic development agencies should be involved — notably the Department of State, USAID, the Council of Economic Advisors, the Department of the Treasury, and the EPA.

No indelible line can be drawn between environmental relations between nations (described in this chapter) and environmental policies for the whole Earth as geosphere-biosphere (detailed in chapter 6 following). Most of the international issues discussed in this chapter are area-specific, or do not immediately affect all nations. Global issues affect all nations and people, although not always directly, equally, or simultaneously (e.g. rising sea levels). For modern people to survive in a livable future they will need to think and act in relation to the Earth as a *total system.* This necessity carries with it implications for concepts, values, assumptions, laws, institutions, and behaviors beyond the scope of this book. How humanity will adapt to the climacteric of the 21st century can only be conjectured. To an uncertain degree in the short run mankind may be able to cope incrementally with coercive forces in the environment — often induced by human behavior. However, in the game of survival, nature sets the "rules" by which people and governments must play if they are to stay in the game for the long run. The fundamental concern of international environmental policy today should be an effort to adjust national policies and practices to the world system "rules" and to avoid collision with cosmic forces that cannot be overcome. In placing NEPA in its international context, this chapter has shown how often the Act has not been invoked in issues where it was relevant and how it has been marginalized and misconstrued for political and bureaucratic purposes. NEPA needs reaffirmation and a return to its literal and intended meaning.

6

NEPA and the Global Environment

WHAT IS INVOLVED IS A CONGRESSIONAL DECLARATION THAT WE
DO NOT INTEND, AS A GOVERNMENT OR AS A PEOPLE, TO INITIATE
ACTIONS WHICH ENDANGER THE CONTINUED EXISTENCE OR THE
HEALTH OF MANKIND [OR] WILL DO IRREPARABLE DAMAGE TO THE
AIR, LAND, AND WATER WHICH SUPPORT LIFE ON EARTH . . .

—SENATOR HENRY M. JACKSON, *CONGRESSIONAL
RECORD* 115, OCTOBER 8, 1969.

Environmental policies for the global environment pertain to a special class of transnational issues which differ from customary foreign affairs in that sovereignty is seldom a dominant issue. Even the territorial claims of nations in Antarctica do not appear to be generally accepted as legitimized exclusive sovereign rights. Relations between two or more countries, except where governed by generally accepted international legal principles, tend to be issue-specific between the countries involved, and are governed by country-to-country negotiations. Policies involving reciprocal relationships between sovereign territorial states are distinguishable from international agreements among governments concerning territories over which no nation-state has sovereignty or jurisdiction. The argument against the alleged intrusion of NEPA upon other sovereign states does not pertain, for example, to the high seas, the deep seabed, outer space or, in certain respects, to Antarctica.

Global environmental issues affect all or nearly all countries and are usually negotiated through international conferences. The concept of "commons" applies to those areas of the Earth and outer space that are outside the jurisdiction of any nation, and by extraterrestrial extension to the Moon, and perhaps to the planet Mars. Antarctica is a special case, regarded as an international commons but governed by a Consultative Committee representing twenty-six national governments and sixteen additional states adhering to a 1959 treaty. These distinctions are of course generalities and there are exceptions and situations to which they may not apply. Nevertheless planetary and extraterrestrial issues are of a magnitude and challenge to cooperative and institutional arrangements sufficient to warrant special consideration in relation to NEPA.

Within the latter decades of the 20th century the "global commons" became an object of international policy. Historically the United States adhered to a doctrine of freedom of the seas which allowed each nation to pursue its own interests, unrestrained by claims of other countries but governed by the customary law of the sea. The globalization of economic affairs and the advent of the "space age" were accompanied by an increase in air transport and in maritime activities—especially in movements of natural resources (e.g. petroleum, timber, and metallic ores) and in the development of new technologies enlarging opportunities in outer space, in the deep seas, and in Antarctica. These developments necessitated an extension of national legislation and international agreements, along with new institutional arrangements for the management, use, and protection of those areas beyond national jurisdictions. Order is being brought into the use of the global common spaces, while new issues arise, and much remains to be addressed. Does NEPA provide guidance to U.S. policy affecting global environmental affairs? It does not appear to have done so in the policies of the Reagan and Bush administrations, which advocated mining development in the deep seabed and Antarctica, urged the "star wars" Strategic Defense Initiative, and rejected the Biodiversity Treaty.

This chapter does not argue that NEPA has had a direct or acknowledged influence on U.S. planetary policies, but it does survey the broad and diverse extent of those policies that have reflected assumptions and values declared by NEPA. Although the Supreme Court has restricted the applicability of NEPA on foreign soil beyond U.S. territorial jurisdiction, the magnitude and domestic impact of many of the transnational and global environmental threats make it a near certainty that U.S. environmental policy in the future will recognize a transplanetary context—and this will doubtless hold true for other countries as it has for the United Nations.

In order to provide substance for global policy it seems necessary to consider the environmental issues that have been encountered and how the Federal government has dealt with them. While this provides no forecast of future developments, it does indicate some political consequences of so-called globalization of economic and environmental affairs. NEPA has seldom been invoked in the following global issues, but its principles have often been paralleled in policy decisions—and they may become more explicit in the increasingly interacting world of the future.

U.S. POLICY IN THE COMMON SPACES

Although a declared purpose of NEPA is "to promote efforts which will prevent or eliminate damage to the environment and the biosphere" this intent has not been fully pursued in Federal decision-making. This chapter identifies the broad and complex areas of policy that NEPA's mandate addresses. It demonstrates the difficult task of implementing NEPA's implied global commitment through the politics of American domestic and foreign policy. Future consequences of environmental overstress, which adversely affects human values and options, may lead toward more inclusive and appreciative understanding of the reasons underlying NEPA principles. Meanwhile, transboundary and global environmental problems increase both in magnitude and in compelling significance for the 21st century.

NEPA's commitment "to promote efforts which prevent or eliminate damage to the environment and the biosphere" provides guidance *in principle* to policy and action affecting the world beyond conventional jurisdictional boundaries. But as yet no firm political or legal consensus has been reached as to where, when, how, or to what extent NEPA principles are to guide U.S. global policies. Commitment to any governing environmental principle explicitly derived from NEPA is not evident. A plausible inference is that agency officials are either (a) unaware of the policy intent of NEPA, or (b) are reluctant to challenge the "official" opinion that the environmental impact requirement of NEPA has (almost) no relevance beyond the territorial limits of the United States. The language of NEPA appears intended to guide U.S. global policy on environmental issues requiring international cooperation. However, the Congress does not appear to find the NEPA admonitions obligatory.

The response of recent congresses to Section 102(2)(f) of NEPA has been indifferent to hostile. The "conservative" members, in particular, have declined to

> (f) Recognize the worldwide and long-range character of environmental problems and, where consistent with the foreign policy of the United States, lend appropriate support to initiatives, resolutions, and programs designed to maximize international cooperation in anticipating and preventing a decline in the quality of mankind's world environment.

The United States has agreed to lead or join various international initiatives on behalf of global environmental concerns, but has often declined to sign or to ratify resulting resolutions or agreements. For example, the United States was the only country to vote against the World Charter for Nature adopted in 1982 by the General Assembly of the United Nations. The United States declined to ratify the Law of the Sea Convention (1982) and the Biodiversity Treaty (1992). Although the United States signed the non-binding United Nations Framework Convention on Climate Change (1992), it was highly uncertain as of mid-1998 that the Senate would ratify the Kyoto Protocol negotiated in December 1997, which would establish legally binding limitations or reductions in greenhouse gas emissions in the developed countries. The president and Senate have presumably interpreted the phrases in

(611b) "consistent with other essential consideration of national policy" and "consistent with the foreign policy of the United States" to justify rejection of any international agreement that might prove disadvantageous to U.S. economic and military interests.

The concept of a "global commons" is relatively new to both national and international law. The surfaces of the earth that formerly belonged to no nation are now regarded as of concern to all nations. But nations have few precedents or demonstrated capabilities for governing common spaces and their political and ideological institutions are not easily adapted to collective international responsibility. Present political arrangements for the common spaces (or commons) have been negotiated through conventions or treaties. But the implementation of these agreements remains subject to experience, innovation, and controversy.

The global commons has been defined to include the upper atmosphere, outer space, and the high seas (including the deep seabed) beyond the effective jurisdiction of any nation. For purposes of policy, the boundary between the outermost atmosphere and outer space is not clearly marked but includes the stratospheric ozone layer, the magnetosphere, and the electromagnetic spectrum. The Antarctic continent has a unique legal status, being treated in many respects as if it were an international commons. Public Law 101-620 (November 16, 1990) is a joint resolution of the Congress for protection of the Antarctic environment, titled "Antarctic Treaty – Global Ecological Commons."

In 1991 Antarctica became the focal point of an important judicial interpretation of NEPA in relation to Federal actions occurring beyond U.S. territorial boundaries. The Environmental Defense Fund (EDF) brought suit against Walter Massey, Director of the National Science Foundation (NSF), to enjoin the agency from incinerating refuse in the pristine Antarctic environment in which NSF was engaged in research. The case, resolved in 1993 in the Court of Appeals for the District of Columbia, was decided in favor of EDF, requiring NSF to prepare an environmental impact statement regarding the intent to incinerate. The Congress had already identified Antarctic as belonging to the global commons (e.g. the high seas and outer space), and U.S. action there did not infringe upon the sovereignty of other nations. The Massey decision affirms that in some instances NEPA and the EIS may apply beyond U.S. boundaries. But it does not clarify the difference of opinion as to whether action taken by the responsible Federal official in Washington or the location of the impact of that decision determines the applicability of the EIS requirement. The issues of jurisdiction and national sovereignty will be revisited in greater detail later in this chapter.

Advances in science and science-based technology in the world of commerce and communication, in the mobility of people, and in the popular perception of planetary issues have enlarged the scope of international politics. They have blurred distinctions between customary nation-to-nation international negotiations and more inclusive, less clearly defined, environmental relationships (as in transboundary air pollution and access to oceanic fisheries). Environmental impacts upon the commons may affect most—or indirectly all—nations (e.g. pollution of the air and seas, over-fishing and oceanic contamination, climate change toward warming or cooling of the atmosphere, changes in rainfall and sea levels, and thinning of the protective stratospheric ozone layer).

As previously noted, there has been an unresolved argument in the Federal government regarding the applicability of NEPA to action taking place outside the territorial limits of the United States. However, there appears to be greater judicial latitude for the application of NEPA to U.S. activities in the global commons than in direct relationship to other sovereign states. Many agencies of the United States government have programs and activities in or affecting the global commons, and some of these may have environmental or economic impacts on other states. This is notably true of activities undertaken by the National Oceanic and Atmospheric Administration and by departments of State, Interior, Energy, Commerce and the National Science Foundation. It is especially true of Defense, whose activities beyond U.S. territory are widely dispersed and sometimes conspicuously visible.

As noted in chapter 5, the Department of Defense *Final Procedures* Appendix H, Requirements for Environmental Considerations, *Foreign Nations and Protected Global Commons*, implemented "the requirements of Executive Order 12114 with respect to major Department of Defense actions that do significant harm to the global commons."[1] Executive Order 12114 is itself essentially procedural, supplementing, though not based or dependent upon, the National Environmental Policy Act. Federal decisionmakers are informed of the procedures which they are required to follow, along with the documents that must accompany their decisions. But the effect of EO 12114 may have been to complicate rather than to clarify the responsibilities of Federal agencies abroad.

Unlike the National Environmental Policy Act, EO 12114 does not provide guidance on substantive matters of policy. And yet the principal legal problems of United States agencies in the "global commons" are those of substance—of what a nation may or may not do, and under what conditions. Under EO 12114 the decision-making procedures that Federal agencies are required to follow as published in the *Federal Register* are presumed to be explicit—but in practice may require interpretation. What agency decisionmakers also need to know, and what EO 11214 does not tell them, are the circumstances and trends among nations with respect to the global environment of which account must be taken in the shaping and implementation of national policies. Policy decisions are more than procedures; the context in which action is proposed requires information and understanding before procedures, which may in practice become policies, are invoked. At present, there is no officially designated means for providing this information. Help might come from legislation to establish an office to analyze and forecast trends and futures, but no such legislation has been enacted. This function would seem to be authorized by Title II of NEPA, but the CEQ has never been funded to perform it. Opponents of government forecasting have alleged it to be the first step toward centralized (i.e. socialist) national planning.

COMMONS POLITICS AND POLICY

With respect to those areas of the Earth beyond the territorial jurisdiction of any national state, technological capabilities have enlarged economic opportunities and led to the extension of national politics into issues of international resources development, transnational environmental effects, and governance.[2] Prior to the establishment of the United Nations and the negotiation of treaties relating to the global environment, national governments were generally regarded as free to act beyond their territorial limits where the jurisdiction of no other nation was recognized. This freedom of action on the high seas, in outer space, in the upper atmosphere, and in Antarctica was governed by certain principles of international law. Nations were not legally free to use the international common spaces in ways harmful to other nations. They could not, for example, lawfully lay explosive mines in international waters.[3]

Within recent decades accelerating developments in science, technology, commerce, and communications have changed the concept of a global commons. From relative freedom of national action, nations now recognize the common spaces as areas of common concern. Largely unrestricted national action is giving way to concepts of international collective responsibility. The formulation of this concept as a principle of international relations, if not confirmed as positive international law, gained worldwide attention in 1967 when the ambassador of Malta to the United Nations introduced the proposition that the deep seabed be regarded as "the common heritage of mankind."[4]

Although this proposition was not accepted in principle by the United States nor by most other technologically advanced countries, in practice there has been recognition that international cooperation is necessary to attain objectives of national interest. International telecommunication and aviation could not be carried on without international agreements regarding the uses of the common spaces in the sea and in the air. World War II was followed by unprecedented development of intercontinental weapons and nuclear technologies. The prospect of nuclear wars in space with unavoidable contamination of the planet, military basing on the Moon, and the transboundary fallout from nuclear testing in the atmosphere persuaded nations—especially those lacking advanced technological capabilities—that the option of using the common spaces for military purposes should be prohibited.[5]

These developments were present in the background against which NEPA was conceived.

The evolving concept of a global commons as an international environmental responsibility is by now built into international law and practice. International arrangements have been formalized for assigning radio frequencies and for restraining unilateral national developmental activities in Antarctica. The Law of the Sea Convention places deep-sea mining under the control of an international authority. But the world is in an early stage in the collective governance of the global environmental commons. Global agreements adopted or proposed thus far have been initiated in response to particular national needs or concerns, including those pervasive in the international commons (e.g. living resources of the sea, quarantine of pathogenic organisms, telecommunications, mineral exploitation, atmospheric pollution, climate change, and solar ultra-violet radiation). No all-inclusive authority for governing the commons seems likely in the foreseeable future, but attention continues to be given to possibilities, options, and alternatives.[6]

GLOBAL APPLICATION OF U.S. LAW

Actions under NEPA are required to be consistent with the foreign policy of the United States — a policy not always clear nor consistent — which is subject to change and to determination by the president and Congress that is virtually unchallengeable on legal grounds. Moreover the foreign policies of all nations are confronted by growing evidence that global policies are needed for environmental issues that affect all nations, all peoples, and the biosphere. There is more agreement that international policies are needed for global problems than on how those problems should be addressed. Of course the foreign policies of nations are subject to changes that could affect their cooperation with other states. Yet global commons issues are becoming compelling subjects of international negotiation and may influence national environmental policy in positive ways.

In its ruling on the case of *Greenpeace USA v. Stone* (1990), the Federal District Court of Hawaii declared that "the language of NEPA indicates that the Congress was concerned with the global environment and the worldwide character of environmental problems . . . and may have intended under certain circumstances for NEPA to apply extraterritorially."[7] This opinion did not resolve the question of the application of NEPA beyond U.S. boundaries. "Certain circumstances" seems to refer primarily to issues in the global commons where the sovereignty of other states is not a factor. A direct and literal interpretation of NEPA should make clear that the Act (notably Section 102(2)(c)) applies to action by U.S. Federal officials. Extraterritorial application is a null proposition. Action by U.S. officials may and does affect other countries far more intrusively than the proportion of impact statements.

Imposition of U.S. policies on other countries in its war against drugs is conspicuous among other cases in point.

As previously noted, there is an ambiguity regarding the obligations of Federal agencies' territorial jurisdiction to observe laws (notably NEPA) that are clearly applicable within the United States. Where a statute or a treaty has mandated such obligation, no question may be expected. But where the letter of the law gives no specific indication regarding its applicability in the global commons or on foreign soil, an argument may be raised (as in the case of *Foley Bros., Inc. v. Filardo* and in the DoD general counsel's memorandum of June 21, 1979) that domestic law does not apply.[8] This absence of clear intent might, in some cases, be remedied by the president under his constitutional role in foreign relations—or through executive interpretation of NEPA. Unfortunately President Carter's EO 12114 does not appear to accomplish this objective.

The legitimacy and scope of national and international law relating to the global environment and biosphere have been significantly enlarged by international conferences sponsored by the United Nations and its specialized agencies. The United Nations Conference on Environment and Development (UNCED) meeting in Rio de Janeiro in June 1992 was, in effect, a confirmation of the 1972 United Nations Conference on the Human Environment (UNCHE) which placed environmental policy on the official agenda of international relations. Treaties relating to the law of the sea, protection of the stratospheric ozone layer, global climate change, the Antarctic region, transboundary pollution, and biodiversity have established the global environment as a subject of collective international policy implemented by institutional arrangements.[9] National governments at the Rio Conference took a historic step in declaring policies that should prevail in relation to the commons. But in 1997, a United Nations review of five years' accomplishment after Rio revealed that nations have not yet reached a point of agreement on how, or when, those policies are to be enforced.[10]

International secretariats to assist implementation of environmental conventions have been generally limited to collecting data (sometimes dubiously verifiable) which is provided by adhering states and in published reports. The United States General Accounting Office has found that environmental treaties have not been effectively monitored.[11] Reports by national governments on treaty observance are not reliable indicators of compliance. To determine whether a nation is honoring its treaty commitments, on-the-scene observance is necessary and this, in many nations, would be regarded as an affront to national sovereignty.

National states historically have been jealous of any infringement of their authority, which many states have undertaken to extend as, for example, a 200 mile limit for their jurisdiction over coastal seas. National bureaucracies, military establishments, dominant elites, and political parties characteristically have been resistant to extranational arrangements that would diminish their freedom of action. National governments are concerned that international agreements not work to the disadvantage of politically influential interests. It was such apprehension that caused President Reagan to reject the Law of the Sea Treaty which would have deprived the United States of a unilateral right to authorize mining on the deep seabed. Similarly, President Bush refused to sign the UNCED Convention on Biodiversity because he believed that it threatened the economic interests of American pharmaceutical industries. The Chemical Weapons Convention was publicly opposed in the U.S. Senate in 1997 on grounds of military security, but an industrial economic interest was also involved.

National interests require that all nations assume responsibility to prevent accidents in the global commons which would harm some or all other nations. To obtain coordinated cooperation, national governments negotiate international agreements to establish intergovernmental organizations and secretaries with an extranational identity.[12] The distinction between international agreements and agreements regarding the common spaces is that in the first case some national government usually has jurisdiction over some part of the subject area, whereas in the latter case no national government has complete or confirmed jurisdiction over any part of the common area. The claims of various nations to sections of the Antarctic continent are not valid exceptions, since they are only claims and all claimants have thus far been subject to the superior authority of the multilateral Antarctic treaty of 1959.[13]

The need for multinational (in effect global) institutional arrangements is especially true for the commons where no national government is in a position to assert jurisdiction or to provide governance. In the United States, no general pattern of relationships has been established for diverse United States activities in relation to the commons. Each Federal agency has its own relationships with other governments or with intergovernmental agencies or with both—depending upon the function or issue involved, for example, with respect to radio frequencies, international civil aviation, and marine fisheries. NEPA is not directly involved in these activities but Section 105 states that "the policies and goals set forth in the Act are supplementary to those set forth in existing authorizations of Federal agencies."

In all cases involving environmental policies in the global commons, national politics have been determining factors. Changes in the presidential office and in chairmanship of a congressional committee may result in changes in foreign policy. Thus Section 102(2)(f) of NEPA, requiring that environmental policy abroad be consistent with foreign policy, cannot anticipate what U.S. international or global foreign policy is or may be. Foreign policy characteristically reflects contemporaneous economic, defense, and ethnic agendas, and may help or hinder NEPA objectives.

On environmental issues, interpretations of national interest and of national policy may be changed by scientific evidence and experience, as in the ozone and climate change investigations. Earlier agreements—global rather than confined to the commons—have sought to prevent the transmission of plant and animal disease through international commerce. Pathogenic organisms are not confined by national boundaries and constitute a kind of living commons requiring preventive action from nearly all nations. Phytosanitary regulations for commerce in plants and campaigns against smallpox and malaria are examples.

As previously noted, U.S. activities in the global commons involve numerous Federal agencies: the departments of State, Commerce, Energy, Interior, and Defense (notably Air Force and Navy), the National Oceanic and Atmospheric Administration (NOAA), the National Aeronautics and Space Administration (NASA), the Federal Aviation Administration (FAA), the Federal Communications Commission (FCC), and the Environmental Protection Agency (EPA). The National Science Foundation (NSF) is engaged in various research activities within the global commons especially with respect to Antarctica, the oceans, and the atmosphere—and the National Academy of Sciences has contributed findings and recommendations to policies affecting the atmosphere, the oceans, and outer space. NOAA and NASA carry on significant research activities in the commons, interacting with intergovernmental agencies notably in the United Nations system—for example, with the World Meteorological Organization (WMO) and the Intergovernmental Oceanographic Commission (IOC) in UNESCO.

In addition there are various Federal commissions whose activities are related to international agreements relevant to the global commons—for example, the Nuclear Regulatory Commission, the Marine Mammal Commission, and the National Marine Fisheries Commission. The matrix of interagency and intergovernmental activities pertaining to the global commons is extensive and complex. Where these activities involve a major impact upon the environment of the commons, NEPA presumably applies. The following subsections identify those areas and issues in the global commons having implications for foreign and environmental policy. They indicate the importance of and need for coordination and foresight in national environmental policies abroad, along with a broad interpretation of the relevance of NEPA.

THE OCEANS

Covering the greater part of the Earth's surface, the high seas and deep seabed are international commons beyond the territorial limits now claimed by national governments. Institutional arrangements have been necessary to accomplish international objectives relating to the oceans, but diverse national objectives complicate arrangements for their governance. These objectives relate to navigation on the sea, living "resources" (notably fish and marine mammals), pollution by oil, deep sea mining, and dumping of noxious materials. The marine plant life on and near the surface of the sea is believed to have an important influence on the oxygen balance in the earth's atmosphere. Any threat to its vitality (e.g. from climate change, chemical pollution, sedimentation, or ultraviolet radiation) would be a matter of international concern. A rise in sea level caused by global climate change would affect the coastal areas of many nations—including the United States—and bring about the partial submergence of some island states.[14]

Navigation on the high seas is largely governed by an international body of law evolving out of customary practice. It is not the ocean commons per se that is governed, but rather human action occurring in or affecting the oceans and their resources. International accords pertaining to fisheries and the protection of certain marine mammals (e.g. whales and seals) are governed by international commissions representing governments that adhere to treaty agreements. As previously noted, Federal departments or commissions in the United States cooperate with these intergovernmental bodies consistent with Section 102(2)(a) and (b) of NEPA. At present the principal international institution governing navigation on the high seas is the International Maritime Organization (IMO). This UN Specialized Agency has, in addition to other concerns, responsibility for obtaining concerted national action to prevent pollution of the sea by oil and other contaminants. For international waters in enclosed, coastal, or regional seas, institutional governance has been provided by multilateral treaties which in effect merge national sovereignties to solve common purposes.

The United Nations Regional Seas Programme (now Oceans and Coastal Areas (OCA)) sponsored by the United Nations Environment Programme (UNEP) has assisted the formation of at least 12 multilateral organizations governing the environmental conditions of coastal and regional waters.[15] These waters—coastal and partially enclosed—are hydrologically and ecologically connected to the global open ocean, and the health of oceanic life depends upon their ecological integrity. Although subject to national or multinational jurisdiction, they cannot be segregated environmentally from the ocean commons and are now of international concern. In 1993 the United States hosted the Second International Conference on the Environmental Management of Enclosed Coastal Seas (EMECS).[16] The first conference was held in Japan in 1991. A third conference was held in Sweden in 1997. The United States has been supportive of OCA and is a participant in the Wider Caribbean Regional Program.

International conferences have been convened by the UN Food and Agricultural Organization (FAO) on Living Resources of the Sea (1955), on Marine Pollution and its effects on Living Resources and Fishing (1970), and by the UN General Assembly on the Law of the Sea (1958-1982). In these meetings and in the adoption of the Convention on Whaling (1946) and the Convention on the Conservation of Antarctic Marine Living Resources (Southern Ocean Convention, 1982) the United States has traditionally favored open seas policies and has been ambivalent on international or global agreements that would restrict American economic opportunities such as mining on the ocean floor. The Reagan administration ignored NEPA in its opposition to the Law of the Sea Treaty.

If or when the United States ratifies the Convention on the Law of the Sea, United States policy for this area of the global commons will be structured in conformity with that of other signatories. United States policy already corresponds to many (perhaps most) of the treaty provisions which Americans played a major role in drafting. Generalizations as always have limited applicability, but the principal task for American policy for the ocean common spaces has been to reconcile traditional policies for open spaces, open equally to all nations, with international governance of the commons and inevitable restrictions on what nations may do consistent with interests common to all nations. NEPA's admonition to "prevent or eliminate damage to the environment and the biosphere" and to "encourage productive and enjoyable harmony between man and his environment" would seem to indicate the direction that U.S. policy should take regarding issues in the ocean commons.

THE ATMOSPHERE AND CLIMATE CHANGE

Although the atmosphere has not traditionally been treated as if it were a commons — nations having asserted jurisdiction over their territorial air space — scientific information and science-based communication and transportation technology now preclude the space above the terrestrial boundaries of nations from being regarded as within their exclusive jurisdiction. Upper levels of the atmosphere may be scientifically (but not altogether practically or politically) distinguishable from outer space. Recognition of the outer atmosphere as an international commons has arisen out of recent scientific findings regarding the impact of modern industrial activity relating to climate change and thinning of the ozone layer. Prominent among these findings has been the effect of certain chemical emissions — especially chlorofluorocarbons (CFCs) — upon the stratospheric ozone layer and the prospect of global warming caused by the emission of so-called "greenhouse gases" (notably carbon dioxide and methane, directly and indirectly resulting from human activities).

Evidence of the global flow of pollutants in the atmosphere led to the 1979 Convention on Long-Range Transboundary Air Pollution and the 1985 and 1988 Protocols, along with the Convention on Environmental Impact Assessment in a Transboundary Context, signed in 1991 but not yet in force. Of less significance at present is the intentional modification of weather. The unintentional transport of dust in the atmosphere from areas undergoing desertification and dense smoke from large-scale land transformation activities (as in Indonesia in 1997) have become serious problems of ultimate global significance. Consistent with NEPA, the United States lent air-borne assistance to Indonesia in efforts to extinguish massive forest and brush fires that laid a thick wall of smoke over the Southwestern Pacific region, carried largely by slash and burn land clearance activities during the drought of 1977. The United States is now party to conventions regarding climate change, the ozone layer, and the long range transport of pollutants—but has resisted time tables for their implemention. These agreements have yet to be put into effect through national and intergovernmental action.

The World Meteorological Organization (WMO) is the principal body for coordinating research on the earth's atmosphere and weather. Scientific research efforts and international cooperative inquiry relating to the atmosphere appear to be well-organized and productive. The U.S. National Oceanic and Atmospheric Administration (NOAA) and the National Academy of Sciences have been major participants in global atmospheric research projects sponsored by WMO and the International Council of Scientific Unions (ICSU). In 1988 WMO and UNEP convened the Intergovernmental Panel on Climate Change (IPCC) whose findings led to the Framework Convention on Global Climate Change which was opened for signature at the UN conference in Rio de Janeiro in 1992. The findings of these investigations have influenced legislative action and national policy in the United States positively, respecting the effects of CFCs on the stratosphere ozone layer, and uncertainly, regarding the authenticity, causes, and prevention of global climate change and atmospheric warming.

Difficulties arise when attempts are made to address the causes and implications of global atmospheric trends (e.g. possible anthropogenic climate change) at the national level. Economic, technological, and behavioral problems are encountered when national governments (especially the United States) attempt to contain or reverse atmospheric trends at costs to jobs, economic competitiveness, and consumer convenience. Addressing the United Nations' June 1997 review of Agenda 21, five years after Rio (Environmental Summit +5), President Clinton endorsed the proposition that global climate change was a serious issue which nations should address, but he declined to support a European proposal to reduce greenhouse gas emissions believed to contribute to global warming.[17] Public officials in a democracy cannot easily adhere to NEPA's injunction "to improve and coordinate Federal plans, functions, programs, and resources to the end that the Nation may . . . fulfill the responsibilities of each generation as trustee of the environment for succeeding generations." People live and generally vote for today and their anticipated future—not for a succession of future generations.

The melding of domestic national policies with international commitments will be a challenge to public policy-making in the United States and other countries in the years ahead. To prevent or retard adverse changes in the environment, changes will also need to occur in America's commitment to increasing material consumption and expansive growth. A serious effort would be required to institutionalize an industrial policy for the development of environmentally benign technologies and to avoid or reduce personal and community distress in the phase-out and phase-in of industries and technologies. It is not demonstrable that private enterprise and market forces, as some people believe, can do this.

Discovery of a thinning of the stratospheric ozone layer which has shielded the Earth from harmful ultraviolet radiation led to an international convention to control emissions of chlorofluorocarbons (CFCs) and other gases that disintegrate the ozone layer.[18] This agreement was followed by adoption of a convention on global climate change signed at the 1992 UN Conference at Rio. This agreement and the ozone convention protocol required nations to limit emissions of gases which, in changing the chemical composition of the atmospheric commons, could have serious consequences for the biosphere and the well-being of human populations. National policies have been adopted or proposed to address threats to the planetary life-support systems which could be met only through concerted action. Nevertheless, implementation of the climate change convention has been vigorously opposed in the United States by certain economic and conservative interests—notably in relation to the anticipated effects of less economic growth and more government regulation. The American economy "runs" largely on fossil fuel and insufficient efforts have been made to develop a comparable energy source. President Reagan wanted to abolish the Department of Energy. President Clinton endorsed the Climate Change Treaty in principle but has appeared indecisive regarding measures for remedial action, many of which would impact severely on American lifestyles and the economy. There has been strong opposition in the Congress over any mandatory burden on the American economy. As of 1998, Senate ratification of the 1997 Kyoto Protocol and the Climate Change Treaty was highly uncertain. Conflict over energy sources and uses within and among nations seems a 21st-century certainty. On energy policy there has been little inclination by Americans or the Congress to honor the admonition of NEPA Section 101(b)(1) to "fulfill the responsibilities of each generation as trustee for the environment of succeeding generations." Future generations are not voters in today's congressional elections.

OUTER SPACE

Science and technology have opened the way to treating the outer space environment as a global commons. Three possible uses of the outer space environment have impacts which national governments have addressed and which have become subjects of international concern.

The first has been the use of the electromagnetic spectrum of the magnetosphere for telecommunications and the use of artificial satellites for communications and surveillance.[19] Swift and dependable telecommunication has become a boundary-transcending value in an "information age" society. Unobstructed flow of information through the electromagnetic spectrum is now a major, if unconventional environmental value. The International Telecommunications Union (ITU) is the principal agent of national governments for cooperation in this medium, and the United States is a major participant. The work of the ITU is carried on by a number of committees, boards, and conferences. As of 1990, approximately 7,000 artificial satellites were in orbit around the earth, utilizing electromagnetic waves for communication and observation and involving military as well as civilian purposes.

The principal organization for international telecommunications by satellite is the International Telecommunications Satellite Organization (INTELSAT). The United States participates in Intelsat through COMSAT, a consortium of private telecommunications organizations. There are also regional telecommunications organizations, e.g. the European Conference of Postal and Telecommunications Administrations (CEPT) and the Committee for Inter-American Telecommunications (CITEL). The International Maritime Organization has been concerned with satellites as aides to communication and navigation at sea and acts as the supervisory agency for the International Maritime Satellite Organization (INMARSAT).

A second use of outer space with environmental implication is remote sensing and photography. These uses by the United States Earth Resources Sensing System (LANDSAT) aroused some objection for unwarranted intrusion on the territory of other countries. Remote sensing has obvious military uses involving so-called "spy satellites."[20] Nevertheless many international collaborative arrangements have been undertaken for both utilization and exploration of the space environment. In 1977 an Ad Hoc Committee on Remote Sensing for Development convened by the United States National Research Council recommended that "the United States government should declare soon that remote sensing systems constitute, in effect, an international public utility destined for international governance."[21] Remote sensing provides valuable information respecting changes in the environment (e.g. oceanic currents, temperature, and pollution, cloud cover and weather, deforestation, desertification, and urbanization). It greatly facilitates the globalization of environmental research and could assist the monitoring of performance under international treaties. The advanced space technology of the United States greatly enhances the national ability to fulfill its NEPA commitment to biospheric protection.

A third use of environment-related activity in outer space includes exploration and research. These activities require highly sophisticated and costly technologies, e.g. an orbiting space laboratory and interplanetary space probes. But because most nations lack the capability of employing space technology and, because of international sensibilities, some means to manage its use in the common interest is needed. Among the objectives of extraterrestrial exploration and research are discoveries relating to the formation of the planet Earth, its geological and climatological history—information that could influence present environmental policy and would advance NEPA's purpose "to promote efforts which will prevent or eliminate damage to the environment and the biosphere." Reconnaissance of the planet Mars may provide clues to the geophysical history of Earth and could conceivably influence policies regarding the atmosphere and the oceans.

Artificial objects in outer space become environmental problems created by an inordinate amount of debris—thousands of mostly small items (e.g. screwdrivers)—orbiting the earth. International cooperation is necessary to monitor, reduce, or eliminate these hazards to space navigation. If the projected orbiting space station "Freedom" is actually constructed, it will probably become an international venture. A clean up of the world's own junkyard in space may be a necessary task for the station and, from an American perspective, one consistent with NEPA.

Prior to NEPA and the UN environmental conferences, a strong impetus toward international governance for the upper atmosphere and outer space environment was fostered by the prospect of military activities that might have global consequences. The development of intercontinental ballistic missiles, orbiting satellites, high flying aircraft, and atomic nuclear technology provided means for military operations—defensive and offensive—that were feared could cause irreparable environmental consequences.

International apprehension and criticism followed two pre-NEPA experiments in space undertaken by the U.S. Department of Defense. In 1961, Project West Ford involved a nuclear explosion in the Van Allen Radiation Belts and in 1962, Project Starfish scattered copper dipoles in the upper atmosphere to ascertain in advance their effect upon radio wave transmission.[22] No serious effort appears to have been made to ascertain the consequences of these experiments. In both cases the results appear to have been inconclusive, and did not (as some feared) leave damaging consequences. Nevertheless, they aroused extensive international concern and protest. If NEPA had been in effect in the early 1960s, the question of its applicability to unpublicized defense-related activities undertaken beyond the territorial jurisdiction of the United States should have required resolution. But some congressionally alleged necessities for national defense (notably weapons systems), even though scientifically dubious and environmentally indefensible, seem immune to NEPA.

The development of intercontinental ballistic missiles and high-level supersonic transport (SST) led to further national concerns with uses of the upper atmosphere and outer space environments. From 1969 through 1971, notably in the 91st Congress, American participation in international supersonic transport was hotly debated. Endorsed by President Nixon and supported in the House of Representatives, it was nevertheless defeated in the Senate through failure to fund the project. Senator William Proxmire of Wisconsin led the fight against the SST, emphasizing its environmental risk. But Senators Jackson and Warren Magnuson of Washington State supported the project because of its prospective benefit to the Seattle-based aircraft industry. Both Washington senators were major defenders of the environment, and the SST episode illustrates the difficulty of reconciling economic and environmental values when the consequences of a proposed action are uncertain. Similarly, Congressman John Dingell from Michigan has been a vigorous defender of the environment, except when environmental regulations would impose costs on the automotive industry.

The threat of nuclear war and its probable effect on the global environment hung over the nation from the 1950s through the 1980s. From 1963 through 1965 the Department of Defense Office of Civil Defense commissioned a number of studies on the environmental effects of nuclear war, prepared chiefly by the Hudson Institute and processed for the Defense Documentation Center/Defense Supply Agency.[23] At this time there was a pervasive fear in the United States and elsewhere that the deep seabed, the Moon, or outer space, might become bases for hostile military activity.

In 1983 a Conference on the World After Nuclear War produced the hypothesis of "nuclear winter"—a severe change in the global climate following multiple nuclear explosions. The Conference followed an earlier meeting (April 25-26, 1983) on the Long-Term Worldwide Biological Consequences of Nuclear War.[24] The nuclear winter thesis was subsequently called into question but it probably reinforced international efforts to rid the world of the threat of nuclear warfare and reinforced the concept of the atmosphere as a global commons.

Apprehension regarding uses of the common spaces for international warfare led to the negotiation of the following treaties to prevent this possibility:

- 1963 Treaty Banning Nuclear Weapons Tests in the Atmosphere, in Outer Space and Under Water (Partial Nuclear Test Ban Treaty).

- 1967 Treaty on Principles Governing the Activities of States in the Exploration and Use of Outer Space, Including the Moon and other Celestial Bodies.

- 1978 Convention on Prohibition of Military or Any Other Hostile Use of Environmental Modification Technologies (ENMOD).

Concern over the possibility of nuclear war in outer space and its environmental consequences became a major factor both in support for and opposition to President Reagan's proposed Strategic Defense Initiative (SDI).[25]

Inappropriately labeled "Star Wars" by the news media, SDI was funded for research purposes by the Congress but its implementation has grown ever more doubtful—especially following the collapse of the Soviet Union. Fears of nuclear warfare and of the effects of radiation from nuclear reactors contributed to the upsurge of environmental consciousness in the 1960s which led to NEPA.

ANTARCTICA

The Antarctic Continent politically is a "quasi-commons" governed by a unique institutional arrangement.[26] Seven nations have asserted territorial claims to Antarctica but they have been effectively suspended since signature of an international treaty in 1959 by 12 national governments. The United States claims no territory in Antarctica but has been a leader in scientific investigations on the continent. Although designated by treaty as an international scientific reserve, economic ambition to exploit mineral deposits and sources of energy has led some governments and mining interests to urge the opening of Antarctica to mineral exploration and development. United States policy has oscillated between support of a protected international scientific reserve and the exploitation of natural resources.

On June 2, 1988, representatives of the then 19 Antarctic Treaty Consultative Parties providing a minimal governance of Antarctica, and 13 contracting (i.e. non-Party) states adopted a convention for the Regulation of Antarctic Mineral Resource Activities, in effect, terminating the protected scientific reserve. Advocates of the Convention argued (to many people unconvincingly) that mineral development and environmental protection could coexist and that scientific investigation would not be impeded. Although Presidents Reagan and Bush favored the opening of Antarctica to minerals development, the Congress disagreed. On November 16, 1990, by Joint Resolution (PL 101-620) the Congress reaffirmed support for protecting Antarctica as a global ecological commons consistent with the Antarctic Treaty of 1959. As the issue turned out, presidential-congressional conflict was avoided by dissent within the Antarctic Consultative Committee. For the Convention to become effective, unanimous consent of the Consultative Parties was required. Opposition by nongovernmental groups (especially by the Cousteau Society) resulted in France and Australia declining to ratify—thus killing the proposal.[27]

The future of Antarctica remains uncertain, but if the international environmental movement continues to grow, especially following UNCED '92, it seems unlikely that development in Antarctica will be authorized in the near future. During the 1970s the Department of Defense, the Department of State, and the National Science Foundation apparently assumed that NEPA applied to U.S. activities in Antarctica. But following inauguration of the Reagan administration in 1981 some agencies began to resist applying the environmental impact statement to Antarctica operations. NEPA was invoked by the Environmental Defense Fund to require the National Science Foundation to undertake impact assessment for its activities in Antarctica. Contrary to some agency and judicial interpretations regarding overseas application of NEPA, the Court of Appeals for the District of Columbia required the National Science Foundation to comply with NEPA and the U.S. government did not appeal its decision.[28]

UNCED AND ITS IMPLICATIONS

The 1992 United Nations Conference on Environment and Development (UNCED), attended by representatives of 178 governments, moved the nations of the world closer to a collective responsibility for the global environment.[29] Even though the declarations of UNCED reaffirm the principle of sovereignty over a nation's natural resources, the traditional meaning of this principle has been modified and reduced. The "sovereignty" that enables a national government to make binding commitments in international negotiations also enables it to limit its cooperation or to assume obligations in its own and international interests. The concept of "merged sovereignty" becomes more realistic as nations find their interests to be best served by mutual cooperation.

For its implications to be understood, UNCED should be viewed as a major event in a series of international moves toward collective responsibility for the global environment. The true test of its effectiveness will be in the extent to which it is implemented in the 21st century. Beginning with the Biosphere Conference in Paris in 1968 and especially with the United Nations Conference on the Human Environment (UNCHE) in 1972, global conferences on Population, Food, Human Settlements, Water, Desertification, and Energy followed. Of particular relevance for the global commons were the sequential UN Conferences on the Law of the Sea (1958-1982) and the UN Conferences on the Exploration and Peaceful Uses of Outer Space (1968 and 1982). An effect of these and many other international and regional conferences since establishment of the United Nations in 1945 has been to blur the distinction between international (nation to nation) policies for the environment and global policies intended for observance by all nations.

In the explicit linkage of environment and development and in its greater prescriptive detail, UNCED represented an advance over the declaration and action plan adopted at UNCHE two decades earlier at Stockholm. However, there may be a more important difference in the much greater international attendance at Rio—the presence of 110 heads of state and an estimated 18,000 voluntary, nongovernmental participants. UNCED may also be seen as a reaffirmation and expansion of the declaration and principles adopted at Stockholm. This in no way diminishes the consciousness-raising and globalizing effect of the Rio Conference. Yet UNCED, like UNCHE, obtained its agreements at the price of evading or discounting some of the basic conditions that made these conferences necessary—notably exponential population increase and national sovereignty over natural resource exploitation. Moreover, as the 1997 UN "Environmental Summit +5" and the controversy over the Global Climate Change Treaty demonstrated, the nations are more ready to declare policies than to implement them.[30]

To the extent that the so-called common spaces are brought under international agreement and policy control they cease to be ungoverned "common spaces" in a traditional sense. The distinction among national, international, and global environments is lost, at least in logic, in the Biodiversity Treaty and the conventions regarding Climate Change, the Ozone Layer, and to a lesser extent the Law of the Sea. We are still trying to describe 21st-century realities with 19th-century institutional language. What do these developments in global and international environmental policy indicate regarding a national environmental policy for the United States?

Two points seem clear. *First,* a plurality of Americans appear to value protection of the planetary environment, although there are contrarians who deny that the environment needs protecting. Nevertheless the Preamble to NEPA declaring U.S. policy to "prevent or eliminate damage to the environment and the biosphere" should be read with recognition of reservations which may arise when environmental protection conflicts with economic, ethnic, military, or diplomatic interests. Where these interests are congruent with, or not in apparent conflict with environmental protection, NEPA principles are politically acceptable and are endorsed by nongovernmental environmental organizations.

Second, international policies hitherto adopted by the U.S. government have been taken mostly on specific strategic considerations, although environmental factors are now being recognized—as in the environmental agreements supplementary to NAFTA. It might be argued that the environmental content in U.S. international agreements might have been there even if NEPA had never been adopted—but this argument misses the point which is that NEPA affirms a national value, recognized in international and global affairs. Interpreted in this way NEPA can be read as making explicit a policy emerging out of a changing American ethos.

Did NEPA establish a new policy for American government or did it give official expression and statutory status to a policy that, at least for the time, was emerging in American society? The thesis of this book is that NEPA represents a long-term reconfiguration of assumptions and values in American society and government and is representative of a trend emerging throughout the world.[31] The process has been evolutionary and often with anomalies. NEPA provides explicit, visible expression of policy for an environmentally (and hence economically) sustainable future. It articulates values latent and emerging in American society. It also reflects a recognition, now beginning to spread throughout high-information level society, that the bio-sphere is a total interactive system, and whatever significantly affects any part of it may ultimately affect it all.

Throughout public economic and environmental affairs, reinforced in recent decades by international enterprise, science, communications, and mass tourism, recognition that the "environment" extends inseparably from local to global and beyond has become widely accepted. It grows ever clearer that the futures of nations and the world are inextricably linked. Yet national environments and economies are still largely and necessarily administered within the territorial and legal confines of bounded sovereign states. But regional arrangements have emerged in North America, Europe, and South-east Asia in which economic and environmental considerations are brought together. World government is not a realistic option in today's world.

Finding a viable, reliable institutional structure through which global issues can be safely and effectively addressed is a challenge for the 21st century. Toward this task, NEPA has made a major strategic contribution. Arrangements to internationalize environmental impact analysis have not yet been institutionalized. Yet the North American Commission for Environmental Cooperation, paralleling the North American Free Trade Agreement, may lead toward this result. The European Union and the Economic Commission for Europe appear to be moving in the same direction. Efforts to institutionalize the impact assessment process on a worldwide basis seem likely to eventually achieve success. The integrative tendencies of globalization, the impact of powerful new technologies, and a recognition of inter-connectedness of the world as a total system push nations toward ways to live together in the biosphere without destroying its vitality or diminishing its future through ignorance or inattention. The unanswered question is whether the "push" will be firm enough and fast enough to avert a common environmental disaster.

Were NEPA's principles realized in action, a model could be provided for the world. NEPA principles universalized summarize a great part of the United Nations Agenda 21. Constructive response to the global challenges identified by two United Nations conferences (1972, 1992) must begin at the national level before collective action can occur. This is why it is important that NEPA be fully implemented in the United States. Symbolic or rhetorical response alone will not provide a credible model for the rest of the world. The emulation of NEPA in more than 80 countries indicates that it indeed has transnational significance. We do not yet know how to integrate NEPA-like principles and process into world affairs, but the United States could make a great contribution toward order and economic-ecological sustainabil-ity, were it to lead by example and advocacy toward this goal.

Unfortunately for the global environment, the example of the United

States has been ambiguous. Legislative bodies, such as the United States Congress, respond to many demands, many of which in the daily lives of people have priorities higher than environmental concerns as they perceive them. The constituencies to which most elective officials respond are the "effective constituencies" that placed them in office, as distinguished from their much larger "legal constituencies," which provided neither funds nor footwork for their election. Foreign policies respond to "effective" domestic pressures, and environmental policies are seldom of compelling concern to the more "effective" domestic constituents.

But the world economy functions within a global environment. If human populations double in the next century, the resulting pressure on all aspects of the environment will cumulate geometrically, not arithmetically. Raising living standards throughout the world would add to the pressure of numbers. At some point people and governments everywhere will be compelled to somehow reconcile population growth and economic purposes with environmental parameters. NEPA provides a timely and far-sighted agenda for leadership among nations to forestall the consequences of unsustainable demographic and economic trends.

7

Future Directions: Beyond NEPA

HISTORY IS UNLIKELY TO PROVIDE ANOTHER OPPORTUNITY AS OPEN
AND PROMISING AS TODAY'S, SO IT IS ESSENTIAL FOR HUMANITY TO
FIND THE WISDOM TO EXPLOIT IT.

—ALEXANDER KING AND BERTRAND SCHNEIDER,
THE FIRST GLOBAL REVOLUTION (1991).

This concluding chapter restates the thesis of this book, recaps its principal arguments, and suggests the implications of NEPA for the environmental future. Not fully appreciated at the time of its enactment, NEPA was and is a manifestation of a fundamental change in perspective that has been spreading throughout the world during the last half of the 20th century.[1]

Although its purpose has not yet been fully realized, the National Environmental Policy Act has had a significant influence on public policy in the United States and abroad. The procedural reform required by the environmental impact statement (EIS) provision has improved the quality of public planning and decision-making in many places. But the EIS alone is insufficient to achieve the intent declared in NEPA. Title II of NEPA has yet to be fully implemented. The Council on Environmental Quality has done what it could with unduly limited resources—but active presidential and congressional support is needed for it to play the role indicated under Title II. In default of positive White House initiatives, the courts have been the principal interpreters of NEPA but the Supreme Court has limited its adjudication under the Act to procedure.[2] If the NEPA intent is to be realized, consistent with its substantive goals, a basis in constitutional law may be necessary. After nearly three decades, sufficient time has elapsed to permit an interim assessment of the difference NEPA has made and, retrospectively, to consider what we have learned that might guide environmental policy for the future.

Four general propositions regarding NEPA have been introduced in the foregoing chapters. *First*, NEPA articulates core values in American society which, although long latent, are now finding expression. It also expresses new values in environmental stewardship, largely lacking in America's pioneering past. It does not seek to impose values—it reflects them and declares goals for their implementation. *Second*, the substantive goals of NEPA have been only partially internalized in government agencies in consequence of bureaucratic and judicial conservatism and equivocal political support. *Third*, NEPA has nevertheless had a positive impact on policy and administration in the United States and a catalytic effect on the policies of nations abroad. *Fourth*, the role of government in the inseparable relationship among the environment, the economy, and the quality of life is of a magnitude deserving recognition in the fundamental law of the nation—its Constitution. To achieve the NEPA intent will require real commitment—political, institutional, scientific, legal, and not least, moral. To understand why new initiatives are necessary, we need to review how the primary intent of NEPA became subordinated to important but limited procedural considerations and why the changing concepts of the presidency have affected the implementation of NEPA. Finally, it is important to consider the underlying implications of the Act for the future, which in the long run may hold its greatest significance.

THE NEPA CONTEXT

If present economic and social demands upon the environment continue to grow, the policy issues addressed in NEPA seem almost certain to reach a point of urgency early in the 21st century. The quality of life in America's future will depend upon the extent to which the government and people of the United States understand the basic and inclusive nature of the environment and make the principles declared in NEPA a practiced reality—applying its principles in actual public administration. Indicators of environmental troubles ahead are all too strong to be dismissed as "alarmist."

Environmental protection policy has now attained worldwide significance, and NEPA recognizes the worldwide and long-range character of environmental problems. But the environmental actions taken by the Federal government are often inconsistent with NEPA's declared principles. The relevance of NEPA beyond U.S. territorial jurisdiction has been both denied and affirmed in Federal courts. Positions taken by the Federal agencies have not been mutually consistent. The goals and principles forcefully declared in Section 101 have largely been treated as postulates having little practical effect. So as the nation moves into the 21st century, in anticipation of problems now being forecast, the welfare of the nation requires that the principles and goals declared by NEPA receive reaffirmation and reinforcement toward conditions that permit attainment of high qualities of personal and civic life and are sustainable.

To vitalize NEPA as an expression of national intent, it is necessary to understand why it has not become a visible centerpiece of American environmental policy. Why has this statute, which has had worldwide influence and been described as America's environmental Magna Carta, not achieved greater recognition in the United States? NEPA is perhaps no less understood than is any other Federal statute—many of which are lengthy, complex, and subject to periodic reinterpretation by the judiciary. NEPA, however, is relatively short, straightforward and, as a policy act, its precepts are not "vague" (as some commentators have alleged).

There are at least five possible explanations for the difference between the policy declared by NEPA and what actually happens or does not happen in government and the economy. The first is marginalization in the executive branch; the second is judicial misinterpretation; the third is popular indifference to matters of principle when no compelling event arouses concern; the fourth is incomprehension of the scope and pervasiveness of the environment; and fifth (and most important) is that no great unifying goal and strategy has activated NEPA's long-range purpose. Principles declared by NEPA have yet to be reaffirmed as a national agenda for action.

These explanations are generalizations and hence there are exceptions. NEPA has been invoked on occasion by Federal officials and has been correctly interpreted in some of the lower Federal courts. In 1975 a commentator found that "after five years, NEPA as a vehicle creating and maintaining environmental integrity and reforming the process of environmental decision making has had only a modicum of success."[3] Twenty years later a more positive assessment would have been warranted. But except for the effects of the environmental impact statement requirement, it would be difficult to demonstrate that NEPA has been unqualified national policy. Yet this does not diminish the importance of the Act. It provides a standard by which action may be evaluated. It is uncertain as to how future American opinion will rate environmental concerns in relation to national priorities. I read the weight of evidence as supporting the probability that coercive environmental change, along with the growth of knowledge, will raise environmental priorities. But this may not happen. Humans have demonstrated an ability to deny what is apparent and to adapt to a diminishing quality of life and environment.[4]

INTENT REVIEWED

In the Washington National Cemetery there is a tombstone on which the letters NEPA are inscribed. Doubtless it marks the burial of a soldier, but can it also be seen as symbolic of the demise of the National Environmental Policy Act as a credible expression of national policy?

There have been numerous evaluations of NEPA, and assessments have differed.[5] Yet despite dismissive evaluations and outspoken hostility the statute remains intact, its provisions essentially unchanged although various exemptions to its application have been enacted (for example, in relation to specific projects such as the Alaska Pipeline). Yet its direct application has been limited largely to the action-forcing provision—Section 102(2)(c)—the preparation of a detailed statement on the impact of Federal actions having a major effect upon the environment and to collateral actions relating to this requirement—the so-called NEPA or EIS Process.

To the extent that the Process informs decision-making and has modified long-standing agency practices, the Act must generally be accounted a success. It has caused reconsideration, redesign, and even withdrawal of Federal projects that previously would have gone forward without effective challenge. It has forced the public disclosure of plans and proposals which previously would have been shielded from public scrutiny. It has required interagency exchange of information on plans and proposals and has facilitated interagency cooperation on environmental projects where competition and exclusiveness were once the practice. Nevertheless, viewed broadly with regard to the intentions of its sponsors, the potential of NEPA has yet to be realized.

The broad intent of the National Environmental Policy Act is stated in its preamble in language appropriate to the declaration of a national policy:

> The purposes of this Act are: To declare a national policy which will encourage productive and enjoyable harmony between man and his environment; to promote efforts which will prevent or eliminate damage to the environment and biosphere and stimulate the health and welfare of man; to enrich the understanding of the ecological systems and natural resources important to the Nation; and to establish a Council on Environmental Quality.

NEPA was a legislative response to an upwelling of public concern in the 1960s over the worsening state of the environment—a general diffuse public anxiety and discontent. Numerous environmental bills were introduced into the 90th and 91st Congresses. Senate Bill 1075, introduced by Senator Henry M. Jackson on February 18, 1969, became, with subsequent additions, the enacted statute intended to declare and implement a national policy for the environment. The Act underwent extensive revisions in the course of its evolution. It received input from many sources, but the enacted statute was basically the work of congressional committees in both houses of Congress—notably in the Senate Committee on Interior and Insular Affairs, and the House of Representatives Subcommittee on Fisheries and Wildlife Conservation of the Committee on Merchant Marine and Fisheries. The emergent statute was not the product of environmental action groups—few of whom appeared to be more than vaguely aware of its enactment until discovering its potential for blocking specific Federal projects to which they were opposed. The Conservation Foundation was a notable exception to this early lack of interest, making available my assistance to Senator Jackson and the Senate Interior Committee in the development of the legislation.

The legislative history of NEPA explains some of the difficulties in its implementation. The NEPA intent was to affirm a national policy for environmental quality by redirecting Federal decision-making toward outcomes supportive of environmental quality values and transgenerational equity. Its substantive principles were general—appropriate to a declaration of national policy. Directives for agency planning and decision-making were stated in clear language but required translation and interpretation, which were provided in 1978 as *Regulations* under President Carter's Executive Order 11991 (1977). For some issues, supplementary legislation would be needed—some of it as yet highly controversial (e.g. for population, land use, and energy policy). For other issues legislation had already been enacted (e.g. Historic Preservation Act of 1966 and the Wilderness Act of 1964). Unlike most environmental statutes enacted during the 1970s, NEPA had no militant organized activists with a possessive concern comparable to advocates on behalf of clean air, water quality, wilderness, endangered species, or civil rights. NEPA was thrust upon a reluctant president and a bureaucracy committed to mission policies which traditionally regarded environmental values (when regarded at all) as subordinate to mission-specific statutory goals. In effect, NEPA amended all Federal agency authorizations—but to accommodate the new mandate to the old was neither automatic nor easy.

LAW OR POLICY?

Law in its traditional sense reflected the long-standing, widely shared consensus or acceptance in communities. It was concerned largely with the communal sense of justice and with the definition of rights and duties of those who governed and were governed. As of today it seems fair to say that in the minds of most Americans, law is also synonymous with rights, regulations, and officially required procedures and duties. In a highly diversified individualistic society, civic responsibilities not required by law seldom influence social behavior. In an ever more complex world, law becomes increasingly specialized, technical, and less comprehensible to ordinary citizens. In a pluralist, diversifying nation a sense of community and a consensus over civic priorities diminishes.

NEPA is relatively simple, but science-based legislation regulating air and water quality, toxic substances, and ecosystem management can be very complex and accessible only to experts. People may argue over whether there should or should not be a law, but the making of positive law has become the near-exclusive province of lawyers, judges, and professional politicians. Laws no longer necessarily conform to popular consensus, and not all legislative acts—including statutes resembling laws—are regarded as real law if their declared intent is unenforceable.

NEPA is Public Law 91-190. But to what extent does calling a statute a law make it one in fact? That NEPA is a declaration of policy by the republic's highest legislative authority is hardly debatable. That the environmental impact statement requirement is good law is evidenced by the litigation and adjudication that it has engendered. But what of those substantive provisions of the Act which impose no judicially enforceable procedural mandate or specific outcome on Federal administrators? The language of NEPA is explicit in relation to its purpose—but to activate it requires congressional and executive action that has not been consistently forthcoming.

If NEPA is indeed real law—not merely declared policy—then the constitutional obligation of the president "to take care that laws be faithfully executed" would appear to be applicable. It is obvious that there are far more positive laws and regulations of the United States government than any president can personally oversee. Thus the politics of the moment displaces oversight of the execution of the law. Institutional arrangements have been devised to strengthen the role of the president as administrator but they cannot compel him to play the role. As has been noted, the Reorganization Act of 1939 (53 Stat. 561) during the Franklin Roosevelt presidency established the Executive Office of the President (EOP); provided for the White House Staff; and enabled the central managerial functions of budget, personnel, and planning to be brought under presidential control.

The Reorganization Act of 1939 implemented recommendations of the President's Committee on Administrative Management (Brownlow Committee) which identified distinctive differences between the Executive Office and the White House Staff.[6] The Executive Office was the principal agent of the managerial (i.e. executive) responsibilities of the institutional presidency. Its nominated officers were subject to confirmation by the Senate. The White House Staff, in contrast, were personal assistants to the president, selected politically without confirmation, and without policy-making or decision-making authority.

Today these functional differences are generally lost on journalists, regularly confused in the news media, and unappreciated in the Federal agencies and the Congress. The managerial functions of the presidency have largely been displaced by an emphasis on the political, symbolic, and especially personal activities of the incumbent president.[7] The Executive Office of the president has not been used as intended by the Brownlow Committee. This, together with the condescension toward NEPA among some influential members of the so-called Washington establishment, have prevented the CEQ from fully fulfilling its statutory functions. Nevertheless, despite political limitations, the CEQ has performed an important and successful role in the implementation of NEPA.

In recognition of the policy-shaping power of the Office of Management and Budget and to modify its economic bias, a proposal was made during the drafting of NEPA to place certain responsibilities for overseeing compliance with its mandates on the OMB (and on the General Accounting Office as well). These proposals may have been functionally realistic if the NEPA intent were to be vigorously pursued. They were politically unrealistic, however, since there was little expectation in either the Congress or the White House that NEPA principles (regarded as symbolic) would be fully supported by political action—at least not in the near future.

The power of the OMB to question expenditures gave it an authority over administrative agencies unavailable to the CEQ. In political affairs, as in life generally, power over money commands respect. The OMB may lack affection but it does not lack respect. The agencies need not fear the CEQ unless it unmistakably speaks for the president—which has seldom been apparent. The CEQ has no institutional authority over the agencies comparable to the OMB other than that provided by President Carter's Executive Order 11991 giving legal status to the CEQ *Regulations*.

Yet beyond the *Regulations* there are other instruments of presidential authority sufficient to allow more latitude in advancing NEPA principles. Over the past three decades, the environment has found an occasional place on the list of proclaimed presidential priorities but it has never really been near the top and is below where public opinion, in principle, appears to prefer it. Because of the ways in which leadership and control are acquired, legitimized, and retained in political parties, it is often difficult for political leaders to know how to deal with new public opinion realities that conflict with conventional political assumptions. When a show of action seems called for, but consequences are uncertain, the politically prudent response is symbolism.

On certain issues of concern to influential congressmen and particular congressional committees, presidents often have deferred to Congress. Presidential preferences are sometimes displaced for tactical reasons—White House action on one set of issues deferred in exchange for votes in Congress on other issues of higher presidential priority. Thus the president's obligation to see to the faithful execution of the laws depends upon his priorities, circumstantial pressures, and his sense of personal reputation and legacy. For elected officials, presidential and congressional, it seems fair to generalize that politics takes precedence over inconvenient constitutional obligations.

In recent years, established political parties in both America and Europe have become alienated from substantial numbers of citizens. The rise of "green" parties in Europe and, to some extent, the decline of voting in America reflect disaffection with conventional politics.[8] The "greens" are better adapted to the multiparty systems of Europe than to traditionally bipartisan America. But an inclusive, focused, and aggressive political movement with the environment as a core (but not exclusive) concern might force the two major parties into competition for its support. Elements of such an environmental coalition presently exist but have not yet achieved the leadership, scope, and coherence needed to offset the influence of big-money electoral

campaign funding, preoccupation with local economic concerns, vote-mobi-
lizing minorities in political elections, and equivocal treatment in the news
media. The intent of NEPA is widely shared among the American people but
has not yet received the integrated and focused political action needed to
move it closer to realization. Its goals have not yet been featured in any
presidential candidate's agenda.

If determined environmental action were to emerge as major policy
within a political party, would it be accounted "liberal" or "conservative"
with the conventional but ambiguous meanings of these words? In response
to ecological/economic catastrophe, the politics of an authoritarian radical
center might gain dominance, fulfilling Robert Heilbroner's conjecture that
transition from present priorities to a sustainable society might be characterized by an era of "iron governments." Heilbroner has reluctantly foreseen
the emergence of "a far more coercive exercise of national power" to bring
the socio-ecological disruptive processes of an unsustainable industrial society under control. He does not foresee "a willing acquiescence of humankind, individually or through its existing social organizations, in the alter-
ations of lifeways that foresight would dictate. If then, by the question 'Is
there hope for man?' we ask whether it is possible to meet the challenges of
the future without the payment of a fearful price, the answer must be: No,
there is no such hope."[9] Heilbroner is not alone in a pessimistic conjecture
for the future. An extensive bibliography of similar assessments could be
assembled.

I cannot evaluate the probability of these projections, but I believe them to
be supported by evidence. Trends referenced elsewhere in these chapters give
them plausibility—but perhaps not inevitability. Serious implementations of
NEPA might go far toward alleviating or possibly avoiding a socioecological
breakdown. But NEPA as presently conceived—even by its friends—is primarily preventative. Merely to reaffirm NEPA is essential but insufficient. In a 1973
EPA National Conference on Managing the Environment, I argued the need
for "The Positive Role of Environmental Management" and for the statutory
establishment of the Environmental Reconstruction Agency (ERA)—to parallel
the Environmental Protection Agency. But under conditions of virtually full
employment and widespread antigovernment sentiments there is little prospect for such an agency. Were the nation to experience a substantial downturn
in the economy, the prospect for an environmental reconstruction effort could
be greater.

In the late 1960s, when the first wave of the environmental movement
was cresting, the absence of a comprehensive legal basis for environmental
policy caused some concerned citizens and congressmen to consider the
possibility of an environmental bill of rights. Assertions of "rights" pervaded
the political atmosphere of the 1960s, but comparatively few persons saw a
constitutional amendment as an answer to environmental complaints. Given

the persistence of judicial legislating in the United States, constitutional protection of the environment may be needed, although not in the form of a bill
of rights. I will return to the constitutional question toward the end of this
chapter. But a constitutional amendment alone would not answer the need
for a positive agenda of environmental reconstruction, enhancement, and
maintenance. NEPA declares principles and articulates values. But beyond
NEPA, constructive programs, projects, and rationalization of existing law
would be necessary to achieve the Act's intent to improve quality of life. To
be of lasting public benefit, a carefully conceived coordinative program
would be necessary. The integrity of such an effort should be protected, so
far as possible, from the abuses and deceptions that historically have characterized Federal natural resources and public works projects.

TO ACHIEVE THE INTENT

Along with a large number of environmental protection statutes,
NEPA has brought about measurable improvement in many aspects of the
environment. But these achievements look best when compared with past
abuse and neglect. They are much less impressive when viewed in relation
to present and future needs. To achieve the NEPA intent is now seen to be
a task far more formidable and costly (sociopsychologically as well as mon-
etarily) than was perceived in 1969. Science is arousing apprehensions for
the environmental future by announcing new findings regarding environmental sources of disease (e.g. contamination of food and water), global
climate change, stratospheric ozone depletion, acidic precipitation, exposure
to toxic substances and radiation, soil degradation, and worldwide deforestation. The adverse environmental consequences of unprecedented increase
in human populations are recognized by an informed minority but are
widely ignored or denied by many governments, religious doctrinaires, and
some intellectual contrarians, and are uncomprehended by a large sector of
the general public.[10] Thus, how our achievements in environmental law are
evaluated depends upon the direction in which one looks—backward at
what has been done, or forward to what needs to be done.

The goals of NEPA will not be more than partially realized in the absence
of popular will sufficient to the NEPA intent. But for popular will to be
effective, it must be politically audible and visible. Political response requires
more than the indicated preference of opinion poll majorities. In democracies
with the social diversity of the United States, pluralities of minorities rather
than majorities tend to dominate politics. Minorities (economic, ethnic, religious, etc.) that are well-organized, militant, and directed may successfully
impose policies that majorities might not prefer but are unable to effectively
oppose. If popular preference is accurately indicated by opinion polls, environmental values, where widely held, could be expected to have a more

prominent place in American politics than is actually the case. In fact, quality of environment, although pervasive, is a mobile value in American society. It is routinely overlayed by other values and has most often come to the surface of politics when events have aroused sufficient numbers of people to active concern.

Budget allocations are one indicator of the relative importance of issues in American politics. For environmental goals, however, public spending is only a partial indicator of political commitment. For many aspects of the natural environment, NEPA goals could be achieved not by public expenditure but simply by abstaining from developments harmful to the environment as revealed by the NEPA Process. Some "costs," however, might be imposed upon the private sector, for example, in foregone profits from resource development or speculation in land. As of the 1990s, militant advocates of private property rights are among the most vigorous opponents of "environmentalism."

A revealing test of commitment is congressional response to politically influential economic interests on developments with adverse environmental impacts. For example, when Congress authorizes or funds projects for dams, highways, airports, power lines, and industrial development, or when it subsidizes mining, timbering, grazing, or agricultural production (e.g. sugar) in which the net effect is a degraded environment, public expenditure contradicts NEPA. Projects that have negative impacts on some aspects of the environment may sometimes have short-term benefits for particular beneficiaries—but not for society in the long run.

If NEPA's intent is to be achieved and a declared national policy realized, means must be found to bring the political will closer to what appear to be growing environmental values in American society. Governance occurs when policies are implemented through institutionalized arrangements. Where these are inadequate for the policies to be pursued, results will fall short of intentions. In reviewing the adequacy of politics and law toward achieving the goals of NEPA, three deficiencies are apparent. The *first* appears in the structured behavior of the American political system; the *second* appears in the legal foundation of environmental policy. Both must be remedied in efforts to achieve the NEPA intent. But for remedial action to occur there must be evidence of popular environmental concern that politicians cannot afford to ignore. A *third* and fundamental deficiency in the circumstances needed to implement NEPA is the insufficiency of civic commitment. A political will has not been mobilized to support positive measures—public and private—or to achieve and maintain a renewing high public quality of life throughout the nation. This opinion in no way undervalues important private ecosystem preservation such as those of land trusts, the Nature Conservancy, and national, State, and local environmental protection associations.

NEPA provides a foundation upon which environmental policy can be integrated within the full scope of human values. But the foundation must be strong enough to support an implementing structure adequate to meet growing challenges to the future of humanity and the biosphere. NEPA principles must be asserted with a clarity and force sufficient to energize action toward achieving a sustainable quality of life on Earth. For this reason both a reaffirmation and a reinforcement of NEPA are necessary toward activating its declared intent.

ALTERNATIVES TO STRENGTHEN NEPA

While there are not an indefinite number of ways to revitalize NEPA, there are at least seven possible approaches. They are not mutually exclusive but all of them are operationally dependent on the first two. In brief they are to

(1) Enlarge public understanding of the need for an effective environmental policy, which is also policy for people in relation to the environment, and of the importance of NEPA principles for America's future.

(2) Ensure that the importance of NEPA principles are present in the attention span of political party leaders and the shapers of public opinion.

(3) Provide institutional nonjudicial means for the appropriate resolution or mediation of conflicts over issues of environmental quality.

(4) Reform the committee structure of the Congress to provide for a more responsible consideration of environmental issues and possibly to establish a congressional Joint House-Senate Committee on the Environment.

(5) Revise NEPA to clarify and strengthen its statutory provisions.

(6) Restore the Council on Environmental Quality to its intended role in the Executive Office of the President as provided by Title II of NEPA.

(7) Amend the U.S. Constitution to give environmental protection the status of fundamental law.

1. Raising the level of popular awareness and concern is an obvious strategy for revitalizing NEPA, but the routes to success in consciousness-raising are not obvious. The experience of disaster has often aroused environmental awareness but has not always led to environmentally rational results. The prospect of possible and deferred disaster is much less moving. People often defy predictable natural disasters by building and rebuilding houses and communities on flood plains, coastal barrier islands, and unstable terrain. Relocation efforts by the government have often been opposed by fiscal conservatives and regarded as invasive of public choice and private

property rights. A greater hazard to the future is that subtle threats to the environment and the future of humanity are unperceived "creeping catastrophes" — climate change, stratospheric ozone degradation, depletion of fresh water, deforestation, soil erosion, extinction of plant and animal species, and human overpopulation. People are either unaware of the trends, misled by professional optimists, or are unimpressed and decline to take the dangers seriously until irreversible damage is imminent. But then it may be too late to avert irretrievable loss or disaster. Americans have a preference for upbeat news and they tend to discount so-called "doom and gloom" scenarios. The effectiveness of NEPA as a policy agenda could be enhanced by increasing public awareness of the reality and significance of national trends harmful to the environment, the economy, and the quality of life.

Underutilized means to this end are provided, indeed mandated, under Title II of NEPA, establishing the Council on Environmental Quality. Section 204 states that, among other responsibilities, "It shall be the duty and function of the Council"

> (2) to gather timely and authoritative information concerning the conditions and trends in the quality of the environment both current and prospective, to analyze and interpret such information for the purpose of determining whether such conditions and trends are interfering, or are likely to interfere, with the achievement of the policy set forth in title I of this Act, and to compile and submit to the President studies relating to such conditions and trends;
>
> (3) to review and appraise the various programs and activities of the Federal Government in the light of the policy set forth in title I of this Act for the purpose of determining the extent to which such programs and activities are contributing to the achievement of such policy, and to make recommendations to the President with respect thereto;
>
> (4) to develop and recommend to the President national policies to foster and promote the improvement of environmental quality to meet the conservation, social, economic, health, and other requirements and goals of the Nation;
>
> (5) to conduct investigations, studies, surveys, research, and analyses relating to ecological systems and environmental quality;
>
> (6) to document and define changes in the natural environment, including the plant and animal systems, and to accumulate necessary data and other information for a continuing analysis of these changes or trends and an interpretation of their underlying causes.

There are several reasons why those functions have not been effectively performed or have not been performed at all. Responsibility for nonfeasance rests with the Congress, the president, and the council, in that order. With only few exceptions, NEPA and the CEQ have been treated as symbolic by the political branches. Had the CEQ the resources of money, personnel, and presidential encouragement to fulfill Section 204 functions and to identify, track, and interpret important trends and report on them in ways likely to obtain public attention, NEPA might have a greater impact upon public policy. There is no lack of public attention to indices of leading economic indicators that possess less enduring significance than trends shaping the environmental future.

As noted in chapter 1, a conventional and necessary route toward public environmental comprehension is through environmental education in the schools and through nongovernmental environmental protection organizations (e.g. North American Environmental Education Association, the National Audubon Society, the Wilderness Society, the Nature Conservancy, North American Wildlife Federation, Sierra Club, and the World Wildlife Fund, among others). Environmental studies appears to have achieved a permanent place in a large number of colleges and universities. And there is now a large environmental literature of books and magazines and numerous television documentaries. Nevertheless, the strength and extent of popular understanding of environmental relationships and trends is as yet uncertain. Membership-supported environmental organizations might have a more persuasive rationale if they reinforced their particular and important agendas by referring to NEPA as basic national policy. But they understandably appeal to their clientele primarily on environment-specific issues such as endangered species, wetlands, forestry, and national parks—and these efforts should not be diminished. The broad policy goals of NEPA appear to be less amenable to direct citizen action and to funding appeals but they could add to the significance of more specific environmental causes.

2. Election of an environmentally concerned Congress and president is an obvious strategy for implementing the NEPA intent. This requires keeping environmental protection in the forefront of political party agendas. But if election candidates don't see the votes, they won't espouse the cause. Reduction in the partisan and ideological polarization of environmental policy that has developed since the mid-1970s would obviously be beneficial. Neither major political party is wholly committed for or against environmental protection measures. "Antienvironmentalism" has been associated with political "conservatives," especially those representing private land owners and economic development interests, but this is only a tendency, with exceptions. Nongovernmental environmental and public interest organizations could play a more effective role in elective politics by broadening their agendas to include the related concerns of a more inclusive number of Americans.

3. Mediation among concerned parties is one approach toward defusing political contention on some environmental issues. The Environmental Policy and Conflict Resolution Act of 1998 established the United States Institute for

Conflict Resolution to assist in implementing national environmental policy, by providing an official Federal facility that could reduce litigation and political conflict in environmental, land use, and resource disputes.[11] While there are issues that probably cannot be mediated, the process might clarify the values and interests involved and reconcile many differences. The CEQ would be involved in both Federal agency requests to use the Institute's services and in interagency disputes resolution.

4. A congressional Joint Committee on the Environment was considered in the course of drafting NEPA but was not adopted, presumably because of the predictable opposition of the committee chairman who claimed jurisdiction over particular aspects of environmental affairs. Moreover, a joint committee would not protect the integrity of NEPA if it were chaired by congressmen unresponsive to environmental issues. A Joint Committee on Environmental Quality was authorized as Title III of S.1752, the Resources, Conservation, and Environmental Quality Act of 1969 sponsored by Senator Gaylord Nelson of Wisconsin. This act closely resembled Jackson's S.1075 in many respects but differed in its designation of the Department of the Interior as the principal focus of ecological research. S.1752 was not reported out of the Interior Committee for consideration by the Congress.

The joint committee provision was included in a number of environment and resource protection statutes preceding NEPA. The model was the Joint Economic Committee of the Congress, a provision of the Employment Act of 1946 (essentially to review the president's economic report and to guide the Congress on economic issues). Because the environment (like the economy) impinges on a wide range of issues, the jurisdiction of a joint environmental committee would need to be carefully defined.

5. A more frequent proposal to strengthen NEPA has been through statutory amendment. On October 11, 1989, Representative Gerry Studds introduced H.R. 1113 (101st Congress, 1st Session), which authorized appropriations for the Office of Environmental Quality (CEQ) and included a number of amendments intended to clarify and extend NEPA provisions. H.R. 1113 would have added a subsection (7) to Section 101(b) to "provide world leadership in ensuring a healthy and stable global environment." A corresponding bill was introduced into the Senate by John H. Chafee, but this legislation found insufficient support in the Congress.

Amendments were also proposed by Philip M. Ferester in the *Harvard Environmental Law Review* (1992).[12] The author would require the agencies to justify their failure to seriously consider the least damaging options, curb agency inclination to minimize or evade mitigation of environmental damage, and resolve the procedure v. substance debate.

Amending NEPA to reinforce agency observance of its substantive provisions as judicially reviewable and obligatory on the Executive branch and to confirm its applicability to Federal actions having environmental impacts beyond United States territorial jurisdiction might allow the NEPA intent to be more fully realized. But, under the ideological partisanship in the congresses of the 1990s, opening the door to revision would risk whatever protection the Act now provides. NEPA was enacted with clear bipartisan support. Since 1994 the conservative wing of the Republican Party, in control of the committees of the Congress, has been hostile to environmental legislation generally and to NEPA in particular. In the 104th and 105th Congresses, numerous exemptions from NEPA have been passed or attempted. These quasi-amendments ("riders") are surreptitiously slipped into the text of bills having no bearing whatever on environmental issues. Sponsors of the "riders" hope that, without notice or hearing, the exemptions will pass as parts of the bills which they have "parasitized." The item veto would enable presidents to prevent this abuse of legislative power. It is not clear to what extent the mere fact of statutory law can influence the assumptions and priorities of politicians and public administrators. There are few rules, regulations, or procedures that government agencies, given time and public inattention, cannot turn to their own preferences. While amendment of NEPA should not be precluded, alternative ways to strengthen NEPA might best be explored, for example, statutes that obstruct the Act's implementation might be amended. The Government in the Sunshine Act of 1976 could be amended to relieve the Council for Environmental Quality from crippling strictures that effectively prevent its functioning as the deliberative body intended by NEPA. The Office of Management and Budget might be directed to examine agency spending proposals for conformity with NEPA and to refer doubtful cases to the CEQ for review.

6. As previously noted, the CEQ after the mid-1970s has had a tenuous existence. Repeated attempts have been made in the Congress to defund it, and proposals to abolish it were made in the Carter and Clinton administrations. One explanation may be found in the persisting perception that environmental policy is important primarily in relation to antipollution measures being administered by the EPA. Another has been that environmental problems were essentially contemporary, limited in scope and significance, and correctable by a few new laws. Moreover, vigorous defense of the environment is not in the political interest of congressmen sensitive to interests of patrons who are indifferent or even unfriendly to environmental values.

For the CEQ to be more effective it should be adequately funded and staffed and should be utilized by the president as the statute intends. New legislation might be helpful but is not essential. The president, by Executive Order and budgetary support, could enable the CEQ to function according to NEPA's intent. Although the chair of the CEQ exercises important administrative functions, the three-member council is an important instrument of policy if the CEQ is to provide the deliberative and coordinative role originally contemplated. As previously noted, a post-Watergate reactive Congress passed the Government in the Sunshine Act of 1976 (P.L. 94-409) which, as interpreted by the courts, complicates and obstructs the deliberative and advisory functions of the three-member Council.[13] Discussions by this Council have been construed as "meetings" requiring advance notice in the Federal Register, and Congress should exempt the CEQ from the handicaps imposed by this Act. Reducing the "Council" to one member seems an unnecessary retreat. The Congress has at least temporarily sought to legitimize this departure from the statute by stipulating that notwithstanding Title II of NEPA, there will be for fiscal year 1998 just one member of the Council instead of three. Similar language may be anticipated in future appropriations.

The First Hoover Commission recommended replacing the three-member Council of Economic Advisers by a single head but the proposal was not accepted by the Congress. Abolishment of the CEQ was recommended in 1988 by a panel of the National Academy of Public Administration.[14] In 1992 a joint commission of the Carnegie Endowment for International Peace and the Institute for International Economics made a similar recommendation. Both reports were advisory to the president-elect on organizational changes in the executive branch. There is no apparent evidence that the staff who prepared these reports or the "blue-ribbon" commissions which endorsed them understood the reasoning behind the establishment of the CEQ. The Carnegie report regarded the environment as a major national policy issue but did not distinguish between the deliberative and coordinative functions for which the CEQ was intended and the direct managerial responsibilities of a cabinet level department or a regulatory agency such as the EPA.

7. The ambivalent and often marginalizing treatment of NEPA in the courts has been a factor in proposals to establish a special court to adjudicate environmental controversies especially in which scientific and technical questions are critical.[15] The scientific and technical issues and concepts involved are alleged to be alien to the educational background of most lawyers and judges. Critics of this proposition point out that more than science and technology are involved in cases in which they are factors. Richard B. Stewart of the Harvard Law School asserted that "environmental problems are not solely or even primarily technical." Science and technology may be highly relevant—but the problem is inevitably one of human preference or behavior.[16] Appointment of a master or specialist advisor to the court where the issues in a case require clarification beyond the ordinary competence of the judiciary may be a practicable solution—although one not without risks.

There remains the most fundamental, but some might say least plausible, alternative to reinforce NEPA and environmental legislation in general—a constitutional amendment. This alternative presently appears beyond feasibility. But it merits consideration for three reasons. *First*, examination of the arguments for and against an amendment opens the way to a broad appraisal of the relative importance, effects, and limitations of environmental policy in law and administration in general and with reference to NEPA in particular. *Second*, the debate over an environmental amendment could lead to examination of the role of law in relation to foreseeable environmental risks and unwanted consequences with which society is presently unprepared to cope. *Third*, the issue raises the question of what policies are appropriate to a written constitution that is intended to declare the fundamental responsibilities and limitations of government. To answer this question, consideration of criteria for constitutional status would be desirable. A benefit from this particular inquiry could be the reduction of numerous proposed amendments inappropriate to fundamental principles of public law.

Whether a constitutional amendment would widen the door to litigation over environmental issues is conjectural. Americans are a litigious people in a society that appears governed by lawyers and judges. If a constitutional amendment clarified the respective public and private rights and duties relating to the environment, the volume of litigation might be reduced, but depending on the language of the amendment and its interpretation by the Supreme Court, recourse to lawsuits might be encouraged. As the law now stands, property rights and civil rights are accorded constitutional protection; the environment has not comparable status. But property rights and civil rights pertain chiefly to identified individuals or directly affected groups. Environmental law applies collectively, as does national defense. But unlike defense, responsibility for the integrity of the environment has not been internalized in the ethos, ethics, and folkways of the American people.

The following pages elaborate the argument for constitutional protection of the environment. They provide a brief history of efforts to obtain an environmental amendment, an analysis of differences between declarations of rights and of duties, an example of what the substance of a government obligations amendment might contain (not a proposed amendment), and finally international implications of the constitutional issue. The argument here is that the legal status of the environment, as a basic collective social fact of life, deserves consideration, especially in a society in which the focus of law has been almost exclusively upon individuals. The issue deserves serious consideration by persons with breadth of competence in constitutional law (not only U.S. law) and in environmental policy issues.

THE CASE FOR A CONSTITUTIONAL AMENDMENT

The case for a constitutional amendment for the environment is not a call for early action; rather, it is a case for continuing consideration of the nation's preparedness to cope with an environmentally troubled future. There are international as well as domestic reasons for building environmental concern into the nation's fundamental law, for declaring the responsibilities of government rather than the environmental rights of individuals. There are cumulative reasons for taking seriously the developing dangers in the world environment, as noted in the Carter administration's *Global 2000 Report* (1980/81), in international declarations, in numerous books and articles, and reiterated in the *World Scientists' Warning to Humanity* (1993). These warnings have been rejected by underinformed optimists who regard them as apocalyptic doomsday scenarios unsupported by "sound science." Nevertheless there is reason to believe that conjoint problems of population, resources, economy, and environment will converge early in the 21st century—the "problematique" of the Club of Rome. While the timing is uncertain, the trends seem unmistakable. America (and the world in general) is poorly prepared conceptually as well as institutionally to cope with them. Bills to establish a national forecasting capability have been uniformly rejected by the Congress. Proposals for a constitutional status for the environment (i.e. environmental rights) heretofore have gone nowhere. Nevertheless the issue should be kept alive and considered so that the nation can be prepared to adopt an effective resolution of the constitutional issue when its time comes.

Differences in viewpoint over a constitutional amendment come down to differences over values, the relative importance of issues, and the role and responsibilities of government. The large number of proposals inappropriate for constitutional amendment that continue to be introduced diminish the prospects of amendments for basic questions of policy. Constitutional amendments for prayer in schools, for budget balancing, for congressional term limiting, and against flag burning are regarded as important by the people who propose them. But are these issues more urgent and more important than the state of the natural systems of air, water, land, and biota upon which the future of life and the economy depends?

The effects of a constitutional amendment on legislation and litigation are uncertain. Much would depend upon the wording of the amendment, especially as it would affect the courts. Present divisions of opinion over the extent of public trust for the environment invites litigation particularly where private rights are claimed against environmental restraints regarding land use, endangered species, natural resources exploitation, and industrial production methods. If the Institute for Environmental Conflict Resolution fulfills the hopes of its sponsors, a constitutional provision for environmental protection might channel more disputes into mediation, reducing recourse to potentially costly litigation of uncertain outcome.

Most proposals for constitutional reinforcement of environmental law have hitherto sought to declare environmental rights.[17] As early as December 11, 1967, a constitutional amendment was proposed in the House of Representatives by Congressman Charles E. Bennett in the form of a House Joint Resolution (H.J. Res. 954). A similar proposal was made on June 13, 1968, by Representative Richard Ottinger (H.J. Res. 1321), and in April 1970 by Morris Udall (H.J. Res. 1205). These proposed amendments specifying "rights" were not acted upon by Congress. An attempt to establish environmental rights by statute was undertaken in the drafting of NEPA. A provision in Senate Bill 1075 that "each person has a fundamental and inalienable right to a healthful environment" was deleted in the House-Senate Conference on NEPA. Subsequently, on January 19, 1970, Senators Gaylord Nelson, Alan Cranston, and Claiborne Pell introduced S.J. Res. 169, an amendment to NEPA which declared that "every person has the inalienable right to a decent environment. The United States and every State shall guarantee this right." Had any of these provisions been adopted, it is doubtful that the intent would have been achieved but, if civil rights are analogous, the volume of litigation would probably have been increased. Defining a practicable and generally acceptable definition of "decent" might be an impossible task.

Environmental rights proposals have been criticized by professional conservatives, by market-choice political economists, and by some legal scholars with primary concern for property rights. It has not always been clear whether the objections are to the idea of an environmental amendment per se, or to the form of the proposals as a "bill of rights." The focus upon rights has been inspired by, although not necessarily dependent upon, a philosophy of natural rights derived from natural law. One may, of course, take a utilitarian view of rights—understanding rights to be socially derived, not inherent in the nature of things and hence never inalienable.

There might be great difficulty in interpreting and applying a constitutional amendment declaring environmental rights. There are fewer difficulties and a more enforceable mandate in an amendment that establishes a governmental obligation to administer and adjudicate the laws and policies in ways that avoid unnecessary damage to the environment, its species, and ecosystems. Compliance in such cases could be more objectively determined, in contrast to the subjectivity of individual claims of rights infringed. But the "obligations" approach would necessitate the right of "standing" in citizen (class action) suits to compel the government to obey the law. Judicial limitation of the courts' access to a common law show of personal injury would limit many complaints to possible enforcement by presidential action or, with doubtful prospects, by the Congress.

Whether one seeks protection of the environment through declared individual rights or public responsibilities might be regarded as a tactical option. In fact, the difference is fundamental. The argument advanced here is that a more reliable route to sustainable environmental relationships is not through rights—not easily defined or defended—but through responsibilities, affirmed through fundamental law. The concept of "rights" is not eliminated however, because citizens do have (at least in theory) a civil right to require their public officials to enforce the law and be accountable for nonfeasance.

How, then, might this concept of environmental responsibility through governmental obligation be written? Following is a brief illustrative (hypothetical) draft amendment to the Constitution that declares the responsibility of the government for protecting the quality and integrity of the environment:

> In all acts authorized or enforced by all governments of the United States, the integrity of natural systems shall not be impaired except as necessary to protect public health, safety, and welfare, or in response to emergencies where no socially acceptable alternative exists. Sustainability and renewal of natural systems, enhancement of environmental quality and human habitat, and fairness to present and future generations shall be governing principles of policy.

This draft is for illustrative purposes only. Until precise language of a proposed amendment is formulated, its interpretations by the Federal courts cannot be foreseen. As with the amendments that form the constitutional Bill of Rights, judicial "creativity" in interpretation often exceeds or distorts the intentions of the sponsors. The mere adoption of a constitutional amendment does not guarantee its effectiveness. A profile of U.S. state constitutional environmental provisions ranges from the moderately effective to the unenforceable. Many of the national constitutional provisions are strictly rhetorical, having no effect whatever upon how the environment is treated.

The argument that the individual states would never ratify an environmental amendment is at best conjectural. During the 1960s and early 1970s there was an upsurge of environmental protection legislation among the states. By 1965 at least sixteen states, the District of Columbia, and Puerto Rico had environmental policy acts or little NEPAs.[18] Other estimates place the number of states that have enacted environmental policy laws at twenty-eight. The difference appears to be that the larger number of states have NEPA-like impact statement procedures whereas the sixteen states have fully developed policy acts.

At least sixteen of the states have environmental provisions in their constitutions.[19] Some are largely rhetorical in effect. But some (e.g. New York, Pennsylvania, and Virginia) invoke the doctrine of public trust and declare the obligation of government to protect the public interest in the environment. Some states have statutory provisions which in certain respects (notably regarding land use) provide more environmental protection than does Federal legislation (e.g. California, Washington, Florida, Vermont). A bipartisan coalition of legislators in forty states have agreed to sponsor resolutions requesting Congress to send a proposed Environmental Rights Amendment to the states for ratification.[20] The proposal continues the effort to require the Federal government to "guarantee present and future generations the right to a clean and healthful environment." How such a guarantee could be honored in practice is far from clear.

The proposed environmental amendment to the Constitution would not preempt the functions of the states that enforce environmental protection measures and could strengthen their position against invasive action by Federal agencies and by out-of-state solid-waste dumpers and resource developers. State discretion would be reduced only where State governments sought to accommodate economic or other interests pursuing projects that were unnecessarily destructive of environmental values. The states may, and some do, provide important protections for environmental circumstances bounded locally. Among these are provisions governing land use, urban and regional planning, and preservation of important ecological assets—scenic, scientific, and cultural. But the larger environmental issues transcend artificial human boundaries and are increasingly discovered to be transnational and even global.

TRANSNATIONAL CONSIDERATIONS REVIEWED

A growing understanding of the transnational character of environmental problems has led toward a convergence of national and international environmental law. A growing body of positive international law and soft law (charters, declarations, resolutions) has been adopted or recognized by international organizations, especially those associated with the United Nations system.[21] International conventions (i.e. treaties) are the principal expressions of universal international environmental law. Under the Constitution of the United States, an international treaty, when ratified by the Senate, becomes analogous in important respects to a constitutional amendment.[22] In 1916 through this device, birds migrating between Canada and the United States were brought under Federal protection whereas previously all wildlife fell under the jurisdiction of the separate states. International efforts to establish environmental protection as positive (i.e. fundamental) international law have been divided, as in the United States, between declaring governmental obligations and individuals' rights. The approach involving governmental obligation has been more inferential than direct. The United Nations' World Charter for Nature (1982) in principle imposed obligations on governments but provided no way to secure compliance. Although overwhelmingly endorsed by the UN General Assembly (the U.S. casting the only dissenting vote), few nations intended to honor its precepts. The occasion had as much to do with the internal politics of the General Assembly as with concern for the global environment.

An indirect approach to national obligations has been through the internationally proposed requirement of environmental impact assessments modeled after NEPA. A resolution proposing a treaty to require signatory governments to prepare environmental assessments and to consult with other governments on potentially harmful proposals was introduced in the Senate on January 24, 1977 (S. Res. 49) by Senator Claiborne Pell of Rhode Island. The Resolution passed the Senate by voice vote on July 21, 1978, but no further advance was taken. The treaty proposition was still alive in April 1979 when the concept was presented to the Governing Council of the United Nations Environment Programme. A Convention on Environmental Impact Assessment in a Transboundary Context was signed on February 25, 1991, in Espoo, Finland.[23] The United States signed the treaty but has not ratified it. As of 1997 the treaty had not received sufficient ratifications to enter into force. That the concern expressed in NEPA "to promote efforts which will prevent or eliminate damage to the environment and the biosphere" is shared in other countries (apart from UN conferences) was demonstrated in 1989 by an International Conference on A More Efficient International Law on the Environment and Establishing an International Court for the Environment Within the United Nations System. The Conference, convened in Rome by the Italian Supreme Court, was attended by representatives from 27 countries. Among the Final Recommendations adopted by the Conference were the following:

(1) The drafting of a universal International Convention proclaiming the duty of all States to conserve and protect the environment, both within and outside the limits of international jurisdiction;

(2) the creation of an international body within the United Nations system to guarantee the supervision, planning, and management of the world environment;

(3) the appointment of a United Nations High Commissioner for the Environment with adequate support facilities;

(4) the creation by the United Nations of the International Court for the Environment, which will be accessible to States, United Nations organs, and private citizens. The court should have the power to decide on the infringements of the right to the environment, international ecological violations, and possibly the issues to be dealt with in an International Convention on the Environment.

Commenting on the universal International Convention, a distinguished Italian jurist declared that it "should specify an individual's inalienable rights and establish an adequate level of information, participation and actions necessary to maintain those rights, . . . and should also define the main obligations of the individual States [and] . . . must identify the people responsible for promoting and protecting his human rights."[24] The concept of a European constitutional law for the environment, justiciable throughout the European Union, has been under consideration since 1990, when the Economic Commission for Europe proposed a Charter on Environmental

Rights and Obligations.[25] An acceptable version is still under consideration. In addition Jacques Cousteau proposed an amendment to the United Nations Charter for transgenerational environmental equity. As of mid-1997 none of these efforts had succeeded, but they express an international concern which, while possibly premature for realization, may become realizable in the future. NEPA places the United States in a position to collaborate and even to lead in these efforts.

The concept of global international environmental responsibility has been advanced by United Nations conferences on the environment and by resolutions adopted by the UN General Assembly. The *Declaration of Principles* adopted by the 1972 United Nations Conference at Stockholm asserted the fundamental human right to "an environment of a quality that permits a life of dignity and well-being;" it also asserted "a solemn responsibility to protect and improve the environment for present and future generations." But emphasis of the twenty-five principles declared at Stockholm was clearly on responsibilities rather than upon rights. The shorter Stockholm *Declaration on the Human Environment* was foremost a statement of duties and responsibilities. After setting forth the imperative to defend and improve the human environment, paragraph 7 declared:

> To achieve this environmental goal will demand the acceptance of responsibility of citizens and communities and by enterprises and institutions at every level, all sharing equitably in common efforts. Individuals in all walks of life as well as organizations in many fields, by their values and the sum of their actions, will shape the world environment of the future.
>
> Local and national governments will bear the greatest burden for large-scale environment policy and action within their jurisdictions. International cooperation is also needed in order to raise resources to support the developing countries in carrying out their responsibilities in this field. A growing class of environmental problems, because they are regional or global in extent or because they affect the common international realm, will require extensive cooperation among nations and action by international organizations in the common interest. The Conference calls upon governments and peoples to exert common efforts for the preservation and improvement of the human environment, for the benefit of all people and for their posterity.

During the 1970s and 1980s, international commitment to environmental sustainability grew significantly. At Stockholm in 1972 less-developed nations suspected that their economic development would be retarded by the environmental agenda proposed by the developed nations. In contrast, the 1992 UN Conference at Rio de Janeiro marked, at least rhetorically, a near global consensus on the necessity for environmental protection as a condition for sustainable development. Principles of the Rio *Declaration on Environment and Development* adopted on June 14, 1992, by the United Nations Conference on Environment and Development declared that states shall cooperate in a spirit of global partnership to conserve, protect, and restore the health and integrity of the Earth's ecosystem. In view of the different contributions to global environmental degradation, states have common but differentiated responsibilities. The developed countries acknowledge the responsibility that they bear in the international pursuit of sustainable development in view of the pressures their societies place on the global environment and of the technologies and financial resources they command.

The significance of these statements is that the conferences felt obligated to declare them. They have more than rhetorical significance, however, because they officially declare beliefs about how nations ought to behave in relation to environmental and transnational affairs. It is common for nations, like people, to acknowledge moral principles which they are unable to practice. Yet acknowledgment of a moral imperative to environmental stewardship may be a necessary first step toward effective international action. Political statements today may become legal obligations tomorrow.

In efforts to actualize these moral principles the developed nations thus far have failed to provide consistent leadership. Disagreement over the application of NEPA to American involvement in on-the-ground action beyond national territory has permitted the United States to pursue an ambivalent course in international environmental cooperation. Yet no nation can wholly escape the disasters (directly or indirectly) that threaten the world's environment. The United States has led in many aspects of environmental protection but it has not given this protection a place in its fundamental law. Despite NEPA, it is still possible for the Federal government to ignore, finesse, or reverse commitments and, where there is no clear constitutional substantive mandate, to disregard the constitutional obligation of the president to take care that the laws be faithfully executed. An eminent professor of international law, Quincy Wright, cited numerous commentators who he declared had clearly shown the importance of national constitutions in determining the actual capacity of states to exercise power and meet responsibilities under international law.[26] At least 44 countries have been identified as having some form of environmental protection provision in their national constitutions.[27]

If the United States is to lead in world environmental affairs, or even to join in common efforts, it will be necessary to arrive at national consensus upon some basic priorities. If the United States is unable or unwilling to place environmental protection among its constitutional obligations it could diminish its prospects as a credible leader among nations in this aspect of public and international policy. Its credibility in international affairs has not been strengthened by its negative response to United Nations initiatives. It was the one country voting against the UN resolution on Protection Against Products Harmful to Health and Environment (1981) and the World Charter for Nature (1982), it declined to ratify the Law of the Sea Treaty, and rejected the Convention on Biodiversity at the 1992 UN Conference in Rio (subsequently signed by President Clinton but not ratified by the Senate).

More than NEPA is necessary to put into action and perhaps to extend the principles declared in NEPA. Recognition of the fundamental importance of the environment in national and world affairs written into the United States Constitution would set an example that could facilitate the movement toward universal environmental protection. The frequently negative position of the United States on United Nations initiatives does not encourage the expectation of its leadership performance in international environmental affairs.

BEYOND NEPA: ADJUSTING TO REALITY

A distinguishing feature of any society is its prevailing assumptions about its relationship to the Earth. The history of cultures—especially of religions—reveals a great number of cosmologies, or mankind's perceived relationships to its planetary environment. Today the future of the human species depends heavily upon the degree to which the prevailing concept of its environmental situation corresponds to biophysical realities and upon what humans value and how they behave in relation to this reality. Some philosophers (or skeptics) may deny the knowability of reality. But humans, in common with other life forms, must know it well enough to survive. Archaeology has recorded the degradation or collapse of societies that have misread the requirements for environmental/economic sustainability.

During the earlier centuries of human history the impact of society on its environment was relatively light and local. If an environment became unsustainable—for whatever reason—people could often move to new lands. When attrition of the environment was slow or scarcely perceptible, the consequences of its decline often were not felt until they were irreversible. Where human numbers were small relative to space, migration permitted impaired environments to recover—or partially recover. But in a world filled with people and settlements, this option is becoming no longer available. Recognition of narrowing environmental options has led in recent decades to conservation practices assisted by the growth of science, the comparative measurement of environmental change, and forecasts of the probable consequences of present trends.

The conservation of natural resources movement had a paradoxical effect upon human perceptions of environmental realities. The conservation movement contributed both to the emergence of applied ecology and to environmental concerns but also tended to reject environmentalism as "uneconomical," misguided, and antipeople. Economy and efficiency in the wise use of resources has been the essence of "conservation." Many resource conservationists saw the environment as indefinitely manageable—capable of sustained and even growing productivity under the guidance of science-informed technical experts.[28] Conservationism was fundamentally consistent with the way the world was viewed in Western society in the late 19th and early 20th centuries. The concept of the environment as infinitely malleable still has its followers. In 1977 a professor of environmental resources policy wrote that "most of the constraints under which we live are modifiable by human action. They are mere inhibitions."[29] It is "nature" that must be modified, not human behavior.

Environmentalism emerged in the latter half of the 20th century from a convergence of changing perceptions of the human condition in fields as diverse as ecology, public health, demography, climatology, cosmology, and ethics. When its full dimensions, assumptions, and expectations are understood, environmentalism is, as Robert Nisbet observed, in essence, revolutionary. Its effect upon human society is comparable to the changed views of reality inherent in the Copernician cosmic revolution in the 17th century, the Darwinian evolution revolution in the 19th century, and the theories of Albert Einstein in the early 20th century.[30]

To some, this conclusion may seem to be an exaggerated and unrealistic assessment of the influence of environmentalism and its future prospects. The counterintuitive behavior of social systems makes any forecast of the future tentative and uncertain. Nevertheless there are ascertainable, measurable trends in today's world that strongly suggest the joint impact of cognitive change and coercive environmental events upon human society in the 21st century. Adherence to NEPA principles may become more a matter of necessity than of voluntary choice. The way in which people and their governments respond to the prospect of these coercions will shape the world's future. The timing of effective response is equally important. The longer the delay the more difficult the task and the greater the possibility of irreparable damage. We do not need to invent a precautionary strategy for the future. In NEPA we already have one.

In view of the numerous agendas and prescriptions for the future it seems redundant for me to propose another agenda. The issues to be addressed and what must be done to sustain an environmentally/economically sustainable future of quality have been stated in reports of the United Nations conferences relating to the environment (1972-1982); in the UN World Charter for Nature (1982); the Bruntland Commission report, on *Our Common Future* (1987); publications sponsored by the Club of Rome; and, for America, by the *Global 2000 Report* (1980-1981). Whether or when an effective program for action can be adopted for the United States is uncertain. The effort—or failure to make it—would be a test of national integrity. I have proposed two parts of an action plan.[31] But I concede the improbability of their acceptance in the economically booming consumer society of the mid-1990s. Because the future of the world in the 21st century cannot be foreseen, we can only conjecture the place of NEPA on the trajectory of history. I offer the following assessment of the significance of NEPA, fully realizing that the world is capable of unpredictable turns.

NEPA is most fully understood today as *a national policy for henceforward into the future.* "Environment" may be understood as a surrogate term for a concept more comprehensive than is usually appreciated. Our language tends to lag behind new insights. Our most persistent social misconception may be the artificial dichotomy of economy/ecology (i.e. the environment). Their true relationship might be suggested by the time-space concept in physics. The concepts of environment and economy in relation to values are not the same—they are distinguishable—but paradoxically they are ultimately inseparable. In mundane reality there are obvious conflicts within and between the "domains" of economy and the environment. Yet both these aspects of our world are in actuality inextricable—separable by cultural convention and for analytic purposes. Ultimately the reality of earthly limits to the growth of populations and the economy will have to be faced, however unwillingly. Better that this occur as choice, not necessity. The *Global 2000 Report* depicted a world "more crowded, more polluted, less stable ecologically, and more vulnerable to disruption than the world we live in now."[32] The test of human character under conditions recognized as morally and rationally civilized depends upon action taken in time to prevent or reverse foreseeable adversities. The alternative is a resolute attempt by a later generation to make the best of a damaged world. The task may be a test for survival, and as Philip Shabecoff concludes in his book *A New Name for Peace,* "it is this generation's duty to do all in our power to spare our grandchildren that test."[33] NEPA as an agenda for the future lays the test of a sustainable future on this generation. Its first principle (Section 101(b)(1)) is to "fulfill the responsibilities of each generation as trustee of the environment for succeeding generations." But illustrative of my contention of an absence of institutional memory in Washington is the absence of any reference to NEPA in the *Global 2000 Report* and, notably, in its recommendation for a comprehensive U.S. national strategy.

Achievement of a national policy for the environment requires awareness of the environment/economy interrelationship, recognition of the direction toward which the world appears to be moving, growth of consensus on the kind of future that is desired and sustainable, and acceptance of the need to adjust expectations and behaviors to those conditions that humans cannot change. The significance and importance of environment in human life and public policy cannot be fully appreciated unless its ultimate dimensions and practicable aspects are recognized and distinguished. The ultimate (i.e. cosmic) environment sets the outer limits to human material achievement. It sets the parameters within which human actions may satisfy human needs and purposes. The universe, Earth and biosphere included, appears to be a self-organizing feedback system. Its controls over human life and behavior are as yet imperfectly understood. To discover and take account of the feed-back consequences of human impact upon the environment is the function of environmental analysis.

A national policy for the environmental future cannot be achieved in isolation from other major societal issues. Issues of population, material growth, property rights and obligations, and basic civil rights and social equities involve choices which many people would prefer not to make. But the world today is not a "new age of Aquarius" free from ultimate account-ability. Regardless of what we may deny or resist, our society will in one way or another be compelled to accommodate to the way the world inexo-rably works. But apocalypse need not be a foreordained outcome for a society that marshals and moves its moral, material, intellectual, technical, and or-ganizational capabilities toward attainment of a preferred and sustainable future. The National Environmental Policy Act may be seen as a major mile-stone on this road—or as an agenda and foundation for the future.

APPENDIX

Public Law 91-190 91st Congress, S.1075
January 1, 1970

AN ACT

83 STAT. 852

To establish a national policy for the environment, to provide for the establishment of a Council on Environmental Quality, and for other purposes.

Be it enacted by the Senate and House of Representatives of the United States of America in Congress assembled, That this Act may be cited as the "National Environmental Policy Act of 1969".

National Environmental Policy Act of 1969.

PURPOSE

SEC. 2. The purposes of the Act are: To declare a national policy which will encourage productive and enjoyable harmony between man and his environment; to promote efforts which will prevent or eliminate damage to the environment and biosphere and stimulate the health and welfare of man; to enrich the understanding of the ecologocial systems and natural resources important to the Nation; and to establish a Council on Environmental Quality.

TITLE I

DECLARATION OF NATIONAL ENVIRONMENTAL POLICY

Sec. 101. (a) The Congress, recognizing the profound impact of man's activity on the interrelations of all components of the natural environment, particularly the profound influences of population growth, high-density urbanization, industrial expansion, resource exploitation, and new and expanding technological advances and recognizing further

Policies and goals.

the critical importance of restoring and maintaining environmental quality to the overall welfare and development of man, declares that it is the continuing policy of the Federal Government, in cooperation with State and local governments, and other concerned public and private organizations, to use all practicable means and measures, including financial and technical assistance, in a manner calculated to foster and promote the general welfare, to create and maintain conditions under which man and nature can exist in productive harmony, and fulfill the social, economic, and other requirements of present and future generations of Americans.

(b) In order to carry out the policy set forth in this Act, it is the continuing responsibility of the Federal Government to use all practicable means, consistent with other essential considerations of national policy, to improve and coordinate Federal plans, functions, programs, and resources to the end that the Nation may—

(1) fulfill the responsibilities of each generation as trustee of the environment for succeeding generations;

(2) assure for all Americans safe, healthful, productive, and esthetically and culturally pleasing surroundings;

(3) attain the widest range of beneficial uses of the environment without degradation, risk to health or safety, or other undesirable and unintended consequences;

(4) preserve important historic, cultural, and natural aspects of our national heritage, and maintain, wherever possible, an environment which supports diversity and variety of individual choice;

(5) achieve a balance between population and resource use which will permit high standards of living and a wide sharing of life's amenities; and

(6) enhance the quality of renewable resources and approach the maximum attainable recycling of depletable resources.

(c) The Congress recognizes that each person should enjoy a healthful environment and that each person has a responsibility to contribute to the preservation and enhancement of the environment.

Administration.

SEC. 102. The Congress authorizes and directs that, to the fullest extent possible: (1) the policies, regulations, and public laws of the United States shall be interpreted and administered in accordance with the policies set forth in this Act, and (2) all agencies of the Federal Government shall—

(A) utilize a systematic, interdisciplinary approach which will insure the integrated use of the natural and social sciences and the environmental design arts in planning and in decisionmaking which may have an impact on man's environment;

(B) identify and develop methods and procedures, in consultation with the Council on Environmental Quality established by title II of this Act, which will insure that presently unquantified environmental amenities and values may be given appropriate consideration in decisionmaking along with economic and technical considerations;

(C) include in every recommendation or report on proposals for legislation and other major Federal actions significantly affecting the quality of the human environment, a detailed statement by the responsible official on—

(i) the environmental impact of the proposed action,

(ii) any adverse environmental effects which cannot be avoided should the proposal be implemented,

(iii) alternatives to the proposed action,

(iv) the relationship between local short-term uses of man's environment and the maintenance and enhancement of long-term productivity, and

(v) any irreversible and irretrievable commitments of resources which would be involved in the proposed action should it be implemented.

Prior to making any detailed statement, the responsible Federal official shall consult with and obtain the comments of any Federal agency which has jurisdiction by law or special expertise with respect to any environmental impact involved. Copies of such statement and the comments and views of the appropriate Federal, State, and local agencies, which are authorized to develop and enforce environmental standards, shall be made available to the President, the Council on Environmental Quality and to the public as provided by section 552 of title 5, United States Code, and shall accompany the proposal through the existing agency review processes;

Copies of statements, etc.; availability.

81 Stat. 54.

(D) study, develop, and describe appropriate alternatives to recommended courses of action in any proposal which involves unresolved conflicts concerning alternative uses of available resources;

(E) recognize the worldwide and long-range character of environmental problems and, where consistent with the foreign policy of the United States, lend appropriate support to initiatives, resolutions, and programs designed to maximize international cooperation in anticipating and preventing a decline in the quality of mankind's world environment;

(F) make available to States, counties, municipalities, institutions, and individuals, advice and information useful in restoring, maintaining, and enhancing the quality of the environment;

(G) initiate and utilize ecological information in the planning and development of resource-oriented projects; and

(H) assist the Council on Environmental Quality established by title II of this Act.

Review.   SEC. 103. All agencies of the Federal Government shall review their present statutory authority, administrative regulations, and current policies and procedures for the purpose of determining whether there are any deficiencies or inconsistencies therein which prohibit full compliance with the purposes and provisions of this Act and shall propose to the President not later than July 1, 1971, such measures as may be necessary to bring their authority and policies into conformity with the intent, purposes, and procedures set forth in this Act.

SEC. 104. Nothing in Section 102 or 103 shall in any way affect the specific statutory obligations of any Federal agency (1) to comply with criteria or standards of environmental quality, (2) to coordinate or consult with any other Federal or State agency, or (3) to act, or refrain from acting contingent upon the recommendations or certification of any other Federal or State agency.

SEC. 105. The policies and goals set forth in this Act are supplementary to those set forth in existing authorizations of Federal agencies.

TITLE II

COUNCIL ON ENVIRONMENTAL QUALITY

Report to Congress.   SEC. 201. The President shall transmit to the Congress annually beginning July 1, 1970, an Environmental Quality

Report (hereinafter referred to as the "report") which shall set forth (1) the status and condition of the major natural, manmade, or altered environmental classes of the Nation, including, but not limited to, the air, the aquatic, including marine, estuarine, and fresh water, and the terrestrial environment, including, but not limited to, the forest, dryland, wetland, range, urban, suburban, and rural environment; (2) current and foreseeable trends in the quality, management and utilization of such environments and the effects of those trends on the social, economic, and other requirements of the Nation; (3) the adequacy of available natural resources for fulfilling human and economic requirements of the Nation in the light of expected population pressures; (4) a review of the programs and activities (including regulatory activities) of the Federal Government, the State and local governments, and nongovernmental entities or individuals, with particular reference to their effect on the environment and on the conservation, development and utilization of natural resources; and (5) a program for remedying the deficiencies of existing programs and activities, together with recommendations for legislation.

SEC. 202. There is created in the Executive Office of the President a Council on Environmental Quality (hereinafter referred to as the "Council"). The Council shall be composed of three members who shall be appointed by the President to serve at his pleasure, by and with the advice and consent of the Senate. The President shall designate one of the members of the Council to serve as Chairman. Each member shall be a person who, as a result of his training, experience, and attainments, is exceptionally well qualified to analyze and interpret environmental trends and information of all kinds; to appraise programs and activities of the Federal Government in the light of the policy set forth in title I of this Act; to be conscious of and responsive to the scientific, economic, social, esthetic, and cultural needs and interests of the Nation; and to formulate and recommend national policies to promote the improvement of the quality of the environment. *Council on Environmental Quality.*

SEC. 203. The Council may employ such officers and employees as may be necessary to carry out its functions under this Act. In addition, the Council may employ and fix the compensation of such experts and consultants as may be necessary for the carrying out of its functions under this Act, in accordance with section 3109 of title 5, United

80 Stat. 416.
Duties and
functions.

States Code (but without regard to the last sentence thereof).

SEC. 204. It shall be the duty and function of the Council—

(1) to assist and advise the President in the preparation of the Environmental Quality Report required by section 201;

(2) to gather timely and authoritative information concerning the conditions and trends in the quality of the environment both current and prospective, to analyze and interpret such information for the purpose of determining whether such conditions and trends are interfering, or are likely to interfere, with the achievement of the policy set forth in title I of this Act, and to compile and submit to the President studies relating to such conditions and trends;

(3) to review and appraise the various programs and activities of the Federal Government in the light of the policy set forth in title I of this Act for the purpose of determining the extent to which such programs and activities are contributing to the achievement of such policy, and to make recommendations to the President with respect thereto;

(4) to develop and recommend to the President national policies to foster and promote the improvement of environmental quality to meet the conservation, social, economic, health, and other requirements and goals of the Nation;

(5) to conduct investigations, studies, surveys, research, and analyses relating to ecological systems and environmental quality;

(6) to document and define changes in the natural environment, including the plant and animal systems, and to accumulate necessary data and other information for a continuing analysis of these changes or trends and an interpretation of their underlying causes;

(7) to report at least once each year to the President on the state and condition of the environment; and

(8) to make and furnish such studies, reports thereon, and recommendations with respect to matters of policy and legislation as the President may request.

SEC. 205. In exercising its powers, functions, and duties under this Act, the Council shall—

(1) consult with the Citizens' Advisory Committee on

Environmental Quality established by Executive order
numbered 11472, dated May 29, 1969, and with such representatives of science, industry, agriculture, labor, conservation organizations, State and local governments and
other groups, as it deems advisable; and

34 F. R. 8693.

(2) utilize, to the fullest extent possible, the services,
facilities, and information (including statistical information) of public and private agencies and organizations,
and individuals, in order that duplication of effort and
expense may be avoided, thus assuring that the Council's
activities will not unnecessarily overlap or conflict with
similar activities authorized by law and performed by
established agencies.

SEC. 206. Members of the Council shall serve full time
and the Chairman of the Council shall be compensated at
the rate provided for Level II of the Executive Schedule Pay
Rates (5 U.S.C. 5313). The other members of the Council
shall be compensated at the rate provided for Level IV or
the Executive Schedule Pay Rates (5 U.S.C. 5315).

Tenure and
compensation.
80 Stat. 460,
461.

81 Stat. 638.

SEC. 207. There are authorized to be appropriated to
carry out the provisions of this Act not to exceed $300,000
for fiscal year 1970, $700,000 for fiscal year 1971, and
$1,000,000 for each fiscal year thereafter.

Appropri-
ations.

Approved January 1, 1970.

LEGISLATIVE HISTORY:

HOUSE REPORTS: No. 91-378, 91-378, pt. 2, accompanying H. R. 12549
(Comm. on Merchant Marine & Fisheries) and 91-765
(Comm. of Conference).

SENATE REPORT No. 91-296 (Comm. on Interior & Insular Affairs).

CONGRESSIONAL RECORD, Vol. 115 (1969):

July 10: Considered and passed Senate.

Sept. 23: Considered and passed House, amended, in lieu of H. R.
12549.

Oct. 8: Senate disagreed to House amendments; agreed to conference.

Dec. 20: Senate agreed to conference report.

Dec. 22: House agreed to conference report.

NOTES

INTRODUCTION

1. Carl Sagan, *Cosmos* (New York: Random House, 1980), xii.
2. Herman E. Daly, *Growth: The Economics of Sustainable Development* (Boston: Beacon Press, 1996), 6.
3. Statement in *National Environmental Policy: Hearing before the Committee on Interior and Insular Affairs, United States Senate*, 91st Congress, 1st Session, April 16, 1969, Appendix 2, p. 206.
4. Organization for Economic Cooperation and Development, *Environmental Performance Reviews: United States* (Paris: OECD, 1996).

CHAPTER 1 ENVIRONMENTAL POLICY: VALUES AND PERCEPTIONS

1. Statement by Senator Henry M. Jackson on *National Environmental Policy: Hearing before the Committee on Interior and Insular Affairs, United States Senate*, 91st Congress, 1st Session, April 16, 1969, Appendix 2, p. 205.
2. For example see Laurence H. Tribe, Corinne S. Schelling, and John Voss, *When Values Conflict: Essays on Environmental Analysis, Discourse, and Decision* (Cambridge, Mass.: Ballinger, 1976).
3. Remarks concerning Conference Committee Report on S.1075 *Congressional Record* 115, 40416 (December 20, 1969).
4. *Background Materials relating to the Environmental Policy and Conflict Resolution Act of 1997 Recently Introduced as S.399 by U.S. Senator John McCain (R-AZ), March 5, 1997* (Tucson: Udall Center for Studies in Public Policy, University of Arizona, 1997); and *A Report on the Proposed U.S. Institute for Environmental Conflict Resolution (S.399)* (Tucson: The Morris K. Udall Foundation, May 15, 1997). McCain's bill was enacted on February 11, 1998, and signed that same day by President Clinton. On environmental mediation see Lawrence S. Bacow and Michael Wheeler, *Environmental Dispute Resolution* (New York: Plenum Press, 1984); Gail Bingham, *Resolving Environmental Disputes: A Decade of Experience* (Washington, D.C.: The Conservation Foundation, 1986); and John K. Gamman, *Overcoming Obstacles to Environmental Policy-Making: Creating Partnerships through Mediation* (Albany: State University of New York Press, 1994).
5. *Congressional Record* 115, 29056 (October 8, 1969).
6. Ronald Inglehart, *Culture Shift in Advanced Industrial Societies* (Princeton: Princeton University Press, 1989); and "Value Change in Industrial Societies," *American Political Science Review* 81 no. 4 (December 1987): 1289-1303; Marvin E. Olson, Dora Lodwick, and Riley E. Dunlap, *Viewing the World Ecologically* (Boulder: Westview Press, 1992); and Max Nicholson, *The Environmental Revolution: A Guide for the New Masters of the World* (New York: McGraw-Hill, 1970).
7. Calvin W. Stillman, "On Saving Places," *Environmental Law* (1977): 485.
8. *A National Policy for the Environment. A Report on the Need for a National Policy for the Environment: An Explanation of Its Purpose and Content; An Exploration of Means to Make It Effective; and a Listing of Questions Implicit in Its Establishment, A Special*

Report to the Committee on Interior and Insular Affairs, United States Senate, Together with a Statement by Senator Henry M. Jackson, 90th Congress, 2nd Session, July 11, 1968.

9. Willett Kempton, James S. Boster, and Jennifer A. Hartley, *Environmental Values in American Culture* (Cambridge: MIT Press, 1995); Richard N. L. Andrews and Mary J. Waits, *Environmental Values in Public Decisions: A Research Agenda* (Ann Arbor: School of National Resources, 1978); Milton Rokeach, *Beliefs, Attitudes, and Values: A Theory of Organization and Change* (San Francisco: Jossey-Bass, 1968); and *The Nature of Human Values* (New York: Free Press, 1973). Lawrence C. Becker and Charlotte B. Becker eds., "Value Theory," *Encyclopedia of Ethics* (New York: Garland, 1992), 1269-1272; and Leo Marx, "American Institutions and Ecological Ideals," *Science* 170 (November 27, 1970): 945-952.

10. Michael S. Greve, *The Demise of Environmentalism in American Law* (Washington, D.C.: AEI Press, 1996). There is a large and often vitriolic literature attacking the environmental movement and Federal ownership and management of land and resources. Many of these publications are sponsored and financed by conservative foundations and "think tanks."

11. *Final Report of the Intergovernmental Conference of Experts on the Scientific Basis for Rational Use and Conservation of the Resources of the Biosphere—Paris, 4-13 September 1968* (Paris: UNESCO SC/MD/9, January 9, 1969).

12. Ernest Becker, *The Revolution in Psychiatry—A New Understanding of Man* (New York: The Free Press of Glencoe, 1964), 222.

13. For a more comprehensive development of this theme see Kristin Shrader-Frechette, *Environmental Ethics* (Pacific Grove, Cal.: Boxwood Press, 1981) and Lynton K. Caldwell, "Environmental Management as an Ethical System," *Environment: A Challenge to Modern Society* (Garden City: Anchor Books-Doubleday, 1971), 204-221. For a "resource book" for this subject with emphasis on ethics in the United States see Clare Palmer, *Environmental Ethics* (Santa Barbara: ABC-CLIO, 1997).

14. James Moffett, *An Introduction to the Literature of the New Testament.* 3d ed. (New York: Charles Scribner's Sons, 1918), 519.

15. Robert Gillette, "National Environmental Policy Act: Signs of Backlash are Evident," *Science* 176 (April 7, 1972): 30-33; Karen F. Schmidt, "Green Education Under Fire," *Science* 274 (December 13, 1996): 1828-1830; Jacqueline Vaughan Switzer, *Green Backlash: The History and Politics of Environmental Opposition in the U.S.* (Boulder: Lynne Rienner, 1997); David Helvarg, *The War against the Greens: The "Wise Use" Movement, the New Right and Anti-Environmental Violence* (San Francisco: Sierra Club Books, 1997); Carl Deal, *The Greenpeace Guide to Anti-Environmental Organizations* (Berkeley: Odonian Press, 1993); and Andrew Rowell, *Green Backlash: Global Subversion of the Environmental Movement* (New York: Routledge, 1996). Note "Conclusion: Environmentalism in Balance," 281-297.

16. Harold Coward, ed., *Population, Consumption and the Environment: Religious and Secular Responses* (Albany: State University of New York Press, 1995). There are chapters on environmental ethics in aboriginal societies and in Judaism, Christianity, Islam, Hinduism, Buddhism, as well as in China.

17. Barry A. Turner, *Man-Made Disasters* (London: Wyeham Publications and New York: Crane, Russak, 1978); also Gilbert F. White and J. Eugene Haas, *Assessment of Research on Natural Disasters* (Cambridge: MIT Press, 1975); and Gilbert F. White, *Natural Disaster: Local, National, Global* (New York: Oxford University Press, 1974).

18. Lyndon B. Johnson, "Conference Call—Message from the President of the United States to the Congress, February 8, 1965," *Public Papers of the Presidents: Lyndon B. Johnson, 1965,* Book I, 155-165. It ought not be assumed that a president's published remarks express personal values or priorities. Presidential speeches serve political purposes and today are drafted by professional writers.

19. Supra, n. 1, 206.

20. Lester W. Milbrath, *Environmentalists: Vanguard for a New Society* (Albany: State University of New York Press, 1984).

21. Robert Nisbet, *Prejudices: A Philosophical Dictionary* (Cambridge: Harvard University Press, 1982), 101. For a more detailed critique see T. O'Riordan, *Environmentalism*, 2nd ed. (London: Pion Ltd. 1981).

22. Amitai Etzioni, "The Wrong Top Priority," *Science* 168 (May 22, 1970): 921 (his objection was to an overemphasis on pollution); and Anthony Downs, "Up and Down with Ecology: The Issue Attention Cycle," *The Public Interest* 28 (1972): 38-50.

23. Joseph M. Petulla, *American Environmentalism: Values, Tactics, Priorities* (College Station: Texas A&M University Press, 1980); Riley E. Dunlap and Angela G. Mertig eds., *American Environmentalism—U.S. Movement, 1970-1990* (Philadelphia: Taylor and Francis, 1992); and Mark Davies, *Losing Ground: American Environmentalism at the Close of the Twentieth Century* (Cambridge: MIT Press, 1995).

24. Reported in *The New York Times* (January 2, 1970). Nixon's comment was apparently verbal; for his official statement see *Weekly Compilation of Presidential Documents* 6, no. 1 (January 5, 1970). For a short-term, quick-fix interpretation of the "environmental crisis" see John C. Whitaker, *Striking a Balance: Environment and Natural Resources Policy in the Nixon-Ford Years* (Washington, D.C.: American Enterprise Institute, 1976), especially pp. 50-52. See also Downs, supra. n. 18.

25. Eric Ashby, *Reconciling Man with the Environment* (Stanford: Stanford University Press, 1978). For a holistic interpretation of environment see Gilbert F. White, "Environment," *Science* 209 (July 4, 1970): 183-190.

26. Garrett J. Hardin, *Living Within Limits: Ecology, Economics, and Population Taboos* (New York: Oxford University Press, 1993); Donald N. Michael, *On Learning to Plan and Planning to Learn.* Rev. ed. (Alexandria, Va.: Miles River Press, 1997); Lester Milbrath, *Envisioning a Sustainable Society: Learning Our Way Out* (Albany: State University of New York Press, 1984); and David W. Orr, *Ecological Literacy: Education and the Transition to a Postmodern World* (Albany: State University of New York Press, 1992).

27. Issued by the Union of Concerned Scientists, 26 Church Street, Cambridge, Mass. 02238-9105.

28. Thomas Princen and Mathias Finger, *Environmental NGOs in World Politics* (New York: Routledge, 1994); and Julie Fisher, *The Road from Rio: Sustainable Development and the Nongovernmental Movement in the Third World* (Westport, Conn.: Praeger, 1993).

29. Richard N. L. Andrews, "The Unfinished Business of the National Environmental Policy Act" in Ray Clark and Larry Canter, eds., *Environmental Policy and NEPA: Past, Present, and Future* (Boca Raton: St. Lucie Press, 1997), 85-97. Many other articles in this volume reach similar conclusions.

CHAPTER 2 NEPA:
ENACTMENT AND INTERPRETATION

1. The National Environmental Policy Act of 1969, PL 91-190, 42 U.S.C. 4321-4347, January 1, 1970, as amended by PL 94-52, July 3, 1975, and PL 94, 83, August 9, 1975. 42 U.S.C. Sec. 4371 (1976); and Executive Office of the President, *Regulations for Implementing the Procedural Provisions of the National Environmental Policy Act*, 43 Fed. Reg. 55978-56007 (November 29, 1978).

2. Nicholas C. Yost, "NEPA's Promise: Partially Fulfilled," *Environmental Law: Northwestern School of Law of Lewis and Clark College* 20 (1990): 533-549; Richard N. L. Andrews, "The Unfinished Business of the National Environmental Policy Act." Ray Clark and Larry Canter, eds. "Chapter 6," *Environmental Policy and NEPA: Past, Present, and Future* (Boca Raton: St. Lucie Press, 1997) 85-97.

3. For prior accounts see Richard A. Liroff, *A National Policy for the Environment:*

NEPA and Its Aftermath (Bloomington: Indiana University Press, 1976). More recently, a Ph.D. dissertation was written on the subject by Matthew Lindstrom (Northern Arizona University, 1997).

4. Terence T. Finn, *Conflict and Compromise: Congress Makes a Law: The Passage of the National Environmental Policy Act*, Doctoral Dissertation, Georgetown University, 1972, unpublished. For congressional deliberations preceding NEPA see Bryce Nelson, "Congress: Toward a National Policy for the Environment," *Science* 161 (August 2, 1968): 445-446. There is a very large literature on NEPA, far exceeding what can be referenced here. Publications are of five types: (1) case books on environmental law; (2) government documents (e.g. hearings and reports); (3) handbooks and guidebooks on the NEPA process—some by agencies, some nongovernmental; (4) books; (5) articles (there are at least 28 journals or law reviews on environmental, natural resources, or land use law); and (6) university doctoral dissertations. Two bibliographies cover roughly the first decade of NEPA: Robert Lazear, *The National Environmental Policy Act and Its Implementation: A Selected, Annotated Bibliography* (Madison: Wisconsin Seminars on Resource and Environmental Systems, Institute for Environmental Studies, University of Wisconsin, 1978); and John P. Worsham, *The National Environmental Policy Act and Related Materials: A Selected Bibliography* (Monticello, Ill.: Vance Bibliographies, 1978).

5. *Beauty for America: Proceedings of the White House Conference on Natural Beauty, May 24-25, 1965* (Washington, D.C.: U.S. Government Printing Office, 1965).

6. International Symposium on Man's Role in Changing the Face of the Earth, *Man's Role in Changing the Face of the Earth* (Chicago: University of Chicago Press, 1955). See also I. G. Simmons, *Changing the Face of the Earth: Culture, Environment, History* (New York: Blackwell, 1989).

7. F. Fraser Darling and John P. Milton, *Future Environments of North America: Transformation of a Continent* (Garden City: Natural History Press, 1966).

8. Advisory Commission on Intergovernmental Relations (ACIR), *The Federal Role in the Federal System: The Dynamics of Growth—Protecting the Environment: Politics, Pollution, and Federal Policy* (Washington, D.C.: ACIR, March 1981); Rosemary O'Leary and Tae Soon Lah, "Progressive Ratcheting of Environmental Law: Implications for Public Management," *Environmental Policy: Transnational Issues and National Trends*, Lynton K. Caldwell and Robert V. Bartlett, eds. (Westfort, Conn.: Quorum Books, 1997), 19-36.

9. U.S. National Academy of Sciences—National Research Council, Committee on Natural Resources, *Natural Resources: A Summary Report to the President of the United States* (Washington, D.C.: N.R.C. Publication 1060, 1962).

10. U.S. Department of Health, Education, and Welfare, *A Strategy for a Livable Environment: A Report to the Secretary of Health, Education, and Welfare by the Task Force on Environmental Health and Related Problems* (Washington, D.C., June 1967).

11. *Managing the Environment*, Report of the Subcommittee on Science, Research, and Development to the Committee on Science and Astronautics, U.S. House of Representatives, 1968.

12. *A National Policy for the Environment: A Report on the Need for a National Policy for the Environment: An Explanation of Its Purpose and Content; An Explanation of Means to Make It Effective; and a Listing of Questions Implicit in Its Establishment. Special Report to the Committee on Interior and Insular Affairs, United States Senate*, 90th Congress, 2nd Session, July 11, 1968.

13. *Joint House-Senate Colloquium to Discuss A National Policy for the Environment: Hearing before the Committee on Interior and Insular Affairs, United States Senate, and the Committee on Science and Astronautics, U.S. House of Representatives*, 90th Congress, 2nd Session, July 17, 1968.

14. *Congressional White Paper on a National Policy for the Environment: Submitted to the United States Congress under the auspices of the Committee on Interior and Insular*

Affairs, United States Senate, and the Committee on Science and Astronautics, United States House of Representatives, 90th Congress, 2nd Session, October 1968.

15. *National Environmental Policy: Hearing before the Committee on Interior and Insular Affairs, United States Senate,* 91st Congress, 1st Session on S.1075, S.237, and S.1752, April 16, 1969.

16. *Hearing,* p. 116.

17. *Environmental Quality: Hearings before the Subcommittee on Fisheries and Wildlife of the Committee on Merchant Marine and Fisheries, United States House of Representatives,* 91st Congress, 1st Session on Bills to Establish a Council on Environmental Quality, and for Other Purposes, May 7 and 26; June 13, 20, 23, 26 and 27, 1969.

18. U.S. House of Representatives, *Conference Report, National Environmental Policy Act of 1969,* H. Report 91-765. 91st Congress, 1st Session, 1969.

19. *Calvert Cliffs Coordinating Committee v. Atomic Energy Commission,* United States Circuit Court of Appeals of the District of Columbia Circuit, 1971, 449 F.2d. 1109.

20. *Abolishing the Council on Environmental Quality: Hearing before the Committee on Environment and Public Works, United States Senate,* 103rd Congress, 1st Session, Section 112 of S.171-Termination of the Council on Environmental Quality and Transfer of Functions, April 1, 1993.

21. Supra, n. 12.

22. "Nixon Promises an Urgent Fight to End Pollution; Signs Measure to Establish a 3-Member Council on Environmental Quality," *The New York Times* (January 9, 1970): 1; and "Nixon Appoints 3 in Pollution War," *The New York Times* (January 30, 1970): 1, 7.

23. Dinah Bear, "NEPA: Substance or Merely Process?" *Forum for Applied Research and Public Policy* (Summer 1993): 86-88.

24. For an early assessment of the CEQ, see Richard A. Liroff, "The Council on Environmental Quality," *Environmental Law Reporter* 3 (1973): 50051-50070.

25. Cases in which the Supreme Court of the United States held that CEQ's interpretation of NEPA was entitled to "substantial deference" are:

   Andrus v. Sierra Club, 442 U.S. 347 (1979) at 358.

   Robertson v. Methow Valley Citizens Council, 490 U.S. 332 (1989).

   Marsh v. Oregon Natural Resources Council, 490 U.S. 360 (1989).

26. *The President's Committee on Administrative Management: Report of the Committee with Studies of Administrative Management. Submitted to the President and to the Congress in accordance with Public Law No. 739,* 74th Congress, 2nd Session, 1937 (note p. 5, *I. The White House Staff,* and p. 31, *V. Administrative Reorganization in the Government of the United States*).

27. Section 103 requires Federal agencies to report anything in their statutory authority that would prevent "full compliance" with NEPA and to propose remedial measures when needed. Section 104 states that "the policies and goals set forth in this Act are supplementary to those set forth in existing authorizations." In effect, NEPA amended all relevant authorizing legislation.

28. Sections 204 and 205 specify ten functions and duties of the CEQ. Owing to White House parsimony, caution, or indifference, many of these functions have never been fulfilled. Proposals have been made to establish a capability for forecasting interactive trends in population, resources, and environment, overlooking the charge to the CEQ under Section 204 to undertake investigations in this area. See Lindsay Grant, *Foresight and National Decisions: The Horseman and the Bureaucrat* (Lanham, Maryland: University Press of America, 1988), 48-53.

29. Supra, n. 19.

30. *Environmental Defense Fund, Inc. v. Corps of Engineers,* U.S. Court of Appeals, Eighth Circuit, 1972, 470 F.2d. 289 (the *Gillham Dam* case). The court ruled that the Corps must satisfy the requirements of NEPA before completing the dam even though

"the overall project was authorized by Congress eleven years prior to the passage of NEPA and was sixty-three percent completed at the date this action was instituted."

31. D. W. Shindler, "The Impact Statement Boondoggle" (editorial), *Science* 192 (7 May 1976): 509; Sally K. Fairfax, "A Disaster in the Environment Movement," *Science* 199 (17 February 1978): 743-748. Michael S. Greve, *The Demise of Environmentalism in American Law* (Washington, D.C.: AEI Press, 1996).

32. *National Environmental Policy: Hearing before the Committee on Interior and Insular Affairs, United States Senate,* 91st Congress, 1st Session, April 16, 1969, p. 31.

33. Ronald C. Moe, "Traditional Organization Principles and the Managerial Presidency: From Phoenix to Ashes," *Public Administration Review* 50 (March-April, 1990): 129-140; "The Institutional Presidency: A Tale of Retreat and Decline," *25 Years from the Bureaucrat to the Public Manager* (Spring 1996): 9-12; and Ronald C. Moe and Robert S. Gilmour, "Rediscovering Principles of Public Administration: The Neglected Foundation of Public Law," *Public Administration Review* 55 (March-April, 1995). For the institution of the presidency in historical perspective see Edward S. Corwin, *The President, Office and Powers: History and Analysis of Practice and Opinion,* 2nd edition (New York: New York University Press, 1941), and Clinton Rossiter, *The American Presidency,* 2nd edition (New York: Harcourt Brace, 1960).

34. For the president as personal leader see Richard Neustadt, *Presidential Power: The Politics of Leadership* (New York: Wiley, 1960).

35. William J. Clinton, "Remarks Announcing a New Environmental Policy, February 8, 1933," *Weekly Compilation of Presidential Documents* Monday, February 15, Vol. 29-No. 6, 159-160. Vice President Gore was acknowledged as a major participant in the reorganization of environmental policy-making.

36. Robert V. Bartlett, "The Rationality and Logic of NEPA Revisited," *Environmental Policy and NEPA: Past, Present, and Future,* Ray Clark and Larry Canter, eds. (Boca Raton: St. Lucia Press, 1997), 51-60.

37. Judge Skelly Wright in *Calvert Cliffs* opinion, supra, n. 19.

CHAPTER 3
ENVIRONMENTAL IMPACT ASSESSMENT

1. There is a large literature on impact assessment, the implementation of NEPA, and international applications for exceeding the representative citations listed here. But see *Impact Assessment* (1981-), published quarterly by the International Association for Impact Assessment. Note especially vol. 6, no. 2—"Update on: International Study of the Effectiveness of Environmental Assessment, including the Results of the International Summit on Environmental Assessment." There are frequent articles on assessment in *The Environmental Professional* (1979-) and *Project Appraisal: the Journal* (1986- U.K.). See also Alan Gilpin, *Environmental Impact Assessment (EIA): Cutting Edge for the Twenty-First Century* (Cambridge: Cambridge University Press, 1995), a detailed survey of various international applications, especially in Australia and New Zealand; Daniel A. Dreyfus and Helen M. Ingram, "The National Environmental Policy Act: A View of Intent and Practice," one of a five-article symposium published in the *Natural Resources Journal* 16, no. 2 (April 1976); Lynton K. Caldwell, *Science and the National Environmental Policy Act: Redirecting Policy through Procedural Reform* (University: University of Alabama Press, 1982); Serge Taylor, *Making Bureaucracies Think: The Environmental Impact Statement Strategy of Administrative Reform* (Stanford: Stanford University Press, 1984); Robert V. Bartlett, "Rationality and the Logic of the National Environmental Policy Act," *The Environmental Professional* 8 (1986): 105-111; "Environmental Impact Assessment and Administrative Theory," *Managing Leviathan: Environmental Politics and the Administrative State,* Robert Paehlke and Douglas Torgerson, eds. (Petersborough, Ontario:

Broadview Press, 1990); and Robert V. Bartlett, ed., *Policy Through Impact Assessment: Institutionalized Analysis as a Policy Strategy* (Westport, Conn.: Greenwood Press, 1989). See also Richard N. L. Andrews, *Environmental Policy and Administrative Change: Implementation of the National Environmental Policy Act* (Lexington, Mass.: D.C. Heath, 1976). For manuals on the NEPA process see Keshava S. Murthy, *National Environmental Policy Act (NEPA) Process* (Boca Raton: CRC Press, 1988) and Valerie M. Fogleman, *Guide to the National Environmental Policy Act: Interpretations, Applications, and Compliance* (New York: Quorum Books, 1990). See also the *Environmental Series* published by the United Nations for the Economic Commission for Europe, and numerous casebooks on environmental law.

2. 43FR 55978-56001, November 29, 1978. 40 CFR Parts 1500-1508.

3. David Sive and Mark A. Chertok, *"Little NEPAs" and their Environmental Impact Assessment Processes.* American Law Institute-American Bar Association Course of Study, June 23, 1997 (available in WESTLAW ALI-ABA database).

4. Michelle S. Wiseman, "Consideration of Alternatives in the NEPA Process." Paper presented at the National Association of Environmental Professionals 16th Annual Conference: NEPA Symposium, April 30, 1991, Baltimore, Maryland.

5. On the judicial history of NEPA see Frederick Anderson, *NEPA in the Courts: A Legal Analysis of the National Environmental Policy Act* (Baltimore: Johns Hopkins Press, 1973); Lettie M. Wenner, *The Environmental Decade in Court* (Bloomington: Indiana University Press, 1982); Daniel A. Farber, "Environmental Law: Disdain for 17-Year-Old Statute Evident in High Court Rulings," *The National Law Journal* (May 4, 1987): 20-23; and Frederic P. Sutherland and Roger Beers, "Supreme Indifference: The National Environmental Policy Act Has Not Had a Friend on the Supreme Court since the Retirement of William O. Douglas," *The Amicus Journal* 13, no. 2 (Spring 1991): 38-42.

6. John Lemons, ed., *Scientific Uncertainty and Environmental Problem-Solving* (Cambridge: Blackwell Science, 1996).

7. Council on Environmental Quality, *Considering Cumulative Effects under the National Environmental Policy Act* (Washington, D.C.: CEQ, January 1997); and L. W. Canter, "Cumulative Effects and Other Analytic Challenges of NEPA," *Environmental Policy and NEPA: Past, Present, and Future,* Ray Clark and Larry Canter, eds. (Boca Raton: St. Lucie Press, 1997), 115-137.

8. Richard A. Carpenter, "The Adequacy of Scientific Information for the Implementation of the National Environmental Policy Act," *Workshop on the National Environmental Policy Act.* A Report . . . by the Environment and Natural Resources Division Congressional Research Service, Library of Congress for House of Representatives Committee on Merchant Marine and Fisheries, February 1976, 52-62; and "The Case for Continuous Monitoring and Adaptive Management Under NEPA," *Environmental Policy and NEPA: Past, Present, and Future,* Ray Clark and Larry Canter, eds. (Boca Raton: St. Lucie Press, 1997), 163-180. See also *The National Environmental Policy Act: A Study of Its Effectiveness after Twenty-Five Years* (Washington, D.C.: Council on Environmental Quality, January 1997).

9. Jon D. Miller, *The American People and Science Policy: The Role of Public Attitudes in the Policy Process* (New York: Pergamon Press, 1983).

10. Antienvironmentalists allege that environmental laws and regulations, and NEPA impact statements in particular, are based on "bad science," e.g. George Claus and Karen Bolander, *Ecologist Sanity: A Critical Examination of Bad Science, Good Intentions and Premature Announcements of Doomsday by the Ecology Lobby* (New York: David McKay, 1977). For response to these allegations see Paul R. Ehrlich and Anne H. Ehrlich, *The Betrayal of Science and Reason: How Anti-Environmental Rhetoric Threatens Our Future* (Washington, D.C.: Island Press, 1996).

11. *World Scientists Warning to Humanity.* Published by the Union of Concerned Scientists, 26 Church St., Cambridge, Mass., 1993.

12. "Problems of Applied Ecology: Perceptions, Institutions, Methods, and Operational Tools," *BioScience* 16 (1966): 524-527.

13. Owen L. Schmidt, *Checklists for Preparing National Environmental Policy Act Documents*. Monographs Series No. 5, Natural Resources Law Section, American Bar Association and the National Energy Law and Policy Institute, University of Tulsa College of Law, 1987.

14. *Public Policy and Natural Environment: An Opportunity for National Leadership. A Report to the Citizens Advisory Committee on Recreation and Natural Beauty,* November 21, 1968 (unpublished).

15. Letter of September 27, 1968, transmitting report, supra, n. 14. *The Congressional White Paper* was prepared at the Congressional Research Service for the Senate Committee on Interior and Insular Affairs and the House Committee on Science and Astronautics, 90th Congress, 2nd Session, October 1968.

16. *Public Policy and Natural Environment,* supra, n. 14, p. 13.

17. *Public Administration Review* 23 (September 1963): 132-139, and especially "Administrative Possibilities for Environmental Control," *Future Environments of North America,* F. Fraser Darling and John P. Milton, eds. (New York: Natural History Press, 1966), 648-671.

18. *National Environmental Policy: Hearing before the Committee on Interior and Insular Affairs, United States Senate,* 91st Congress, 1st Session on S.1075, S.237, and S.1752, April 16, 1969, p. 116.

19. *Time* (August 1, 1969): 42.

20. Edward S. Corwin, *The President: Office and Powers. History and Analysis of Practice and Opinion.* 2nd ed. Revised. (New York: New York University Press, 1941).

21. "Note: Retroactive Laws—Environmental Law—Retroactive Application of the National Environmental Policy Act of 1969," *Michigan Law Review* 69 (March 1971): 732-761.

22. *Environmental Defense Fund, Inc. v. Corps of Engineers,* U.S. Court of Appeals, Eighth Circuit, 1972, 470 F.2d. 289 (the *Gillham Dam* case). The court ruled that the Corps must satisfy the requirements of NEPA before completing the dam even though "the overall project was authorized by Congress eleven years prior to the passage of NEPA and was sixty-three percent completed at the date this action was instituted."

23. See Robert Cahn, "Impact of NEPA on Public Perception of Environmental Issues—NEPA as a Focus for Anti-Environment Forces," *Workshop on the National Environmental Policy Act,* supra, n. 8, p. 68. See also *Mobil Oil Corp. et al. v. Federal Trade Commission* 430 F Supp. (1977) on failure to prepare an EIS on regulations for distribution of petroleum products.

24. Martin Healy, "The Environmental Protection Agency's Duty to Oversee NEPA's Implementation: Section 306 of the Clean Air Act," *Environmental Law Reporter* 3 (August, 1973): 50071-50084.

25. *New Engineer* 5 (June 1976): 11.

26. D. W. Shindler, "The Impact Statement Boondoggle" (Editorial), *Science* 192 (7 May 1976): 509. Contrary to the intentions of the framers and inconsistent with its proper administration, the impact requirement was seen as an opportunity by consulting firms around the Washington Beltway.

27. U.S. Environmental Protection Agency, *Introduction to the Environmental Review Process under Section 309 of the Clean Air Act,* July 1992. Also supra, n. 24. See also U.S. Code Annotated, Title 42. The Public Health and Welfare, Chapter 85, Air Pollution Prevention and Control, Subchapter III—General Provisions (enacted as Section 306 of the Clear Air Act of 1970).

28. Comment, "The Environmental Court Proposal. Requiem, Analysis, and Counterproposal," *University of Pennsylvania Law Review* 123 (January 1975): 676-696.

29. Since 1991 six reports have been issued in the *Environment Series:* No. 1,

Application of Environmental Impact Assessment: Highways and Dams; No. 2, *National Strategies for Protection of Flora, Fauna and their Habitats;* No. 3, *Post-Project Analysis in Environmental Impact Assessment;* No. 4, *Policies and Systems of Environmental Impact Assessment;* No. 5, *Application of Environmental Impact Assessment Principles to Policies, Plans and Programmes;* and No. 6, *Current Policies, Strategies and Aspects of Environmental Impact Assessment in a Transboundary Context.*

CHAPTER 4

INTEGRATING ENVIRONMENTAL POLICY

1. "Integration in Concept and Practice," chapter 5. Council on Environmental Quality, *21st Annual Report,* 1991, 189–220; and Odelia Funke, "Prospects for Integrating Environmental Policy," *Environmental Policy: Transnational Issues and National Trends,* Lynton K. Caldwell and Robert V. Bartlett, eds. (Westport, Conn.: Quorum Books, 1997), 173–200.

2. *National Environmental Policy: Hearing before the Committee on Interior and Insular Affairs, United States Senate,* 91st Congress, 1st Session on S.1075, S.237, and S.1752, April 16, 1969, p. 31.

3. *Public Administration Review* 28 (July-August 1968): 305.

4. *Setting Priorities, Getting Results: A New Direction for the Environmental Protection Agency* (Washington, D.C.: National Academy of Public Administration, April 1995), 47.

5. *A National Policy for the Environment: A Report on the Need for a National Policy for the Environment: An Explanation of its Purpose and Content; an Explanation of Means to Make it Effective; and a Listing of Questions Implicit in its Establishment. Special Report to the Committee on Interior and Insular Affairs, United States Senate,* 90th Congress, 2nd Session, July 11, 1968.

6. *Hearing,* April 16, 1969, p. 117.

7. National Science and Technology Council, *Integrating the Nation's Environmental Monitoring and Research Networks and Programs: A Proposed Framework* (Washington, D.C.: NSTC Committee on Environment and Natural Resources, March 1997).

8. J. Skelly Wright, "New Judicial Requisites for Informal Rulemaking: Implications for the Environmental Impact Statement," *Administrative Law Review* 29 (Winter 1977): 59–60, 64.

9. Ronald C. Moe, *The Hoover Commissions Revisited* (Boulder: Westview Press, 1982).

10. "Autobiography," *The Works of Thomas Jefferson,* Paul Leicester Ford, ed., Federal ed., vol. I (New York: G. P. Putnam's Sons, 1904-1905), 122.

11. Woodrow Wilson, *Congressional Government: A Study in American Politics* (New York: Meridian Books, 1885). Reprint.

12. *The President's Committee on Administrative Management: Report to the Committee with Studies of Administrative Management. Submitted to the President and to the Congress in accordance with Public Law No. 739,* 74th Congress, 2nd Session, 1937 (Note p. 5, *I. The White House Staff* and p. 31, *V. Administrative Reorganization in the Government of the United States.*)

13. Executive Office of the President. Under authority of the Reorganization Act of 1939 (5 U.S.C. 133-133r, 133t note), various agencies were transferred to the Executive Office of the President by the President's Reorganization Plans I and II of 1939 (5 U.S.C. app.), effective July 1, 1939. Executive Order 8248 of September 8, 1939, established the divisions of the Executive Office and defined their functions. Numerous changes in the EOP agencies have subsequently occurred.

14. Ronald C. Moe, "Traditional Organization Principles and the Managerial Presidency: From Phoenix to Ashes," *Public Administration Review* 50 (March-April

1990): 129–140, and "The Institutional Presidency: A Tale of Retreat and Decline," *25 Years from the Bureaucrat to the Public Manager* (Spring 1996): 9–12.

15. Council on Environmental Quality, *NEPA Reinvention Workshop: Rediscovering and Implementing the National Environmental Policy Act* (June 19, 1997). *Proceedings.*

16. The most informative source on the interactive and collaborative environmental management of Federal agencies is the *Federal Facilities Environmental Journal* published by John Wiley & Sons, New York (1990-).

17. U.S. Department of Defense, *Legacy Resources Management Program: Report to Congress,* September 1992 (Washington, D.C.: Office of the Deputy Assistant Secretary of Defense for the Environment, 1992).

18. Judith Landry Lee, "NEPA is a Powerful Collaborative Process" *Federal Facilities Environmental Journal* 8, no. 1 (Spring 1997): 85–79.

19. National Academy of Public Administration (NAPA), *Resolving the Paradox of Environmental Protection: An Agenda for Congress, EPA, and the States* (Washington, D.C.: The Academy, September 1977), 95–74. See also *Setting Priorities, Getting Results: A New Direction for the Environmental Protection Agency,* April 1995.

20. NAPA, 1995 Panel report, 65.

CHAPTER 5
INTERNATIONAL ENVIRONMENTAL POLICY

1. For an account of the rise of a transnational environmental movement with implications for national laws and policies see Lynton K. Caldwell, *International Environmental Policy: From the Twentieth to the Twenty-First Century* (Durham: Duke University Press, 1996); John McCormick, *Reclaiming Paradise: The Global Environment Movement* (Bloomington: Indiana University Press, 1989); Andrew Harrell and Benedict Kingsbury, eds., *The International Politics of the Environment* (Oxford: Clarendon Press, 1992); Gareth Porter and Janet Welsh Brown, *Global Environmental Politics* (Boulder: Westview Press, 1992); Max Nicholson, *The Environmental Revolution* (London: Hodder & Straughton, 1970); and Edith Brown Weiss, ed., *International Change and International Law* (Tokyo: United Nations Press, 1992).

2. Nicholas C. Yost, "The Road to Rio and Beyond," *Environmental Law* no. 4, American Bar Association (Summer 1992): 6.

3. For a comprehensive in-depth historical account see William L. Thomas Jr., ed., *Man's Role in Changing the Face of the Earth* (Chicago: University of Chicago Press, 1956). Publications on the transformations in the 20th century are numerous and varied to a degree precluding specific citation here. But see Philippe Sands, ed., *Greening International Law* (New York: New Press, 1994).

4. Thomas Princen and Mathias Finger, *Environmental NGOs in World Politics: Linking the Local and the Global* (New York: Routledge, 1994).

5. Stephen Schmidheimy, ed., *Changing Course: Global Business Perspective on Development and Environment* (Cambridge: MIT Press, 1992). Although the scope of multinational business is potentially worldwide, the focus of environmental concern is largely international because international business activities are affected by the national policies, laws, and practices of numerous countries.

6. For excerpts from numerous national constitutions relating to environmental protection see Edith Brown Weiss, *In Fairness to Future Generations: International Law, Common Patrimony, and Intergenerational Equity* (Ardsley-on-Hudson, New York: Transnational Publishers, 1989), Appendix B: 297–327 and Albert P. Blaustein and Gisbert H. Flanz, *Constitutions of the World,* binders I–XIX (Dobbs Ferry, N.Y.: Oceana Publications, 1992). For the practical implementation of these constitutional provisions see Ernst Brandl and Hastwin Bungert, "Constitutional Entrenchment of Environmental

Protection: A Comparative Analysis of Experiences Abroad," *Harvard Environmental Law Review* 16, no. 1 (1992): 1-100.

7. Richard E. Benedick, *Ozone Diplomacy: New Directions in Safeguarding the Planet* (Cambridge: Harvard University Press, 1991).

8. See "Clinton Defers Curbs on Gases Heating Globe," *The New York Times* (Friday, June 27, 1997): 1, 7 and "Top Aids Urge Clinton to Ease Global Warming Emission Goal," *The New York Times* (Friday, October 10, 1987): 1.

9. See *U.S. Government Participation in International Treaties, Agreements, Organizations and Programs in the Fields of Environment, Natural Resource and Population: An Inventory Prepared at the Request of the Interagency Global Issues Work Group—under the Leadership of the State Department's Bureau of Oceans and International Environmental Affairs, with the Assistance from the Council on Environmental Quality and the Office of International Activities of the Environmental Protection Agency; updated by International Agreements to Protect the Environment and Wildlife,* United States International Trade Commission, January 1991.

10. Jordan J. Paust, *International Law as Law of the United States* (Durham: Carolina Academic Press, 1996).

11. See *GATT: Implications on Environmental Laws: Hearings before the Subcommittee on Health and the Environment of the Committee on Energy and Commerce, House of Representatives,* 102nd Congress, 1st Session, September 27, 1991; *Trade and the Environment: Hearing before the Subcommittee on International Trade, Committee on Finance, Senate,* 102nd Congress, 1st Session, October 25, 1991; also *The National Environmental Policy Act and the North American Free Trade Agreement: Hearing before the Committee on Environment and Public Works, United States Senate,* 103rd Congress, 1st Session, July 22, 1993. See also "George Bush and the Secret Side of Free Trade," *The New York Times* (December 14, 1992): A12; Daniel C. Esty, *Greening the GATT: Trade, Environment, and the Future* (Washington, D.C.: Institute for International Economics, 1994); Kerry Krutilla, "World Trade, the GATT, and the Environment," *International Environmental Policy: Transnational Issues and National Trends,* Lynton K. Caldwell and Robert Bartlett, eds. (Westport, Conn.: Quorum Books, 1997), 87-112; and Mike Meier, "GATT, WTO, and the Environment: To what Extent do GATT/WTO Rules Permit Member Nations to Protect the Environment When To Do So Adversely Affects Trade?" *Colorado Journal of International Environmental Law and Policy* 8, no. 2 (Summer 1997): 241-282.

12. See *Restatement of the Law.* 3rd series. *The Foreign Relations Law of the United States* American Law Institute, 1987, section 402.2. Beyond a few settled principles, primarily relating to individual persons, the applicability of U.S. law beyond U.S. territory appears to defy generalization. The so-called "Foley doctrine" holds that U.S. law does not apply in another country, absent an express intent to give a statute extraterritorial application (*Foley Bros., Inc. v. Filardo,* 336 U.S. 281, 1949). This doctrine is irrelevant to NEPA's application to action by Federal agencies without regard to where an environmental impact occurs. NEPA applied, however, might cause a foreign nation to revise or abandon environment-affecting development projects dependent on U.S. financial or technical assistance. For example see A. Dan Tarlock, "The Application of the National Environmental Policy Act of 1969 to the Darien Gap Highway Project," *New York University Journal of International Law and Politics* 7, no. 3 (Winter 1974): 459-473. See also "Statement by Warren Christopher, Acting Secretary of State on the Panama Canal Treaties and Environmental Protection," reported in *Sierra* 63 (April 1978): 24-25. See also Nicholas A. Robinson, "International Environmental Protection Obligations of Foreign Affairs Agencies: The Unfulfilled Mandate of NEPA," *New York University Journal of International Law and Politics* 7 (1974): 257-270; and Jeffrey E. González-Perez and Douglas A. Klein, "The International Reach of the Impact Statement Requirement of the National Environmental Policy Act," *The George Washington Law Review* 62, no. 5 (June 1994): 757-794.

13. See for example *Lujan, Secretary of the Interior v. Defenders of Wildlife et al.* 505

U.S.555, 1992, 112 *Supreme Court Reporter* 2130–2160 (June 12, 1992). The case involved U.S. financial participation in a dam-building project in Sri Lanka which was alleged to imperil endangered wildlife. The Court denied standing to the Defenders.

14. J. Owen Saunders, "The NAFTA and the North American Agreement on Environmental Cooperation," *Environmental Policy: Transnational Issues and Environment Trends,* Lynton K. Caldwell and Robert V. Bartlett, eds. (Westport, Conn.: Quorum Books, 1997), 61–85.

15. For a negative assessment of NEPA's relevance to U.S. actions affecting environmental impacts abroad see David C. Shilton, "Assessment of Extraterritorial Impacts under NEPA and Executive Order 12114," *Land and Natural Resources Division Journal* 17, no. 4 (September-October 1980): 2–12.

16. *Administration of the National Environmental Policy Act,* Merchant Marine and Fisheries Committee, H.R. Rep., No. 316 92nd Congress, 1st Session (1971): 53; and also Bosire Maragia, "Defining the Jurisdictional Reach of NEPA: An Analysis of the Extraterritorial Application of NEPA in *Environmental Defense Fund, Inc. v. Massey,*" *Widner Journal of Public Law* 4, no. 1 (1994): 129–198.

17. *Export-Import Bank Amendments of 1978: Hearings before the Subcommittee on Resource Protection of the Senate Committee on Environment and Public Works,* 95th Congress, 2nd Session, 1978, p. 220.

18. United Nations Environment Programme. Programme Matters Requiring Guidance from the Governing Council: Report of the Director General. GC14/17 (5 June 1987). Addendum I, Annex III, also Economic Commission for Europe, *Application of Environmental Impact Assessment Principles to Policies, Plans, and Programs* (New York: United Nations, 1992).

19. 44 Fed. Reg. (4 January 1979); 3. *Code of Federal Regulations,* 356–360. Executive Order 12114, 4 January 1979, 356–360.

20. For analyses of EO 12114 see David C. Shilton, "Assessment of Extraterritorial Environmental Impacts under NEPA and Executive Order 12114, *Land and Natural Resources Division Journal* (U.S. Department of Justice) 17, no. 4 (September-October 1980): 2–12, an official administration interpretation; Francis M. Allegra, "Executive Order 12114—Environmental Effects Abroad: Does It Really Further the Purpose of NEPA?" *Cleveland State Law Review* 29, no. 1 (1980): 109–139; Nicholas C. Yost, "American Governmental Responsibility for the Environmental Effects of Actions Abroad," *Albany Law Review* 43 (1979): 528–537, specifically 535–537. A General Accounting Office report declared EO 12114 in need of clarification and its relationship to NEPA ambiguous. See *International Environment: Improved Procedures Needed for Environmental Assessments of U.S. Actions Abroad* GAD/RCED-94-55, February 1994.

21. Statement of Administration Policy, HR 1113—Office of Environmental Quality Appropriations Authorization, October 10, 1989.

22. Supra, n. 12 and 13.

23. Charles Grove Haines, *The American Doctrine of Judicial Supremacy* (New York: Macmillan, 1914); Raoul Berger, *Government by Judiciary: The Transformation of the Fourteenth Amendment* (Cambridge: Harvard University Press, 1977); and Louis Fisher, *Constitutional Dialogues: Interpretation as a Political Process* (Princeton: Princeton University Press, 1988).

24. 44 Fed. Reg. Department of Defense, Final Procedures (April 12, 1979): 21786 and AR 206-2 Update, Appendix H, 86–89.

25. Michael Satchell, "The Mess We've Left Behind," *U.S. News & World Report* (November 30, 1992): 28–31 and John M. Broder, "U.S. Military Leaves Toxic Trail Overseas" and "Pollution 'Hot Spots' Taint Water Sources," *Los Angeles Times* (June 18, 1990). United States General Accounting Office, *Hazardous Waste Management Problems Continue at Overseas Military Bases,* GAO/NSIAD-91-231, August 28, 1991. (Compares effects of NEPA and EO 12114.) But see also *Report of the Delegation to Europe of the Committee on Armed Services: House of Representatives* 102nd Congress,

2nd Session, March 3, 1992. It is hardly extenuating, however, to point out that the record of Soviet occupation in Eastern Europe was worse. Note observations of the Delegation to Europe, pages 48-55, and Ruben A. Mnatsakian, *Environmental Legacy of the Former Soviet Republics* (Edinburgh: Centre for Human Ecology, University of Edinburgh, 1992).

26. James R. Blaker, *United States Basing: An Anatomy of the Dilemma* (New York: Praeger, 1990).

27. See Commission for Environmental Cooperation Secretariate, *North American Agreement on Environmental Cooperation* (unofficial text): 1-40. For "environmentalist" misgivings on NAFTA see "Trading Away the Environment," *The Amicus Journal* 14, no. 4 (Winter 1993): 9-10. See also supra, n. 14.

28. *The Earth in Balance: Ecology and the Human Spirit* (New York: Penguin Books, 1992/1993). The assumptions and conclusions of this book were attacked in *Environmental Gore: A Constructive Response to the Earth in Balance,* edited by John A. Baden (1994), a collection of essays sponsored by the Pacific Research Institute for Public Policy, a conservative organization promoting free enterprise and private rights.

29. Laura A. Strohm and Roy W. Shin, "Policy Regimes for the International Waste Trade," in *Environmental Policy: Transnational Issues and National Trends,* Lynton K. Caldwell and Robert V. Bartlett, eds. (Westport, Conn.: Quorum Books, 1997), 113-129.

30. *U.S. Export of Banned Products. Hearing before a Sub-Committee of the House of Representatives Committee on Government Operations,* July 11-13, 1978. Another effort was made in 1980 in the 96th Congress. H.R. 6587 introduced February 25, 1980; hearing in the House of Representatives June 5, 12, and September 9, 1980. In the 97th Congress H.R. 2439, introduced March 11, 1981; hearing in House, March 19, 1981. In the 98th Congress H.R. 2467 introduced but no hearing reported.

31. David Weir and Mark Shapiro, *Circle of Poison* (San Francisco: Institute for Food and Development Policy, 1981); and Saul Rich, "Interactions of Air Pollution and Agricultural Practices," *Response of Plants to Air Pollution,* J. Brian Mudd and T. T. Kozlowski, eds. (New York: Academic Press, 1975), 335-360.

32. *Review of the Global Environment—10 Years after Stockholm: Hearings before the Subcommittee and Human Rights and International Organizations of the Committee on Foreign Affairs of the House of Representatives,* March 30, April 1, 1982.

33. *U.N. Multilateral Treaties Deposited with the Secretary General: Status at 31 December 1995.* New York United Nations, 1996, 900-901 Doc. E, ECE (Economic Commission for Europe), 1250.

34. For example see *The Independent Sector—Networks* published by the Centre for Our Common Future, Geneva, Switzerland. Not published since 1995.

35. Elizabeth Pinckard, "ISO 14000," *Colorado Journal of International Environmental Law and Policy* 8, no. 2 (Summer 1997): 423-450.

36. Supra, n. 12.

37. United States General Accounting Office International, *Environment: International Agreements are Not Well-Monitored.* D.C.: GAO/RCED-92-43 (January 1992).

38. Victor H. Martinez, "Hacia la creación del sistema interamericano para la conservación de la naturaleza," *Ambiente y Recursos Naturales* 4, no. 2 (abril-junio 1987): 12-34.

CHAPTER 6

NEPA AND THE GLOBAL ENVIRONMENT

1. 447 Fed. Reg. 21786, (April 12, 1979).

2. See Jan Schneider, *World Public Order of the Environment: Toward an International Ecological Law and Organization* (Toronto: University of Toronto Press, 1979),

and any of the more comprehensive treatises on international law, e.g. Ian Brownlie, *Principles of Public International Law.* 4th ed. (Oxford: Clarendon Press, 1990). See also Kenneth Dahlberg, ed., *The Environment in the Global Arena* (Durham: Duke University Press, 1985); Marvin S. Soroos, *Beyond Sovereignty: The Challenge of Global Policy* (Columbia: University of South Carolina Press, 1986); David W. Orr and Marvin S. Soross, *The Global Predicament* (Chapel Hill: University of North Carolina Press, 1979); and Lynton K. Caldwell, *International Environmental Policy: From Twentieth to the Twenty-First Century* (Durham: Duke University Press, 1996); "International Environment Politics: American's Response to Global Imperative," *Environmental Policy in the 1990's: Toward a New Agenda,* Norman J. Vig and Michael E. Kraft, eds. (Washington, D.C.: CQ Press, 1990), 301-321; Oran Young, George J. Demko, and Kilaparti Ramakrishna, eds., *Global Environmental Change and International Governance* (Hanover, N.H.: University of New England Press), 1996.

3. Quincy Wright, "The Corfu Channel Case," *American Journal of International Law* 43 (1949): 491-494 and *Encyclopedic Dictionary of International Law* (1986): 177.

4. Rudolph Preston Arnold, "The Common Heritage of Mankind as a Legal Concept," *International Lawyer* 9, no. 1 (1975); 153-58. See also James K. Sebenius, *Negotiating the Law of the Sea* (Cambridge: Harvard University Press, 1984).

5. Treaty Banning Nuclear Weapons Tests in the Atmosphere, in Outer Space, and under Water (Partial Nuclear Test Ban Treaty, 1963), and Treaty on Principles Governing the Activities of States in the Exploration and Use of Outer Space, Including the Moon and other Celestial Bodies (1967).

6. See for example *Institutions for the Earth: Sources of Effective International Environmental Protection,* Peter M. Haas, Robert O. Keohane, and Marc A. Levy, eds. (Cambridge: MIT Press, 1993).

7. 7487 F Supp. 749 (September 28, 1990).

8. See "Bases of jurisdiction to prescribe," *Restatement of the Law: The Foreign Relations of the United States.* 3rd series. American Law Institute, 1987 (Section 402.2). Perhaps in adherence to the separation of powers doctrine and the constitutional role of the president in foreign affairs, the courts are reluctant to inject their opinions into the actions of Federal agencies abroad except as required to do so by the specific congressional mandate or by the Constitution or treaty obligations. See also Jordan J. Paust, *International Law as Law of the United States* (Durham: Carolina Academic Press, 1996).

9. For a survey of legal and institutional arrangements for the global commons, see Lynton K. Caldwell, "International Commons: Air, Sea, Outer Space," *International Environmental Policy: From the Twentieth to the Twenty-First Century,* supra, n. 2, 202-241; Susan J. Buck, *The Global Commons: An Introduction* (Washington, D.C.: Island Press, 1988); and Young, Demko, and Kilaparti, supra, n. 2.

10. See assessments of the UN review of RIO and U.S. reservations published in *The New York Times* (Friday, June 27, 1997): Al and A7 and "Half-Hearted Global Warming Conference Closes Gloomily" (Saturday, June 28, 1997).

11. United States General Accounting Office, *International Environment: International Agreements Are Not Well Monitored.* Washington, D.C.: GAO/RCED-92-43 (January 1992); and *International Environment: Strengthening the Implementation of Environmental Agreements.* D.C.: GAO/RCED-92-188 (August 1992).

12. Thaddeus C. Trzyna, ed., *World Directory of Environmental Organizations.* 3rd ed.: *A Handbook of National and International Organizations and Programs—Governmental and Non-Governmental, Concerned with Protecting the Earth's Resources* (Claremont: California Institute of Public Affairs, 1989).

13. F. M. Auburn, *Antarctic Law and Politics* (Bloomington: Indiana University Press, 1982). See also Susan B. Fletcher, *Antarctica: Environmental Protection Issues* (Washington, D.C.: Congressional Research Service, April 10, 1989). See also Public Law 101-620 (November 16, 1990). Antarctic Treaty-Global Ecological Commons.

14. James G. Titus and Vijay K. Narayanan, *The Probability of Sea Level Rise* (Washington, D.C.: U.S. Environmental Protection Agency, 1995).

15. United Nations Environment Programme, *Achievements and Planned Developments of UNEP's Regional Seas Programme and Comparable Programmes Sponsored by Other Bodies. UNEP Regional Seas Reports and Studies* No. 1, 1982, and issues of UNEP's bulletin *SIREN,* a publication of UNEP's program of Oceans and Coastal Areas.

16. L. Anathea Brooks and Stacy D. VanDeveer, eds., *Saving the Seas: Values, Scientists, and International Governance* (College Park: A Maryland Sea Grant Book, 1997).

17. *The New York Times* (Friday, June 27, 1997): supra, n. 10.

18. Richard E. Benedick, *Ozone Diplomacy: New Directions in Safeguarding the Planet* (Cambridge: Harvard University Press, 1991).

19. Marvin S. Soroos, "Telecommunications: Managing A Technological Revolution" *Beyond Sovereignty: The Challenge of Global Policy* (Columbia: University of South Carolina Press, 1986), 323-49; Frances Lyall, *Law and Space Telecommunications* (Aldershot, UK: Gower, 1989); Milton L. Smith, *International Regulation of Satellite Communication* (Dordrecht: Martinus Nijhoff, 1990); and Anne W. Branscomb, *Toward a Law of Global Communication Networks* (New York: Longman, 1986).

20. Ricardo Umali, "Landsat: Uninvited Eye," *East-West Perspectives* 1 (Winter 1980): 12-21. See also Nicholas N. Matte and Hamilton De Sassure, *Legal Implications of Remote Sensing from Outer Space* (Leyden: A.W. Sijthoff, 1976).

21. *Remote Sensing from Outer Space: Prospects for Developing Countries. Report of the Ad Hoc Committee on Remote Sensing for Development* (Washington, D.C.: National Academy of Science, 1977).

22. American Association for the Advancement of Science, Committee on Science in the Promotion of Human Welfare, "The Integrity of Science," *American Scientist* 53 (June 1965): 174-198. This report provides extensive citations to documents of the Department of Defense and various scientific groups.

23. For example, Robert U. Ayers, *Environmental Effects of Nuclear Weapons.* Vol. I, II. Cameron Station, Alexandria, Virginia: Defense Documentation Center for Scientific and Technical Information, December 1, 1965.

24. R. P. Turco, et al. "Nuclear Winter: Global Consequences of Multiple Nuclear Explosions," *Science* 222 (December 23, 1983): 1283-1292 and Paul R. Ehrlich et al., "Long-Term Biological Consequences of Nuclear War," ibid., 1293-1300. See also Anne Ehrlich, "Nuclear Winter—A Forecast of the Climatic and Biological Effects of Nuclear War," *Bulletin of the Atomic Scientists* (April 1984): 16 pp.

25. Seon-ki Park, *Legal Aspects of the Strategic Defense Initiative* (Washington, D.C.: World Peace Through Law Center, 1987).

26. Christopher C. Joyner and Sudkir K. Chopra, *The Antarctic Legal Regime* (Dordrecht: Martin Nijhoff, 1988); and Gillian D. Triggs, ed., *The Antarctic Treaty Regime: Law Environment and Resources* (New York: Cambridge University Press, 1987). See also Tullio Scovazzi, "The Antarctic Treaty System and the New Law of the Sea," *International Law for Antarctica,* Francesco Francioni and Tullio Scovazzi, eds. (Netherlands: Kluwer Law International, 1996), 377-394.

27. Philip Shabecoff, "Development Seen for the Minerals of All Antarctica," *New York Times* (June 8, 1988): 1, 7; Malcolm W. Browne, "French and Australians Kill Accord on Antarctica," *New York Times* (September 25, 1989); also Harry H. Almond, Jr., "Demilitarization and Arms Control: Antarctica," *Journal of International Law* 17, no. 2 (Spring 1985): 229-284.

28. *Environmental Defense Fund v. Walter Massey,* 1991, Court of Appeals for the District of Columbia 772. Fed. Supp. 1296; Fed. Rep. 986, 2nd Series, p. 528, January 29, 1993.

29. For a summary of UNCED see *Bruntland Bulletin* Issue 16 (July 1992 Special Earth Summit Issue). See also Nicholas C. Yost, "Rio and the Road Beyond," *Environmental Law Quarterly Newsletter of the Standing Committee on Environmental Law—*

American Bar Association 11, no. 4 (Summer 1992): 1-6; also whole issues of the *Colorado Journal of International Law and Policy* 4, no. 1 (Winter 1993) and *Environmental Law and Policy* 22, no. 4 (August 1992). For an assessment by the Deputy Secretary General of UNCED, Nitin Desae, see "The Outcome of Rio," *Network '92* (Centre for Our Common Future) 18 (June-July 1992): 1, 18-19.

30. United Nations, *Environmental Summit +5: Special Session of the General Assembly to Review and Appraise the Implementation of Agenda 21. New York, 23-27 June 1997.* New York: United Nations Department for Policy Coordination and Sustainable Development.

31. Riley E. Dunlap, "International Opinion at the Century's End: Public Attitudes Toward Environmental Issues," *International Environmental Policy: Transnational Issues and National Trends,* Lynton K. Caldwell and Robert V. Bartlett, eds. (Westport, Conn.: Quorum Books, 1997), 201-224.

CHAPTER 7 FUTURE DIRECTIONS: BEYOND NEPA

1. Alexander King and Bertrand Schneider, *The First Global Revolution: A Report to the Club Rome* (New York: Pantheon Books, 1991).

2. Frederick Anderson, *NEPA in the Courts: A Legal Analysis of the National Environmental Policy Act* (Baltimore: Johns Hopkins Press, 1973); Lettie M. Wenner, *The Environmental Decade in Court* (Bloomington: Indiana University Press, 1982); Fredric P. Sutherland and Roger Beers, "Supreme Indifference," *Amicus Journal* (Spring 1991): 38-42; and Keith Schneider, "Thwarted Environmentalists Find U.S. Courts are Citadels No More," *The New York Times* (March 23, 1992).

3. Hanna J. Cortner, "A Case Analysis of Policy Implementation: The National Policy Act of 1969," *Natural Resources Journal* 16 (April 1969): 323-338.

4. René Dubos, *Man Adapting* (New Haven: Yale University Press, 1965).

5. See for example Nicholas C. Yost, "NEPA—The Law That Works," *The Environmental Forum* (January 1985): 38, 40; Sally K. Fairfax, "A Disaster in the Environmental Movement," *Science* 199 (17 February 1978): 743-748; Lynton K. Caldwell, "Is NEPA Inherently Self-Defeating?" *Environmental Law Reporter* 9 (January 1979): 50001-07.

6. *The President's Committee on Administrative Management: Report of the Committee with Studies of Administrative Management in the Federal Government* (Washington, D.C.: U.S. Government Printing Office, 1937); and *Administrative Management in the Government of the United States: Report of the President's Committee* (U.S. Government Printing Office, January 8, 1937).

7. For a criticism of this trend see Walter Williams, *Mismanaging America: The Rise of the Anti-Analytic Presidency* (Lawrence: University of Kansas Press, 1990). See also Ronald C. Moe, "Traditional Organizational Principles and the Managerial Presidency: From Phoenix to Ashes," *Public Administration Review* 50 (March-April 1990): 129-140 and "The Institutional Presidency: A Tale of Retreat and Decline," *25 Years from the Bureaucrat to the Public Manager* (Spring 1996): 9-12.

8. Fritjof Capra and Charlene Spretnak in collaboration with Rudiger Lutz, *Green Politics,* rev. ed. (Santa Fe: Bear, 1986); Stephen Rainbow, *Green Politics* (New York: Oxford University Press, 1993).

9. Robert L. Heilbroner, *An Inquiry into the Human Prospect: Updated and Reconsidered for the 1980s* (New York: W. W. Norton, 1980), 158. For similar assessments see Jay W. Forrester, *World Dynamics* (Cambridge: Wright-Allen Press, 1971), "Epilogue," 123-128, and William R. Catton, Jr., *Overshoot: The Ecological Basis of Revolutionary Change* (Urbana: University of Illinois Press, 1980).

10. Lynton K. Caldwell, *Population and Environment: Inseparable Policy Issues, a*

Monograph in Two Parts (Washington, D.C.: The Environmental Fund, 1985); Garrett J. Hardin, *Living Within Limits: Ecology, Economics, and Population Taboos* (New York: Oxford University Press, 1993); and Shridath Ramphal and Steven W. Sinding, *Population Growth and Environmental Issues* (Westport, Conn.: Praeger, 1994).

11. *Background Materials Related to the Environmental Policy and Conflict Resolution Act of 1987. Recently Introduced as S.399 by U.S. Senator John McCain (R-AZ), March 5, 1997* (Tucson, Ariz: Udall Center for Studies in Public Policy, University of Arizona, 1997).

12. Philip Michael Ferester, "Revitalizing the National Environmental Policy Act: Substantive Law Adaptions from NEPA's Progeny," *Harvard Environmental Law Review* 16 (1992): 207-260.

13. See *Pacific Legal Foundation v. CEQ, U.S. Court of Appeals District of Columbia Circuit* (1986). One of the purposes of this foundation is to fight environmental regulations especially as they affect property rights.

14. *The Executive Presidency: Federal Management for the 1990s: A Report by an Academy Panel for the 1988-89 Presidential Transition* (Washington, D.C.: National Academy of Public Administration, September 1988).

15. Scott C. Whitney, "The Case for Creating a Special Environmental Court System," *William and Mary Law Review* 14 (1973): 473-522. See also Harold Leventhal, "Environmental Decisionmaking and the Role of the Courts," *University of Pennsylvania Law Review* 122 (1974): 509-555; Comment, "The Environmental Court Proposal: Requiem, Analysis, and Counterproposal," *University of Pennsylvania Law Review* 123 (1975): 676-696.

16. Richard B. Stewart, "Paradoxes of Liberty, Integrity and Fraternity: The Collective Nature of Environmental Quality and Judicial Review of Administrative Action," *Environmental Law* 7 (1977): 463-484.

17. Texts of many of these proposals were printed in the *Environmental Amendment Circulars* published for the Comprehensive Environmental Project by Marshall Massey of Thornton, Colorado, notably *Circular No. 4, A Gallery of Proposals,* June 1991. Among them, the text of a proposed Environmental Quality Amendment was published in March 1987 by the National Wildlife Federation and revised in September 1989. Similar proposals have been made by concerned citizens (e.g. Marshall Massey and Carolyn Merchant, Richard O. Brooks, and more recently by Rodger Schlickeisen in the *Tulane University Environmental Law Journal* 8 [Winter 1994]: 181-220). Some philosophic proposals (e.g. Richard Cartwright Austin, *Environmental Theology* [1987]; Roderick Nash, *The Rights of Nature* [1989]; and Christopher Stone, *Should Trees Have Standing: Toward Legal Rights for Natural Objects* [1975]) would extend rights to all living species and natural systems. A novel amendment including more than environmental affairs has been proposed by Bruce Tonn. His "Court of Generations" (May 1990, privately circulated) is described as an adjunct of the Supreme Court but separate from the Federal judicial system. It would convene periodically to consider issues of transgenerational justice. It would not declare judgments but acting as a grand jury would issue indictments for the political branches to consider. For a critical review of the environmental rights concept see J. B. Ruhl, "An Environmental Rights Amendment: Good Message, Bad Idea," *Natural Resources and Environment* (American Bar Association) 11, no. 3 (Winter 1997): 46-49.

18. David Sive, "National Environmental Policy Act, Little NEPAs, and the Environmental Impact Process," American Law Institute—American Bar Institute Course of Study 1995, available in WESTLAW, ALI-ABA database (there is a 1997 revision); Nicholas A. Robinson, "SEQRA's Siblings: Precedents from Little NEPAs in the Sister States," *Albany Law Review* 46 (1982): 1155-1176. See also Elizabeth H. Haskell and Victoria S. Price, *State Environmental Management: Case Studies of Nine States* (New York: Praeger, 1973).

19. Richard J. Tobin, "Some Observations on the Use of State Constitutions to

Protect the Environment," *Environmental Affairs* 3 (1974): 473-485. See also A. E. Dick Howard, "State Constitutions and the Environment," *Virginia Law Review* 58 (February 1972): 192-229; Oliver A. Pollard III, "A Promise Unfulfilled: Environmental Provisions in State Constitutions and the Self-Executive Question," *Virginia Journal of Natural Resources Law* 5 (1986): 351-370; and José L. Fernandez, "State Constitutions, Environmental Rights Provisions, and the Doctrine of Self-Execution: A Political Question?" *Harvard Environmental Law Review* 17, no. 2 (1993): 333-387. Also Sheldon M. Nosick et al., "State Law and Programs (b) State Constitutional Provisions," *Law of Environmental Protection* (Environmental Law Institute) (St. Paul: West, 1998, 601(2)(b)).

20. See Coalition of Legislators for Environmental Action Now (CLEAN), Media Advisory, "Unprecedented National Debate on the Role of the Constitution in Protecting Public Health and the Environment" (1996). See also Richard L. Brodsky and Richard L. Russman, "A Constitutional Initiative," *Defenders* 71, no. 4 (Fall 1996): 37-38.

21. For listing of leading treaties and soft law see Lynton K. Caldwell, *International Environmental Policy. 3rd ed. From the Twentieth to the Twenty-First Century* (Durham: Duke University Press, 1996). Appendices D and E. Comprehensive lists of international environmental treaties may be found in *Environmental Quality: The Twentieth Annual Report of the [U.S.] Council on Environmental Quality* (Washington, D.C.: Council on Environmental Quality, 1990), Appendix C and in *Breakthrough* [Global Education Associates] (Summer-Fall 1989): 18-19. F.

22. For status of treaties in relation to U.S. domestic and international law see Jordan J. Paust, *International Law as Law of the United States* (Durham: Carolina Academic Press, 1996). Cf. *Missouri v. Holland*, 252 U.S. 416 (1916). See also *Sherman S. Hayden, International Protection of Wildlife: An Examination of Treaties and Other Agreements for the Preservation of Birds and Mammals* (New York: Columbia University Press, 1942; reprinted by AMS Press, 1970) and Simon Lyster, *International Wildlife Law: An Analysis of International Treaties Concerned with the Conservation of Wildlife* (Cambridge, U.K.: Grotius, 1985).

23. *International Legal Materials*, vol. 30 (1991): 802. See also Economic Commission for Europe, *Current Policies, Strategies and Aspects of Environmental Impact Assessment in a Transboundary Context.* Environmental Series 6, New York: United Nations, ECE/CEP 19, 1996.

24. Amedeo Postiglione, "A More Efficient International Law on the Environment and Setting up an International Court for the Environment Within the United Nations," *Environmental Law* 20 (1990): 322.

25. Christian Calliess, "Toward a European Constitutional Law," *European Environmental Law Review* 6, no. 4 (April 1997): 113-120.

26. Quincy Wright, "International Law in its Relation to Constitutional Law," *American Journal of International Law* 17 (1923): 234-244.

27. Edith Brown Weiss, *In Fairness to Future Generations: International Law, Common Patrimony and Intergenerational Equity* (Ardsley-on-Hudson, New York: Transnational Publishers, 1989), Appendix B, 247-327.

28. Samuel P. Hays, *Conservation and the Gospel of Efficiency: The Progressive Conservation Movement, 1890-1920.* 2nd ed. (Cambridge: Harvard University Press, 1969); and *Beauty, Health and Permanence: Environmental Politics in the United States, 1955-1985* (Cambridge: Cambridge University Press, 1985).

29. See for a "libertarian" perspective Calvin W. Stillman, "On Saving Places," *Environmental Law* 7 (1977): 485-497.

30. For example see King and Schneider, supra, n. 1; Robert Nisbet, *Prejudices: A Philosophical Dictionary* (Cambridge: Harvard University Press, 1982), "Environmentalism," 101; and Max Nicholson, *The Environmental Revolution: A Guide to the New Masters of the World* (New York: 1970). (The message may be right but the

prospect premature.) Compare with Lester Milbrath, *Environmentalists: Vanguard for a New Society* (Albany: State University of New York Press, 1984).

31. Lynton K. Caldwell, "The Positive Role of Environmental Management," *Final Report on Managing the Environment* (Washington, D.C.: Environmental Protection Agency, Socioeconomic Studies Series, 600-5-73-010, 1973), 130-134 and "Restoration Ecology as Public Policy," *Readings from the Environmental Professional: Natural Resources,* John Lemons, ed. (Cambridge: Blackwell Science, 1995), 134-143.

32. *Global Future: Time to Act. Report to the President on Global Resources, Environment, and Population* (Washington, D.C.: Council on Environmental Quality and the Department of State, January 1981), a consideration of the *Global 2000 Report* which curiously under the section on *A Comprehensive U.S. Strategy* never mentions the National Environmental Policy Act, nor is NEPA included in the index to this report. The full study is reported in three volumes: I Summary, II Technical Report, III Documentation on the Government Global Models. See the *Global 2000 Report to the President: Entering the Twenty-First Century* (Washington, D.C.: U.S. Government Printing Office, 1981).

33. Philip Shabecoff, *A New Name for Peace: International Environmentalism, Sustainable Development and Democracy* (Hanover: University Press of New England, 1996).

INDEX

adaptive environment management, 56

Administrative Procedures Act of 1946, 23, 100

Agenda for Tomorrow (Udall, 1968), xi

air pollution, 17, 27, 33, 100, 127, 134–36. *See also* atmosphere, global concern for; atmospheric depositions; outer space, global concern for; pollution

Alaska oil and gas pipelines, 67, 148

American Bar Association, Natural Resources Law Section, 62

American Enterprise Institute, 7, 43, 58

American Medical Association (AMA), 27

Andrews, Richard N. L., 22

Andrus v. Sierra Club (442 U.S. 347 at 358), 185 n.25

Antarctic Treaty (1959), 140

"Antarctic Treaty—Global Ecological Commons" (PL 101-620), 126

Antarctica: development of, 140–41; protection of, 123, 124, 126, 130, 131, 140–41

anthropocentrism, defined, 13

antienvironmentalism, 7, 9–10, 50, 56, 58, 75, 154, 157

antipollution issues, 4, 27, 28, 33, 37–38, 78

Apollo VIII mission, 27

Army, U.S., 110; Corps of Engineers, 65, 75. *See also* military bases

Ashby, Sir Eric, 17–18

assessment, defined, 48

atmosphere, global concern for, 134–36. *See also* air pollution; global climate change; greenhouse gas emissions; ozone depletion

atmospheric depositions, 113

Austin, Richard Cartwright, 197 n.17

Bacon, Francis, xvi

Barnes, Michael, 115

Base Closure and Defense Authorization Amendments and Realignment Act of 1988, 85

Becker, Ernest, 7

Bennett, Charles E., 162

Bible (New Testament): Book of John, 8

Big Bang theory, 8

biocentrism, defined, 13

Biodiversity Treaty (1992), 100, 124, 125, 130, 131, 142, 169

biosphere, defined, 11, 26. *See also* environ-

ment; global environment, interconnectivity (interactivity) of

Biosphere Conference (Paris, 1968), 7, 141

bird migrations, 165

Boulding, Kenneth, 9

Bowman, Wallace D., 63

British Town and County Planning Acts, 4

Brooks, Richard O., 197 n.17

Brownlow, Louis, 89

Bureau of Land Management, U.S., 85, 94

Bureau of Reclamation, U.S., 62

Bush, George: Antarctic development under, 140; environmental policy under, 37, 72, 115, 124, 131

Caldwell, Lynton K.: national environmental policy formulated by, 5, 29, 36, 59–63, 170

Calvert Cliffs Coordinating Committee v. Atomic Energy Commission (449 F.2d. 1109), 32, 43, 186 n.37

Capra, Fritjof, 16

carbon dioxide emissions, 17

Carnegie Endowment for International Peace, *Memorandum to the President Elect* (1992), 41, 160

Carpenter, Richard A., 63

Carson, Rachel, 15, 26

Carter, Jimmy: environmental policy under, 34, 40, 44, 100, 109–11, 113, 115, 159

Cato Institute, 58

Catton, W. R., Jr., 15

Cautionary Guides (Design and Industries Association of Great Britain), 58

Centre for Religion and Society, University of Victoria (British Columbia), 10

CEQ. *See* Council on Environmental Quality

Chafee, John H., 158

Charter on Environmental Rights and Obligations (proposed), 166–67

checklists, for environmental policy, 61–62

Checklists for Preparing National Environmental Policy Act Documents (American Bar Association, Natural Resources Law Section, 1987), 62

chemical biocides, transport of, 115

chemical spills, 16

Chemical Weapons Convention (1997), 131

Citizens' Advisory Committee on Environmental Quality, 19

LYNTON KEITH CALDWELL is Arthur F. Bentley Professor Emeritus of Political Science and Professor of Public and Environmental Affairs at Indiana University, active in environmental and science policy research. He is noted as one of the principal architects of the National Environmental Policy Act of 1969 and an "initiator" of the environmental impact statement. He has published more than 250 articles and monographs and twelve books, including *In Defense of Earth* (Indiana University Press, 1972), and with Lynton R. Hayes and Isabel M. MacWhirter, *Citizens and the Environment: Case Studies in Popular Action* (Indiana University Press, 1976).